Motivation

R1.15

KU-002-820

Penguin Modern Psychology Readings

General Editor

B. M. Foss

Advisory Board

P. C. Dodwell
Marie Jahoda
S. G. Lee
W. M. O'Neil
R. L. Reid
Roger Russell
P. E. Vernon
George Westby

MOTIVATION

Selected Readings

Edited by Dalbir Bindra and Jane Stewart

Penguin Books

Penguin Books Ltd, Harmondsworth,
Middlesex, England
Penguin Books Inc., 3300 Clipper Mill Road,
Baltimore 11, Md, U.S.A.
Penguin Books Pty Ltd, Ringwood,
Victoria, Australia

First published by Penguin Books 1966

This selection © Bindra and Stewart, 1966
Introduction and Notes © Bindra and Stewart, 1966

Made and printed in Great Britain by
Hazell Watson and Viney Ltd, Aylesbury, Bucks
Set in Monotype Times Roman

Contents

GOAL DIRECTION

V From Purpose to Goal Direction

NATURE OF REINFORCERS

VI Pleasure and Pain as the Basis of Reinforcement

VII Drive Reduction as the Basis of Reinforcement

VIII Reinforcers as Elicitors of Responses

IX Sensory Effects as the Basis of Reinforcement

X Brain Mechanisms and Reinforcement

Introduction

In this volume we have attempted to provide an account of the major theoretical and experimental developments in the study of motivation. The excerpts and articles reproduced here are among the ones that most directly deal with the fundamental questions and issues in this area of psychology.

Chapter headings in psychology, *emotion*, *motivation*, *perception*, *learning*, and the like, designate neither distinctly separate sets of behavioural phenomena nor unique psychological processes. An assumption basic to the work of psychologists is that there exist a few key processes which are responsible for all the variety of behaviour observed in nature. The same processes are assumed to produce behaviour we describe as 'emotional' (e.g., anger, fear, joy), 'motivational' (e.g., eating, maternal behaviour, drug addiction), 'perceptual' (e.g., estimating sizes, shapes, and distances), 'learning' (e.g., response shaping, acquiring motor skills), and 'thinking' (problem solving, reasoning). Thus chapter headings do not clearly subdivide psychological knowledge; they serve merely as convenient guideposts indicating the current areas of search for the basic processes. Chapter headings change as our ideas about the nature of these processes change.

The beginning of the concept of motivation as a basic psychological process is difficult to trace. The term does not seem to have been used by psychologists trained in the Wundtian structuralist tradition. But it crept into the writings of functionally minded psychologists in England and America in the 1880s. This usually happened in chapters on voluntary action or will, midst discussions of desire, impulse, and intention. Sully[1] in 1884 said that the desire that precedes an act and determines it is to be called 'its moving force, stimulus or *motive*'. 'A desire when chosen becomes a *motive*,' wrote Dewey[2] (1886). These definitions indicate that motivation was considered to be an entity that impelled one to action of a particular type. The idea of motivation or impulsion-to-action, which had been implicit in the idea of instinct, was thus extended to voluntary action as well.

McDougall[3] (1908) made this extension of the concept of motivation to 'voluntary behaviour' explicit by suggesting that instincts were the 'prime movers of all human activity'. Avoiding the metaphysical tone of McDougall's doctrine of instinct, Woodworth[4] (1918) proposed the concept of *drive* to refer to 'the motives and springs of action' that arouse a particular type of action. Troland's[5] *The Fundamentals of Human Motivation* (1928) provided a physiological interpretation of the roles of pleasure and pain in human actions and learning. Warden's[6] research monograph, *Animal Motivation*, was published in 1931, and Tolman's[7] *Purposive Behavior in Animals and Men* in 1932. Young[8] brought together much of the early research and provided the first systematic account of the area in his *Motivation of Behavior* (1936). It was during this period, the 1930s, that 'motivation' gained acceptance as a fundamental psychological concept. Since that time textbook writers have viewed motivation as a major subdivision of psychological knowledge.

The questions about behaviour that initially led to the adoption of the motivation concept are evident in psychological discussions today. In contemporary psychology, 'motivation' encompasses three main problems. The first of these is the problem of *drive*: Why are organisms active at all? Given the existence of certain activities (e.g., eating, drinking) in the repertoire of an animal, why does it engage in these activities at certain times but not at others? Once initiated, why is an activity terminated? The second problem is that of purpose or *goal direction*: Behaviour of organisms tends to be directed toward particular ends or goals, but can this goal direction be objectively described and measured? What makes behaviour goal directed? The third problem comprising motivation is that of pleasure and pain or the *nature of reinforcers*: Recognizing that animals tend to repeat activities that lead to certain consequences (rewards) and stop doing what leads to certain other consequencies (punishments), what precisely is the nature of such reinforcers? What are the essential properties that make certain events positive reinforcers (pleasurable) and other events negative reinforcers (painful)?

The excerpts and articles collected in this volume represent attempts by major investigators to answer the above questions. The period covered extends roughly from 1900 to 1960. The selections are collected in three sections: Nature of Drive, Goal Direction, and Nature of Reinforcers. Within each section, the selections bearing on particular issues are grouped together in chapters. Brief notes are provided to introduce each section and each chapter.

Acknowledgement
We wish to thank Miss Lorraine Ford for her generous assistance in all phases of the preparation of this book.

1. Sully, J., *Outlines of Psychology*, D. Appleton & Co., New York, 1884.
2. Dewey, J., *Psychology*, Harper, New York, 1886.
3. McDougall, W., *An Introduction to Social Psychology*, Methuen, London, 1908.
4. Woodworth, R. S., *Dynamic Psychology*, Columbia University Press, New York, 1918.
5. Troland, L. T., *The Fundamentals of Human Motivation*, Van Nostrand, Princeton, 1928.
6. Warden, C. J., *Animal Motivation: Experimental Studies on the Albino Rat*, Columbia University Press, New York, 1931.
7. Tolman, E. C., *Purposive Behavior in Animals and Men*, Century, New York, 1932.
8. Young, P. T., *Motivation of Behavior: The Fundamental Determinants of Human and Animal Activity*, Wiley, New York, 1936.

Part One NATURE OF DRIVE

Organisms have numerous goal-directed activities in their repertoires. Each of these activities is displayed only at certain times; at other times it remains latent. Clearly it is important to know what factors control the occurrence (initiation and termination) of the various potential activities. Why does the organism display a particular activity at a given moment? The common-sense 'explanation' is that the activity serves a motive, the latter being defined in terms of a goal or end result; the goal is considered both an 'incentive' to which an action leads and a 'source of motivation' for the action. Thus, one says that X eats in order not to be hungry, X fights in order to protect his wife, X joins a club in order to be respected, etc. Such statements confuse the motivational and incentive aspects of actions and do not constitute explanation in any rigorous sense. In modern psychology, the term *drive* has come to refer to the motivational factor that makes an activity occur, regardless of what incentive the activity leads to. The term *reinforcer* is used to refer to the incentive factor in the determination of behaviour.

I Drive as Instinctive Energy

The ancient view held that instincts were the determiners of certain primitive types of actions, which could be differentiated from intelligent and voluntary behaviour. McDougall proposed that instincts were the primary source of energy for all varieties of action. This same conception of drive is to be found in the writings of Freud, as well as in the earlier writings of ethologists (zoologists interested in animal behaviour whose work lay outside the mainstream of psychological developments). Some excerpts from the writings of McDougall and Freud, and from the early writings of two ethologists, Lorenz and Tinbergen, are presented in the following pages. This is followed by critiques of instinct-energy models of drive by Hinde and Nissen. (For the current views of ethologists, the reader should consult their more recent writings.)

1 W. McDougall

On the Nature of Instinct

Excerpts from W. McDougall, *An Introduction to Social Psychology*, Methuen, London, 1908, Chapter 2.

The human mind has certain innate or inherited tendencies which are the essential springs or motive powers of all thought and action, whether individual or collective, and are the bases from which the character and will of individuals and of nations are gradually developed under the guidance of the intellectual faculties. These primary innate tendencies have different relative strengths in the native constitutions of the individuals of different races, and they are favoured or checked in very different degrees by the very different social circumstances of men in different stages of culture; but they are probably common to the men of every race and of every age. . . .

In treating of the instincts of animals, writers have usually described them as innate tendencies to certain kinds of action, and Herbert Spencer's widely accepted definition of instinctive action as compound reflex action takes account only of the behaviour or movements to which instincts give rise. But instincts are more than innate tendencies or dispositions to certain kinds of movement. There is every reason to believe that even the most purely instinctive action is the outcome of a distinctly mental process, one which is incapable of being described in purely mechanical terms, because it is a psycho-physical process, involving psychical as well as physical changes, and one which, like every other mental process, has, and can only be fully described in terms of, the three aspects of all mental process – the cognitive, the affective, and the conative aspects; that is to say, every instance of instinctive behaviour involves a knowing of some thing or object, a feeling in regard to it, and a striving towards or away from that object.

We cannot, of course, directly observe the threefold psychical aspect of the psycho-physical process that issues in instinctive behaviour; but we are amply justified in assuming that it invariably accompanies the process in the nervous system of which the instinctive movements are the immediate result, a process which, being initiated on stimulation of some sense organ by the physical impressions received from the object, travels up the sensory nerves, traverses the brain, and descends as an orderly or co-ordinated stream of nervous impulses along efferent nerves to the appropriate groups of muscles and other executive organs. We are justified in assuming the cognitive aspect of the psychical process, because the nervous excitation seems to traverse those parts of the brain whose excitement involves the production of sensations or changes in the sensory content of consciousness; we are justified in assuming the affective aspect of the psychical process, because the creature exhibits unmistakable symptoms of feeling and emotional excitement; and, especially, we are justified in assuming the conative aspect of the psychical process, because all instinctive behaviour exhibits that unique mark of mental process, a persistent striving towards the natural end of the process. That is to say, the process, unlike any merely mechanical process, is not to be arrested by any sufficient mechanical obstacle, but is rather intensified by any such obstacle and only comes to an end either when its appropriate goal is achieved, or when some stronger incompatible tendency is excited, or when the creature is exhausted by its persistent efforts. . . .

An instinctive action, then, must not be regarded as simple or compound reflex action if by reflex action we mean, as is usually meant, a movement caused by a sense-stimulus and resulting from a sequence of merely physical processes in some nervous arc. Nevertheless, just as a reflex action implies the presence in the nervous system of the reflex nervous arc, so the instinctive action also implies some enduring nervous basis whose organisation is inherited, an innate or inherited psycho-physical disposition, which, anatomically regarded, probably has the form of a compound system of sensori-motor arcs.

We may, then, define an instinct as an inherited or innate psycho-physical disposition which determines its possessor to perceive, and to pay attention to, objects of a certain class, to experience an emotional excitement of a particular quality upon perceiving such an object, and to act in regard to it in a particular manner, or, at least, to experience an impulse to such action.

It must further be noted that some instincts remain inexcitable except during the prevalence of some temporary bodily state, such as hunger. In these cases we must suppose that the bodily process or state determines the stimulation of sense-organs within the body, and that nervous currents ascending from these to the psycho-physical disposition maintain it in an excitable condition. . . .

Are, then, these instinctive impulses the only motive powers of the human mind to thought and action? What of pleasure and pain, which by so many of the older psychologists were held to be the only motives of human activity, the only objects or sources of desire and aversion?

In answer to the former question, it must be said that in the developed human mind there are springs of action of another class, namely, acquired habits of thought and action. An acquired mode of activity becomes by repetition habitual, and the more frequently it is repeated the more powerful becomes the habit as a source of impulse or motive power. Few habits can equal in this respect the principal instincts; and habits are in a sense derived from, and secondary to, instincts; for, in the absence of instincts, no thought and no action could ever be achieved or repeated, and so no habits of thought or action could be formed. Habits are formed only in the service of the instincts.

The answer to the second question is that pleasure and pain are not in themselves springs of action, but at the most of undirected movements; they serve rather to modify instinctive processes, pleasure tending to sustain and prolong any mode of action, pain to cut it short; under their prompting and guidance are effected those modifications and adaptations of the instinctive bodily movements which we have briefly considered above.

We may say, then, that directly or indirectly the instincts are the prime movers of all human activity; by the conative or impulsive force of some instinct (or of some habit derived from an instinct), every train of thought, however cold and passionless it may seem, is borne along towards its end, and every bodily activity is initiated and sustained. The instinctive impulses determine the ends of all activities and supply the driving power by which all mental activities are sustained; and all the complex intellectual apparatus of the most highly developed mind is but a means towards these ends, is but the instrument by which these impulses seek their satisfactions, while pleasure and pain do but serve to guide them in their choice of the means.

Take away these instinctive dispositions with their powerful impulses, and the organism would become incapable of activity of any kind; it would lie inert and motionless like a wonderful clockwork whose main-spring had been removed or a steam-engine whose fires had been drawn. These impulses are the mental forces that maintain and shape all the life of individuals and societies, and in them we are confronted with the central mystery of life and mind and will.

2 S. Freud

Source, Aim, and Object of Instinctive Energy

Excerpt from S. Freud, 'Instincts and their vicissitudes' (1915),
Collected Papers, Hogarth, London, 1925, Vol. 4, Chapter 4.

If we apply ourselves to considering mental life from a biological point of view, an 'instinct' appears to us as a borderland concept between the mental and the physical, being both the mental representative of the stimuli emanating from within the organism and penetrating to the mind, and at the same time a measure of the demand made upon the energy of the latter in consequence of its connection with the body.

We are now in a position to discuss certain terms used in reference to the concept of an instinct, for example, its impetus, its aim, its object and its source.

By the *impetus* of an instinct we understand its motor element, the amount of force or the measure of the demand upon energy which it represents. The characteristic of impulsion is common to all instincts, is in fact the very essence of them. Every instinct is a form of activity; if we speak loosely of passive instincts, we can only mean those whose aim is passive.

The *aim* of an instinct is in every instance satisfaction, which can only be obtained by abolishing the condition of stimulation in the source of the instinct. But although this remains invariably the final goal of every instinct, there may yet be different ways leading to the same goal, so that an instinct may be found to have various nearer or intermediate aims, capable of combination or interchange. Experience permits us also to speak of instincts which are *inhibited in respect of their aim*, in cases where a certain advance has been permitted in the direction of satisfaction and then an inhibition or deflection has occurred. We may suppose that even in such cases a partial satisfaction is achieved.

The *object* of an instinct is that in or through which it can achieve its aim. It is the most variable thing about an instinct and is not originally connected with it, but becomes attached to it only in consequence of being peculiarly fitted to provide satisfaction. The object is not necessarily an extraneous one: it may be part of the subject's own body. It may be changed any number of times in the course of the vicissitudes the instinct undergoes during life; a highly important part is played by this capacity for displacement in the instinct. It may happen that the same object may serve for the satisfaction of several instincts simultaneously, a phenomenon which Adler calls a 'confluence' of instincts. A particularly close attachment of the instinct to its object is distinguished by the term *fixation*: this frequently occurs in very early stages of the instinct's development and so puts an end to its mobility, through the vigorous resistance it sets up against detachment.

By the *source* of an instinct is meant that somatic process in an organ or part of the body from which there results a stimulus represented in mental life by an instinct. We do not know whether this process is regularly of a chemical nature or whether it may also correspond with the release of other, *e.g.*, mechanical, forces. The study of the sources of instinct is outside the scope of psychology; although its source in the body is what gives the instinct its distinct and essential character, yet in mental life we know it merely by its aims. A more exact knowledge of the sources of instincts is not strictly necessary for purposes of psychological investigation; often the source may be with certainty inferred from the aims.

Are we to suppose that the different instincts which operate upon the mind but of which the origin is somatic are also distinguished by different qualities and act in the mental life in a manner qualitatively different? This supposition does not seem to be justified; we are much more likely to find the simpler assumption sufficient – namely, that the instincts are all qualitatively alike and owe the effect they produce only to the quantities of excitation accompanying them, or perhaps further to certain functions of this quantity. The difference in the mental effects produced by the different instincts may be traced to the difference in their sources. In any event, it is only in a later connection that we shall be able to make plain what the problem of the quality of instincts signifies.

Now what instincts and how many should be postulated? There is obviously a great opportunity here for arbitrary choice. No objection can be made to anyone's employing the concept of an instinct of play or of destruction, or that of a social instinct, when the subject demands it and the limitations of psychological analysis allow of it. Nevertheless, we should not neglect to ask whether such instinctual motives, which are in one direction so highly specialized, do not admit of further analysis in respect of their sources, so that only those primal instincts which are not to be resolved further could really lay claim to the name.

I have proposed that two groups of such primal instincts should be distinguished: the *self-preservative* or *ego*-instincts and the *sexual* instincts. But this proposition has not the weight of a necessary postulate, such as, for instance, our assumption about the biological 'purpose' in the mental apparatus (*v. supra*); it is merely an auxiliary construction, to be retained only so long as it proves useful, and it will make little difference to the results of our work of description and classification if we replace it by another. The occasion for it arose in the course of the evolution of psychoanalysis, which was first employed upon the psycho-neuroses, actually upon the group designated transference neuroses (hysteria and obsessional neurosis); through them it became plain that at the root of all such affections there lies a conflict between the claims of sexuality and those of the ego. It is always possible that an exhaustive study of the other neurotic affections (especially of the narcissistic psychoneuroses, the schizophrenias) may oblige us to alter this formula and therewith to make a different classification of the primal instincts. But for the present we do not know what this new formula may be, nor have we met with any argument which seems likely to be prejudicial to the contrast between sexual and ego-instincts.

3 K. Lorenz

An Energy Model of Instinctive Actions

Excerpts from K. Lorenz, 'The comparative method in studying innate behaviour patterns', *Symposia of the Society for Experimental Biology*, Cambridge University Press, Cambridge, 1950, Vol. 4, pp. 221–68.

At the level of superficial observation the innate behaviour patterns in question appeared reflex-like in that they were set off by a sort of 'trigger-action' in a very specific stimulus situation. But on closer inspection it became apparent that these activities are, at bottom, to a very high degree independent from external stimulation. Captive animals, deprived of the normal object or releasing situation of an innate behaviour pattern, will persist in discharging the same sequences of movements at a very inadequate substitute object or situation. The longer the normal stimulation is withheld, the less necessary it becomes, in order to set off the reaction, to supply *all* of the stimuli pertaining to it. The longer the reaction does not go off, the finer the trigger that releases it seems to become set. In other words, the threshold of the stimulation necessary to release this type of innate reaction is not a constant, but is undergoing a continuous process of lowering, going on throughout the time during which the reaction is not released. This gradual lowering of threshold does, in a good many cases, actually reach the theoretically possible limit of zero, that is, the activity in question will finally go off *in vacuo*, with an effect somewhat suggestive of the explosion of a boiler whose safety valve fails to function. This occurrence has been termed 'Leerlaufreaktion' in German, vacuum reaction and explosion reaction. I would move the general acceptance of Armstrong's (1942) term 'energy accumulation activity' for reasons discussed later.

The consequences of the 'damming up' of a certain innate activity are, however, not confined to the threshold of the mechanism (whatever that mechanism may be) which releases the activity. It is not only a facilitation of the releasing process, not only an increase of passive excitability that takes place, but, quite on the contrary, an active and peculiar excitation. Any one of these particular innate behaviour patterns, however small and unimportant it may seem in itself, develops into an active source of excitation which influences the whole of the organism whenever it finds its outlet blocked. In this case, the undischarged activity becomes a *motive* in the literal and original sense of the word, derivated from *movere*, 'to move'. In the simplest and most primitive case the organism shows undirected, 'random' loco-motion, *kineses* as we term it. In more highly differentiated types these kineses are interlaced with taxes orienting the organism's locomotion in space, or even with conditioned responses and all the most complicated and least analysed forms of animal and human behaviour, which, for lack of a better term, we are wont to describe as 'intelligent'. Though the activities thus elicited comprise the whole range of behaviour, from its simplest to its most complex form, they have one decisive character in common: they are all *purposive* in the sense which E. C. Tolman (1932) has given to this term, that is to say, they all tend to bring about, by *variable* movements, an *invariable* end or goal, and they go on until this goal is reached or the animal as a whole is exhausted. The invariable end or goal is represented by the releasing stimulus situation and, therewith, the discharge of the specific behaviour pattern that had been dammed up. The purposive behaviour striving for this discharge was called *appetitive* behaviour by Wallace Craig (1918); the behaviour pattern finally discharged was termed *consummatory action*.

The Method of Dual Quantification

A very considerable percentage of all animal activities consists of the typical successive links of appetitive behaviour, attainment of a desired stimulus situation, to which an innate releasing mechanism responds and sets off the discharge of accumulated endogenous action. In the vast majority of cases where we find an organism responding specifically and without previous experience to certain stimulus situations, closer investigation will reveal one or other of the innumerable variations to this theme, always leading up in one way or the other to the final discharge of consummatory actions. What we can objectively observe is exclusively this discharge. But this discharge is dependent upon two absolutely heterogeneous causal factors: (1) the level attained by the accumulated action-specific energy at the moment and (2) the effectiveness of external stimulation. None of these two factors is directly accessible to our observation. Absolutely identical reactions can result, in one case, from an extremely low level of endogenous accumulation and strong stimulation, and, in the other, from a high level of accumulated action-specific energy and a very weak external stimulation, or even, in the case of explosion activity, from internal factors alone, external stimulation not taking any part in the activity at all. . . .

The practical way of proceeding in experiments of dual quantification is obvious, after what has already been said. Presenting the animal with a given stimulus situation and recording the intensity of its reaction presents us, as I have explained, with an equation containing two unknowns: we do not know how much of the intensity recorded is due to internal accumulation of action-specific energy and how much is due to external stimulation. The obvious thing to do is to let *maximal* stimulation impinge upon the organism immediately after the first experiment, in order to see how much specific energy is 'left'. This already gives us a definite notion about the *relative* effectiveness of the stimulation supplied in the first experiment. What we are doing is best illustrated in a hydro-mechanic model which, in spite of its extreme crudeness and simplicity is able to symbolize a surprising wealth of facts really encountered in the reactions of animals. In Fig. 1 the tap *T* supplying a constant flow of liquid represents the endogenous production of action-specific energy; the liquid accumulated in the reservoir *R* represents the amount of this energy which is at the disposal of the organism at a given moment; the elevation attained by its upper level corresponds, at an inverse ratio, to the momentary threshold of the reaction. The cone-valve *V* represents the releasing mechanism, the inhibitory function of the higher centres being symbolized by the spring *S*. The scale-pan *SP* which is connected with the valve-shaft by a string acting over a pulley represents the perceptual sector of the releasing mechanism, the weight applied corresponds to the impinging stimulation. This arrangement is a good symbol of how the internal accumulation of action-specific energy, and the external stimulation are both acting in the same direction, both tending to open the valve. It can also easily and obviously represent the occurrence of explosion activity. The activity itself is represented by the spout discharged from the jet *J*. The intensity of the reaction is symbolized by the distance to which the jet springs, in other words, by the speed of the outflow. This automatically corresponds to the proven fact that the consumption of action-specific energy in the time unit is in direct proportion to the intensity of the reaction. The intensity of the reaction can be read on the scale *G*. To this apparatus we can easily attach a gadget exactly symbolizing the way in which a sequence of different movement patterns belonging to one scale of action-specific excitation is activated. A row of little funnels attached below the gradation will meet the case where, with the attaining of a higher level of excitation, the activities corresponding to lower levels are discontinued (as, for instance, in the taking-to-wing ceremony of the greylag goose). It is, however,

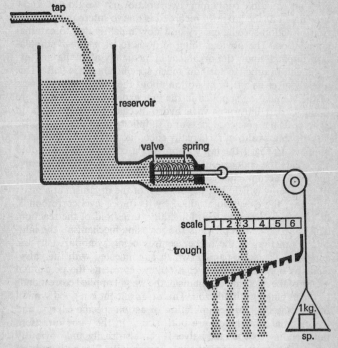

Figure 1

much more usual that the movements activated at the lowest levels of action-specific excitation are continued unceasingly all the while those corresponding to higher levels are discharged. We can symbolize this by fixing below the scale *G* an oblong trough *Tr* which has an oblique bottom perforated by a number of holes. The outflow from these holes then represents the intensity scale of a sequence of different activities, such as fin-spreading, gill-membrane expanding, etc. For reasons subsequently to be expounded, we have arranged the scale tray representing the receiving section of the innate releasing mechanism in such a manner as to let some of the ultimate flowing-out of liquid impinge on it in a diffuse way.

This contraption is, of course, still a very crude simplification of the real processes it is symbolizing, but experience has taught us that even the crudest simplisms often prove a valuable stimulus to investigation. As an instrument for the quantification of external and internal stimulation this model has already proved to be of some value. Let me explain its use. Suppose we present an organism with a stimulus of unknown effectiveness. All we can immediately record is, as already explained, the intensity of the reaction. In the terms of our model, we do not know what weight we have applied to the pan. In order to ascertain it, we must try to get some notion of the pressure pushing on the valve from the inside. The simplest way to do this is to open the valve altogether and record the distance which the spout delivered by the jet will now attain. In other words, we shall present our animal with the *normal* object of the reaction which may be roughly (though not theoretically) identified with its optimal object, and record the intensity of which the reaction is capable at the moment. Out of both data the relative effect of the first stimulus can be roughly calculated, as well as the pressure acting from within. In other words, we have now got two equations with two unknowns.

References

Armstrong, E. A., *Bird display*, Cambridge University Press, 1942.
Craig, W., Appetites and aversions as constituents of instincts. *Biol. Bull.*, Woods Hole, No. 2, 1918, 91–107.
Tolman, E. C., *Purposive behavior in animals and men.* (Century Psychol. Series), New York and London, 1932.

4 N. Tinbergen

Hierarchical Organization of Instinctive Actions

Excerpts from N. Tinbergen, *The Study of Instinct*, Oxford University Press, Oxford, 1951, Chapter 5. (These excerpts are reproduced here because of their historical interest and influence.
Tinbergen has revised his views since the publication of this book. For his recent views, see: Tinbergen, N., 'On aims and methods of ethology', *Zeitschrift für Tierpsychologie*, 20, 4, 1963, pp. 410–33.)

Hierarchical Organization

A closer study of differences in complexity leads us to the conclusion that the mechanisms underlying [instinctive] reactions are arranged in a hierarchical system, in which we must distinguish between various levels of integration.

The reproductive behaviour of the male stickleback may be taken as an example.

In spring, the gradual increase in length of day brings the males into a condition of increased reproductive motivation, which drives them to migrate into shallow fresh water. Here, as we have seen, a rise in temperature, together with a visual stimulus situation received from a suitable territory, releases the reproductive pattern as a whole. The male settles on the territory, its erythrophores expand, it reacts to strangers by fighting, and starts to build a nest. Now, whereas both nest-building and fighting depend on activation of the reproductive drive as a whole, no observer can predict which one of the two patterns will be shown at any given moment. Fighting, for instance, has to be released by a specific stimulus, viz. 'red male intruding into the territory'. Building is not released by this stimulus situation but depends on other stimuli. Thus these two activities, though both depend on activation of the reproductive drive as a whole, are also dependent on additional (external) factors. The influence of these latter factors is, however, restricted; they act upon either fighting or building, not on the reproductive drive as a whole.

Now the stimulus situation 'red male intruding', while releasing the fighting drive, does not determine which one of the five types of fighting will be shown. This is determined by additional, still more specific stimuli. For instance, when the stranger bites, the owner of the territory will bite in return; when the stranger threatens, the owner will threaten back; when the stranger flees, the owner will chase it; and so on.

Thus the effect of a stimulus situation on the animal may be of different kinds. The visual stimulus 'suitable territory' activates both fighting and nest-building; the visual situation 'red male in territory' is specific in releasing fighting, but it merely causes a general readiness to fight and does not determine the type of fighting. Which one of the five motor responses belonging to the fighting pattern will be shown depends on sign stimuli that are still more restricted in effect. The tactile stimulus 'male biting' releases one type of fighting, the visual stimulus 'male threatening' another type. The stimulus situations are not of an essentially different order in all these cases, but the results are. They belong to different levels of integration and, moreover, they are organized in a hierarchical system, like the staff organization of an army or of other human organizations. The facts (1) that at each of the levels an external stimulus can have a specific releasing influence and (2) that each reaction has its own motor pattern mean that there is a hierarchical system of IRMs (Innate Releasing Mechanisms). . . .

Appetitive Behaviour and Consummatory Activity

The distinction between appetitive behaviour and consummatory act separates the behaviour as a whole into two components of entirely different character. The consummatory act is relatively simple; at its most complex, it is a chain of reactions, each of which may be a simultaneous combination of a taxis and a fixed pattern. But appetitive behaviour is a true purposive activity, offering all the problems of plasticity, adaptiveness, and of complex integration that baffle the scientist in his study of behaviour as a whole. Appetitive behaviour is a conglomerate of many elements of very different order, of reflexes, of simple patterns like locomotion, of conditioned reactions, of 'insight' behaviour, and so on. As a result it is a true challenge to objective science, and therefore the discrimination between appetitive behaviour and consummatory act is but a first step of our analysis.

A consideration of the relationships between appetitive behaviour and consummatory act is important for our understanding of the nature of striving in animals. It is often stressed that animals are striving towards the attainment of a certain end or goal. Lorenz has pointed out not only that purposiveness, the striving towards an end, is typical only of appetitive behaviour and not of consummatory actions, but also that the end of purposive behaviour is not the attainment of an object or a situation itself, but the performance of the consummatory action, which is attained as a consequence of the animal's arrival at an external situation which provides the special sign stimuli releasing the consummatory act. Even psychologists who have watched hundreds of rats running a maze rarely realize that, strictly speaking, it is not the litter or the food the animal is striving towards, but the performance itself of the maternal activities or eating.

Holzapfel (1940) has shown that there is one apparent exception to this rule: appetitive behaviour may also lead to rest or sleep. As I hope to show further below, this exception is only apparent, because rest and sleep are true consummatory actions, dependent on activation of a centre exactly as with other consummatory actions.

Whereas the consummatory act seems to be dependent on the centres of the lowest level of instinctive behaviour, appetitive behaviour may be activated by centres of all the levels above that of the consummatory act. As has been pointed out by Baerends (1941), appetitive behaviour by no means always leads directly to the performance of a consummatory act. For instance, the hunting of a peregrine falcon usually begins with relatively random roaming around its hunting territory, visiting and exploring many different places miles apart. This first phase of appetitive behaviour may lead to different ways of catching prey, each dependent on special stimulation by a potential prey. It is continued until such a special stimulus situation is found: a flock of teal executing flight manoeuvres, a sick gull swimming apart from the flock, or even a running mouse. Each of these situations may cause the falcon to abandon its 'random' searching. But what follows then is not yet a consummatory action, but appetitive behaviour of a new, more specialized and more restricted kind. The flock of teal releases a series of sham attacks serving to isolate one or a few individuals from the main body of the flock. Only after this is achieved, is the final swoop released, followed by capturing, killing, plucking, and eating, which is a relatively simple and stereotyped chain of consummatory acts. The sick gull may provoke the release of sham attacks tending to force it to fly up; if this fails the falcon may deftly pick it up from the water surface. A small mammal may release simple straightforward approach and subsequent capturing, &c. Thus we see that the generalized appetitive behaviour was continued until a special stimulus situation interrupted the random searching and released one of the several possible and more specific types of appetitive behaviour. This in its turn was continued until the changing stimulus situation released the swoop, a still more specific type of appetitive behaviour, and this finally led to the chain of consummatory acts.

Baerends (1941) came to the same conclusion in his analysis of the behaviour of the digger wasp *Ammophila campestris* and probably the principle will be found to be generally applicable. It seems, therefore, that the centres of each level of the hierarchical system control a type of appetitive behaviour. This is more generalized in the higher levels and more restricted or more specialized in the lower levels. The transition from higher to lower, more specialized types of appetitive behaviour is brought about by special stimuli which alone are able to direct the impulses to one of the lower centres, or rather to allow them free passage to this lower centre. This stepwise descent of the activation from relatively higher to relatively lower centres eventually results in the stimulation of a centre or a series of centres of the level of the consummatory act, and here the impulse is finally used up.

This hypothesis of the mechanism of instinctive behaviour, though supported by relatively few and very fragmentary facts and still tentative therefore, seems to cover the reality better than any theory thus far advanced. Its concreteness gives it a high heuristic value, and it is to be hoped that continued research in the near future will follow these lines and fill in, change, and adapt the sketchy frame. . . .

Neurophysiological Facts

It is of great importance for our understanding of instinctive behaviour as a whole to realize that the various instincts are not independent of each other. We have rejected the reflex hypothesis of behaviour and we have seen that each instinctive mechanism is constantly primed, that is to say, prepared to come into action. Such a system can only work because blocking mechanisms prevent the animal from performing continuous chaotic movements.

Now chaos is further prevented by another principle, viz. that of inhibition between centres of the same level. As a rule, an animal can scarcely do 'two things at a time'. Although there is a certain amount of synchronous activity of two instincts, this is only possible at low motivation, and, as a rule, the strong activation of instinctive behaviour of one kind prevents the functioning of another pattern. Thus an animal in which the sexual drive is strong is much less than normally susceptible to stimuli that normally release flight or eating. On the other hand, when flight is released, the thresholds of the reproductive and feeding activities are raised. The same relationship of mutual inhibition seems to exist between centres of lower levels. Intensive nest-building, for instance, renders the male stickleback much less susceptible than usual to stimuli normally releasing fighting, and vice versa. . . .

Another set of interrelations, though in itself perhaps not of primary importance in the organization of behaviour, has to be considered now: those revealed by the occurrence of 'displacement activity'. This phenomenon will be discussed in some detail, because it is not generally known and yet seems to be of great importance for our understanding of the neurophysiological background of instinct.

It has struck many observers that animals may, under certain circumstances, perform movements which do not belong to the motor pattern of the instinct that is activated at the moment of observation. For instance, fighting domestic cocks may suddenly pick at the ground, as if they were feeding. Fighting European starlings may vigorously preen their feathers. Courting birds of paradise wipe their bills now and then. Herring gulls, while engaged in deadly combat, may all at once pluck nesting material, &c. In all the observed instances the animal gives the impression of being very strongly motivated ('nervous'). Rand (1943) has called such movements 'irrelevant' movements. Makkink (1936) gave an implied interpretation by using the term 'sparking-over movements', suggesting that impulses are 'sparking over' on another 'track'. Kirkman (1937) used the term 'substitute activities' which I adopted in 1939 (Tinbergen, 1939). Later the term 'displacement activity' was proposed (Tinbergen and van Iersel, 1947; Armstrong, 1948), and this term will be used here.

The phenomenon has been clearly recognized and analysed independently by Kortlandt (1940a) and by Tinbergen (1939, 1940). An examination of the conditions under which displacement activities usually occur led to the conclusion that, in all known cases, there is a surplus of motivation, the discharge of which through the normal paths is in some way prevented. The most usual situations are: (1) conflict of two strongly activated antagonistic drives; (2) strong motivation of a drive, usually the sexual drive, together with lack of external stimuli required for the release of the consummatory acts belonging to that drive.

The fact that a displacement activity is an expression, not of its 'own' drive (of autochthonous motivation 'as Kortlandt (1940) called it) but of a 'strange' drive (of allochthonous motivation), makes it possible for it to act as a signal to fellow members of the same species, provided it can be distinguished from the 'genuine' activity, activated by its 'own' drive. As a matter of fact, many displacement activities are different from their 'models' and do act as signals. Thus displacement digging in sticklebacks is actually understood by other sticklebacks as a threat (as an expression of the fighting drive); it is different from its 'model', true digging, in that the spines are erected.

References

Armstrong, E. A., 1947: Bird Display and Behaviour. Cambridge.

Baerends, G. P., 1941: Fortpflanzungsverhalten und Orientierung der Grabwespe Ammophila campestris. Jur. Tijdschr. Entomol., 84, 68–275.

Holzapfel, M., 1940: Triebbedingte Ruhezustände als Ziel von Appetenzverhalten. Naturwiss. 28, 273–80.

Kirkman, F. B., 1937: Bird Behaviour. London-Edinburgh.

Kortlandt, A., 1940a: Wechselwirkung zwischen Instinkten. Arch. néerl. Zoöl. 4, 442–520.

Makkink, G. F., 1936: An attempt at an ethogram of the European avocet (Recurvirostra avosetta L.) with ethological and psychological remarks. Ardea. 25, 1–60.

Rand, A. L., 1943: Some irrelevant behavior in birds. Auk, 60, 168–71.

Tinbergen, N., 1939a: The behavior of the Snow Bunting in spring. Trans. Linn. Soc. N.Y. 5.

Tinbergen, N., 1940: Die Übersprungbewegung. Zs. Tierpsychol. 4, 1–40.

Tinbergen, N., & J. J. A. van Iersel, 1947: 'Displacement reactions' in the three-spined stickleback. Behaviour, 1, 56–63.

5 R. A. Hinde

Critique of Energy Models of Motivation

An abridged version of R. A. Hinde, 'Energy models of motivation',
Symposia of the Society for Experimental Biology, Cambridge
University Press, Cambridge, 1960, Vol. 14, pp. 199–213.

Introduction

The problem of motivation is central to the understanding of
behaviour. Why, in the absence of learning and fatigue, does the
response to a constant stimulus change from time to time? To
what is the apparent spontaneity of behaviour due? This paper is
concerned with one type of model which has been developed to
help answer such questions – namely that in which changes in the
organism's activity are ascribed to changes in the quantity or
distribution of an entity comparable to physical, chemical or
electrical energy.

Such models have been developed by theoreticians with widely
differing backgrounds, interests and aims, and the frameworks of
ideas built round them diverge in many respects; but in each case
the energy treatment of motivation is a central theme (cf. Carthy,
1951; Kennedy, 1954). They have had a great influence on psychological thought, and although they are unlikely to continue to
be useful, it is instructive to examine their nature, their achieve-
ments and their limitations.

The Models

The four models or theories to be discussed here are those of
Freud, McDougall, Lorenz and Tinbergen. They are only four of
many in which energy concepts are used, but in them the energy
analogy is made explicit in terms of a mechanical model, instead
of being merely implied by a 'drive' variable which is supposed to
energize behaviour. The models were designed to account for
many features of behaviour in addition to the phenomena of
motivation, and here it will be necessary to extract only those
aspects relevant to the present theme.

In the psycho-analytic model (Freud, 1932, 1940) the id is
pictured as a chaos of instinctive energies which are supposed to
originate from some source of stimulation within the body. Their
control is in the hands of the ego, which permits, postpones or

denies their satisfaction. In this the ego may be dominated by the super-ego. The energy with which Freud was particularly concerned – the sexual energy or libido – is supposed not to require immediate discharge. It can be postponed, repressed, sublimated, and so on. The source of this energy lies in different erogenous zones as the individual develops, being successively oral, anal and phallic, and it is in relation to these changes that the individual develops his responses to the external world. The instinctual energy is supposed to undergo various vicissitudes, discussions of which often imply that it can be stored, or that it can flow like a fluid. It may become attached to objects represented by mental structures or processes (libidinal cathexes) and later withdrawn from them in a manner that Freud (1940) likened to protoplasmic pseudopodia: it has also been compared with an electric charge. Thus some of the characteristics of the energy depend on its quantitative distribution.

McDougall (1913) envisaged energy liberated on the afferent side of the nervous system, and held back by 'sluice gates'. If the stimuli necessary to open the gates are not forthcoming, the energy 'bubbles over' among the motor mechanisms to produce appetitive behaviour. On receipt of appropriate stimuli, one of the gates opens, and the afferent channels of this instinct become the principal outlet for all available free energy. Later (1923) he used a rather more complex analogy in which each instinct was pictured as a chamber in which gas is constantly liberated. The gas can escape via pipes leading to the executive organs when the appropriate lock(s) is opened. The gas is supposed to drive the motor mechanisms, just as an electric motor is driven by electrical energy.

The models of Lorenz and Tinbergen have much in common with McDougall's. Lorenz's 'reaction specific energy' was earlier (1937) thought of as a gas constantly being pumped into a container, and later (e.g. 1950) as a liquid in a reservoir. In the latter case it is supposed that the reservoir can discharge through a spring-loaded valve at the bottom. The valve is opened in part by the hydrostatic pressure in the reservoir, and in part by a weight on a scale pan which represents the external stimulus. As the reservoir discharges, the hydrostatic pressure on the valve decreases, and thus a greater weight is necessary to open the valve again.

Tinbergen (1951) pictured a hierarchy of nervous centres, each of which has the properties of a Lorenzian reservoir. Each centre can be loaded with 'motivational impulses' from a superordinated centre and/or other sources. Until the appropriate stimulus is given the outflow is blocked and the animal can show only appetitive behaviour; when the block is removed the impulses can flow into the subordinate centre or be discharged in action.

It is important to emphasize again that the theories of these authors have little in common except for the energy model of motivation – they were devised for different purposes, and the more recent authors have been at pains to emphasize their differences from the earlier ones. For instance, for McDougall the most important feature of instinct was the 'conative-affective core', while for Lorenz it was the stereotyped motor pattern. Furthermore, the models differ greatly in the precision with which they are defined. The Freudian model is a loose one: its flexibility is perhaps necessary in view of the great range of behavioural and mental phenomena it comprehends, but makes it very difficult to test. The other models are more tightly defined, but differ, as we shall see, in their supposed relations to the nervous system.

In spite of such differences, all these models share the idea of a substance, capable of energizing behaviour, held back in a container and subsequently released in action. In the discussion which follows, I shall be little concerned with the other details of the models, or with the ways in which the theories based on them differ. Furthermore, I shall disregard the niceties of terminology, lumping instinctual energy, psychophysical energy, action specific energy and motivational impulses together as, for present purposes, basically similar concepts.

Reality Status of the Models

Until recently, students of the more complex types of behaviour could get little help from physiology, and had to fashion their concepts without reference to the properties of the nervous system. Many, indeed, advocated this course from preference, either on grounds of expediency, suggesting that knowledge of the nervous system was still too primitive and might be misleading, or on principle, claiming that physiology and behaviour were distinct levels of discourse. At present the models and theories used in attempts to understand, explain or predict behaviour range from those whose nature is such that physiological data are irrelevant (Skinner, 1938) to those which consist of a forthright attempt to describe psychological data in physiological terms (Hebb, 1947, 1955). The former type may be applicable over a wide range of phenomena, but only at a limited range of analytical levels: the latter may point the way to analysis at lower levels, but their expectancy of life depends on their compatibility with the phenomena found there.

The originators of all the models discussed here regard them as having some relation to structures in the nervous system, but vary in the emphasis which they lay on this. Tinbergen, although freely emphasizing the hypothetical status of his model, clearly regards his 'centres' as neural structures, and his 'motivational impulses' as related to nerve impulses. He speaks of his hierarchical scheme as a 'graphic picture of the nervous mechanisms involved'. McDougall likewise regards the relationship between model and nervous system as a close one, for he localizes the 'sluice gates' in the optic thalamus. Lorenz, on the other hand, usually treated his model in an 'as if' fashion – he did not suggest that we should look for reservoirs in the body. He did, however, bring forward physiological evidence in its support – quoting, for instance, Sherrington's work (1906) on spinal contrast, and von Holst's (1936) work on endogenous rhythms in fishes; and he sometimes uses such terms as 'central nervous impulse flow' as a synonym for 'reaction specific energy'. His use of physiological evidence was, however, *post hoc* – the model was based on behavioural data and the physiological evidence came later.

Freud's model developed from physiology, in particular from a sensory-excitation–motor-discharge picture of nervous function, and its basic postulates are almost a direct translation of such ideas into psychological terms – excitation into mental energy, the discharges of excitation into pleasure, and so on (Peters, 1958). However, Freudian theory developed far beyond these primitive notions, and then bore little or no relation to physiology, even though the instincts were supposed to have an ultimately physiological source.

Thus two of these models (Tinbergen and McDougall) had explicitly physiological implications; that of Lorenz was usually used in an 'as if' fashion; and Freud's, although it had physiological roots, became divorced from any supposed structures or functions in the nervous system. However, as we shall see, all have been influenced by the covert introduction of existence postulates concerning the explanatory concepts used.

Difficulties and Dangers

In the following paragraphs we shall consider some of the difficulties and dangers inherent in the use of an energy model of motivation. These arise in part from misunderstandings of the nature of the model, and in part from incompatibilities between the properties of the model and those of the original.

(i) *Confusion between behavioural energy and physical energy*

We have already seen that behavioural energy, postulated to account for changes in activity, need share no properties with physical energy. Not only is there no necessary reason why it should be treated as an entity with any of the properties of physical energy, but the question of its convertibility into physical energy is a dangerous red herring. The way in which the properties of the model may be confused with those of the original have been discussed for Freudian theory by Meehl & MacCorquodale (1948). Concepts like libido or super-ego may be introduced initially as intervening variables without material properties, but such properties have a way of creeping into discussion without being made explicit. Thus Meehl & MacCorquodale point out that libido may be introduced as a term for the 'set of sexual needs' or 'basic strivings', but subsequently puzzling phenomena are explained in terms of properties of libido, such that it flows, is dammed up, converted, regresses to earlier channels, and so on. Such properties are introduced surreptitiously as occasion demands, and involve a transition from admissible intervening variables, which carry no existence postulates, to hypothetical constructs which require the existence of decidedly improbable entities and processes.

Such difficulties are especially likely to occur when a model which purports to be close to the original, like that of Tinbergen, develops out of an 'as if' model, like that of Lorenz. This case has been discussed elsewhere (Hinde, 1956). To quote but one example, ethologists have called behaviour patterns which appear out of their functional context 'displacement activities'. These activities usually appear when there is reason to think that one or more types of motivation are strong, but unable to find expression in action: instead, the animal shows a displacement activity, which seems to be irrelevant. Thus when a chaffinch has conflicting tendencies to approach and avoid a food dish, it may show preening behaviour. Such irrelevant activities were explained on the energy model by supposing that the thwarted energy 'sparked over' into the displacement activity – sparking over being a property of (electrical) energy which was imputed to the behavioural energy. This idea hindered an analytical study of the causal factors underlying displacement behaviour. Thus it has recently become apparent that many displacement activities are not so causally irrelevant as they appear to be, for those factors which elicit the behaviour in its normal functional context are also present when it appears as a displacement activity. For example, some displacement activities appear to be due to autonomic activity aroused as a consequence of fear-provoking stimuli or other aspects of the situation. The displacement activity may consist of the autonomic response itself (e.g. feather postures in birds) or of a somatic response to stimuli consequent upon autonomic activity (Andrew, 1956; Morris, 1956). In other cases the displacement behaviour consists of a response to factors continuously present, which was previously inhibited through the greater priority of the incompatible behaviour patterns which are in conflict (van Iersel & Bol, 1958; Rowell, 1959). Of course it remains possible that the intensity of the apparently irrelevant behaviour is influenced by factors not specific to it, including those associated with the conflicting tendencies (see also Hinde, 1959).

Similarly in psychoanalytic theory we find not only that within one category of instincts (e.g. sexual) the constituent instincts can change their aim, but also that 'they can replace one another – the energy of one instinct passing over to another' (Freud, 1940). Explanations of this type may be useful at a descriptive level, but are misleading as analysis proceeds.

(ii) *The distinction between the accumulation and release of energy*

In all energy models, the energy is supposed to build up and subsequently to be released in action. McDougall, Lorenz and Tinbergen, all of whom were influenced by Wallace Craig, compare the releasing stimulus to a key which opens a lock. This apparent dichotomy between releasing and motivating effects is a property of the model, and may not be relevant to the mechanisms underlying behaviour. Although many factors appear to have both a motivating and a releasing effect on the responses they affect – they appear both to cause an increase in responsiveness, and to elicit the response – this does not necessarily imply that two distinct processes are at work. For example, if a given input increased the probability of a certain pattern of neural firing, it might appear in behaviour both that the responsiveness was increased and that the behaviour was elicited.

This sort of difficulty is the more likely to arise, the more precisely the model is portrayed. Thus McDougall, who did not work out his model in such detail as Lorenz and Tinbergen, implied that motivation and release were in fact one process when he wrote 'The evoking of the instinctive action, the opening of the door of the instinct on perception of its specific object, increases the urgency of the appetite'.

(iii) *Implications about the cessation of activity*

In all these theories, the cessation of activity is ascribed to the discharge of energy – the behavioural energy flows away as a consequence of performance. Influenced by the analogy with physical energy, Freud held that the main function of the nervous system is to reduce excitation to the lowest possible level. McDougall, Lorenz and Tinbergen imply a similar view, and the two latter emphasize that it is the performance of more or less stereotyped motor patterns which involve the discharge of the energy.

This view of the cessation of activities comes naturally from models in which the properties of physical energy are imputed to behavioural energy. It is, however, also supported by another type of argument, also involving a *non sequitur*. Much behaviour is related to an increase in stimulation. Therefore, it might be argued, all activity is due to an increase in stimulation, and cessation of activity is related to a decrease. On an energy model, stimulation may increase the energy, and thus a decrease in activity is related to a decrease in energy.

Such a view is incompatible with the data now available on two grounds. First, cessation of activity may be due to the animal encountering a 'goal' stimulus situation, and not to the performance of an activity. If this goal stimulus situation is encountered abnormally early, the behaviour which normally leads to it may not appear at all. McDougall recognized this, and indeed defined his instincts in terms of the goals which brought about a cessation of activity. This, however, made it necessary for him to be rather inconsistent about his energy model. While the energy was supposed to drive the motor mechanisms, it was apparently not consumed in action, but could flow back to other reservoirs or to the general source. The more precisely described Lorenz/Tinbergen models, on the other hand, do not allow for reduction in activity by consummatory stimuli: reduction in responsiveness occurs only through the discharge of energy in action. These models are misleading because they are too simple – energy flow is supposed to control not only what happens between stimulus and response, but also the drop in responsiveness when the response is given. In practice, these may be due to quite different aspects of the mechanisms underlying behaviour:

for instance the energy model leaves no room for inhibition (Kennedy, 1954). Further, even if the cessation of activity is in some sense due to the performance, many different processes may be involved: the mechanism is not a unitary one, as the energy model implies (see below).

Secondly, if activity is due to the accumulation of energy and cessation to its discharge, the organisms should come to rest when the energy level is minimal. In fact, much behaviour serves the function of bringing the animal into conditions of increased stimulation. This has been shown dramatically with humans subjected to acute sensory deprivation – the experimental conditions are intolerable in spite of the considerable financial reward offered (Bexton, Heron & Scott, 1954). Energy theories are in difficulty over accounting for such 'reactions to deficit' (Lashley, 1938).

(iv) *Unitary nature of explanation*

In these energy models, each type of behaviour is related to the flow of energy. Increase in strength of the behaviour is due to an increased flow of energy, decrease to a diminished flow. The strength of behaviour is thus related to a single mechanism. It is, however, apparent that changes in responsiveness to a constant stimulus may be due to many different processes in the nervous system and in the body as a whole – for instance, the changes consequent upon performance may affect one response or many, may or may not be specific to the stimulus, and may have recovery periods varying from seconds to months. Energy models, by lumping together diverse processes which affect the strength of behaviour, can lead to an over-simplification of the mechanisms underlying it, and distract attention from the complexities of the behaviour itself. Similarly, energy models are in difficulty with the almost cyclic short-term waxing and waning of such activities as the response of chaffinches to owls, the song of many birds, and so on.

Kubie (1947) has emphasized this point with reference to the psychoanalytic model. Changes in behaviour are referred to quantitative changes in energy distribution, but in fact so many variables are involved (repression, displacement, substitution, etc.) that it is not justifiable to make easy guesses about what varied to produce a given state. Similar difficulties in relation to other models have been discussed by Hinde (1959).

Precht (1952) has elaborated the Lorenzian model to allow for some complication of this sort. Analysing the changes in strength of the hunting behaviour of spiders, he distinguishes between 'drive' which depends on deprivation, and 'excitatory level', which is a function of non-release of the eating pattern. The distinction is an important one, but it may be doubted whether the elaborate hydraulic system which he produced is really an aid to further analysis.

Tinbergen's model translated the Lorenzian reservoir into nervous 'centres'. Changes in response strength are ascribed to the loading of these centres. Now for many types of behaviour it is indeed possible to identify *loci* in the diencephalon whose ablation leads to the disappearance of the behaviour, whose stimulation leads to its elicitation, and where hormones or solutions produce appropriate effects on behaviour. There is, however, no evidence that 'energy' is accumulated in such centres, nor that response strength depends solely on their state. Indeed the strength of any response depends on many structures, neural and non-neural, and there is no character-by-character correspondence between such postulated centres and any structure in the brain.

Although the greatest attraction of these energy models is their simplicity – a relatively simple mechanical model accounting for diverse properties of behaviour – there is a danger in this, for one property of the model may correspond to more than one character of the original. This difficulty has in fact arisen in many behaviour systems irrespective of whether they use an energy model of motivation. Thus a single drive variable is sometimes used not only with reference to changes in responsiveness to a constant stimulus, but also to spontaneity, temporal persistence of the effects of the stimuli, after-responses (i.e. the persistence of activities after the stimulus is removed), the temporal grouping of functionally related activities, and so on. As discussed elsewhere (Hinde, 1959), there is no *a priori* reason why these diverse characters of behaviour should depend on a single feature of the underlying mechanism: an over-simple model may hinder analysis.

(v) *Independence of activities*

Another difficulty which arises from the use of energy models, though by no means peculiar to them, is due to the emphasis laid on the independence of different activities. Lorenz & Tinbergen (1938) write 'If ever we may say that only part of an organism is involved in a reaction, it may confidently be said of instinctive action'. Activities are interpreted as due to energies acting in specific structures, and not as responses of the organisms as a whole. Both types of attitude carry disadvantages, but an over-emphasis on the independence of activities leads to a neglect of, for instance, sensory, metabolic or temperamental factors which affect many activities.

Is an Energy Concept Necessary?

We have seen that these energy models will account for diverse properties of behaviour, but that they meet with serious difficulties when the behaviour is analysed more closely. They have also been strangely sterile in leading to bridgeheads with physiology. These shortcomings of energy models have been emphasized by a number of other writers (e.g. Kubie, 1947; Deutsch, 1953; Bowlby, 1958). Energy concepts are useful in descriptions of changes in behaviour, but are they necessary? Colby states that 'a dynamic psychology must conceive of psychic activities as the product of forces, and forces involve energy sums. It is thus quite necessary that metapsychology have some sort of energy theory'. Is this really so?

Kubie (1947) has pointed out that psychological phenomena are the product of an interplay of diverse factors. A rearrangement of these factors can alter the pattern of behaviour without any change in hypothetical stores of energy. Such a view is in harmony with the known facts about the functioning of the nervous system. The central nervous system is not normally inert, having to be prodded into activity by specific stimuli external to it. Rather it is in a state of continuous activity – a state supported primarily by the non-specific effects of stimuli acting through the brainstem reticular system. Factors such as stimuli and hormones which affect specific patterns of behaviour are to be thought of as controlling this activity, of increasing the probability of one pattern rather than another. Changes in strength or threshold can thus be thought of as changes in the probability of one pattern of activity rather than another, and not as changes in the level of energy in a specific neural mechanism. This involves some return to a 'telephone exchange' theory of behaviour, but with emphasis on the non-specific input necessary to keep the switch mechanism active, and with switches which are not all-or-none, but determine the probability of one pattern rather than another. Furthermore, switching does not depend solely on external stimuli – i.e. we are not concerned with a purely reflexological model. This is not the place to pursue this view further: it suffices to say that it seems possible and preferable to formulate behaviour theories in which concepts of energy, and of drives which energize behaviour, have no role.

DRIVE AS INSTINCTIVE ENERGY

References

Andrew, R. J. (1956). Some remarks on conflict situations, with special reference to *Emberiza* spp. *Brit. J. Anim. Behav.* 4, 41–45.

Bexton, W. H., Heron, W. & Scott, T. H. (1954). Effects of decreased variation in the sensory environment. *Canad. J. Psychol.* 8, 70–76.

Bowlby, J. (1958). The nature of the child's tie to his mother. *Internat. J. Psychoanalysis*, 39.

Carthy, J. D. (1951). Instinct. *New Biology*, 10, 95–105.

Colby, K. M. (1955). *Energy and Structure in Psychoanalysis*. New York: Ronald Press Co.

Deutsch, J. A. (1953). A new type of behaviour theory. *Brit. J. Psychol.* 44, 304–317.

Freud, S. (1932). *New Introductory Lectures on Psychoanalysis*. London: Hogarth Press, 1946.

Freud, S. (1940). *An Outline of Psychoanalysis*. New York. London: Hogarth Press, 1949.

Hebb, D. O. (1949). *The Organization of Behaviour*. New York: Wiley.

Hebb, D. O. (1955). Drives and the C.N.S. (Conceptual Nervous System). *Psych. Rev.* 62, 243–254.

Hinde, R. A. (1956). Ethological models and the concept of drive. *Brit. J. Philos. Sci.* 6, 321–331.

Hinde, R. A. (1959). Unitary drives. *Anim. Behav.* 7, 130–141.

Holst, E. von (1936). Versuche zur Theorie der relativen Koordination. *Pflüg. Arch. ges. Physiol.* 237, 93–121.

Iersel, J. J. A. van & Bol, A. C. (1958). Preening of two tern species. A study on displacement. *Behaviour* 13, 1–89.

Kennedy, J. S. (1954). Is modern ethology objective? *Brit. J. Anim. Behav.* 2, 12–19.

Kubie, L. S. (1947). The fallacious use of quantitative concepts in dynamic psychology. *Psychoanalytic Quart.* 16, 507–518.

Lashley, K. S. (1938). Experimental analysis of instinctive behaviour. *Psychol. Rev.* 45, 445–471.

Lorenz, K. (1937). Über die Bildung des Instinktbegriffes. *Naturwiss* 25, 289–300, 307–318, 324–331.

Lorenz, K. (1950). The comparative method in studying innate behaviour patterns. *Sym. Soc. Exp. Biol.* IV, 221–268.

Lorenz, K. & Tinbergen, N. (1938). Taxis und Instinkthandlung in der Eirollbewegung der Graugans. *Z. Tierpsychol.* 2, 1–29. Translated in Schiller, C. H. (1957). *Instinctive Behaviour*. London: Methuen.

McDougall, W. (1913). The sources and direction of psychophysical energy. *Amer. J. Insanity.* Not consulted. Quoted in McDougall (1923).

McDougall, W. (1923). *An Outline of Psychology*. London: Methuen.

Meehl, P. E. & MacCorquodale, K. (1948). On a distinction between hypothetical constructs and intervening variables. *Psych. Rev.* 55, 95–107.

Morris, D. (1956). The feather postures of birds and the problem of the origin of social signals. *Behaviour* 9, 75–113.

Peters, R. S. (1958). *The Concept of Motivation*. London: Routledge and Kegan Paul.

Precht, H. (1952). Über das angeborene Verhalten von Tieren. Versuche an Springspinnen. *Z. Tierpsychol.* 9, 207–230.

Rowell, C. H. F. (1959). The occurrence of grooming in the behaviour of

Chaffinches in approach-avoidance conflict situations, and its bearing on the concept of 'displacement activity'. *Ph.D. Thesis*. Cambridge.

Sherrington, C. S. (1906). *Integrative Action of the Nervous System*. New York: Scribner.

Skinner, B. F. (1938). *The Behaviour of Organisms*. New York: Appleton Century.

Tinbergen, N. (1951). *The Study of Instinct*. Oxford.

6 H. W. Nissen

Instinct as Seen by a Psychologist

Reproduced in full from H. W. Nissen, 'Instinct as seen by a psychologist'. In W. C. Allee, H. W. Nissen, and M. F. Nimkoff, 'A re-examination of the concept of instinct', *Psychological Review*, 1953, Vol. 60, pp. 287–97.

As Dr Allee has shown, many animals exhibit complex patterns of behavior, constant for the species and apparently unlearned, which need a name to set them off descriptively from other behaviors. In the first part of my discussion I shall try to relate the term 'instinct,' as designation for these uniformities, to certain other concepts, such as reflex, habit, and drive. These considerations will lead to the conclusion that 'instinct' has real but limited usefulness, and to the suggestion that all behaviors may be ordered on a continuum of possible associations which are more and less readily learned.

My second point will be a criticism of the current tendency to oversimplify the problem of motivation by organizing all behavior under half a dozen biogenic drives or instincts plus a few psychogenic or secondary drives. This part of the discussion will be illustrated by recent observations of the development of sex behavior in chimpanzees.

Terms referring to the dynamic or energizing aspect of behavior must be kept sharply separate from those pertaining to the form or pattern of the behavior itself. Confusion between the two has been responsible for much of the misunderstanding and controversy about instinct and persists even today: Tinbergen, 1951, presents a diagram of 'the hierarchical organization of instincts' which looks like the flow chart of a military chain of command. The top brass – that is, the top instinct – decides the strategy, lower centers direct the tactics, and the lowest-level instincts do the work. The 'instinct of pugnacity' refers both to the motivation to fight, and to the manner or pattern of fighting. The term is useful only in the latter sense, which is the way I shall use it here.

The dynamic factor in behavior has been given various names, the most common one, perhaps, being 'drive'. Morgan has termed it 'the central motive state', or CMS, and I have called it the 'sensitizing component of behavior determination'. The drive or sensitizing factor elicits behavior which is often such as to increase or decrease the amount of a certain kind of stimulation. Thus the earthworm may orient away from the source of light, whereas the Euglena may swim towards the light. Instead of deriving from the external environment, the stimulation may arise internally: the organism sneezes, defecates, or urinates. In other cases, the effective condition is a surplus or deficiency of chemicals in the bloodstream, presumably sensitizing certain parts of the nervous system. In still other cases, the mechanism of the energizing factor is completely unknown. You will note that I am postulating a sensitizing factor in all behavior, whether it is of external or internal origin, and whether it leads to behavior as simple as a reflex or as complicated as nest-building.

Now the behavior which ensues when a sensitizing factor is active may differ in various ways. Most obviously, it may be all over in a moment, or it may last a long time. When the goal or situation which brings relief is immediately present, the response is prompt and brief; we call it an unconditioned or conditioned reflex, tropism or taxis, or automatized habit. When the goal object or situation is not at hand, a more or less prolonged series of acts occurs. Duration in time is therefore one differentiating criterion. Further, a reflex typically is elicited by a specific, localized stimulus, whereas an instinct is usually determined by a combination of internal factors plus a *class* of external stimulus patterns which, in their details, may vary considerably. On the response side, a reflex implies contraction of a particular muscle or muscle group, whereas instinctive behavior allows considerable leeway in the effector mechanisms by which a common effect is achieved.

In the absence of the goal or drive-reducing situation, the organism is forced to an indirect, extended series of acts. These longer sequences may be classified into five categories, in accordance with information available to us regarding *how* the form of that behavior was determined: (a) When little or no direction or selectivity is in evidence, we speak of 'random' or 'spontaneous' activity. (b) When innately determined components are conspicuous, we call the sequence an 'instinct'. (c) When learning has determined the pattern, we call it a 'complex habit'. (d) When there is evidence of reasoning and foresight, we speak of 'purposive striving' or 'goal-directed' activity. (e) When we want to remain neutral about the role of the innate, experiential, and central factors involved, we call it simply 'drive behavior'.

Together with the other terms designating prolonged behavior sequences, 'instinct' implies the sensitizing effect of neural stimulation. An animal behaves differently when hungry than when thirsty. The drive or motivating factor sensitizes the animal to some stimuli and makes it obtuse to others. It both filters and intensifies. This selective action does *not* differentiate among the five classes of long sequences. Nor does the consummatory response, which usually gives the behavior its name, and which may be the same for random, instinctive, rational, and habitual responses. It is in the etiology of the behavior preceding the consummatory response, in the past history of the animal, that the differentiating criteria are to be sought. This demands experimental analysis. Sometimes the data are unambiguous, as when the isolated bird sings the song which is characteristic of its species. Both birds and chimpanzees build tree nests; in the former the behavior pattern is often innate, but in the apes it is evidently learned, being transmitted from one generation to the next. Often the answer is complicated, because the behavior sequence contains both innately determined and learned components. Instinct and intelligence are *not* mutually exclusive. Some of the fastest and most efficient learning that we know of is intimately related to instinctive behavior: the foraging insect must learn and remember, on the basis of a single flight, the direction or the landmarks which guide it back home. According to Baerends, the digger wasp even remembers from day to day how well each of its eight or ten burrows is stocked with provisions.

Finally, I should like to suggest that reflexes, instincts, and the inherited capacity to learn may be distributed on a continuum. What is inherited may be *a more or less specific readiness to learn.* The concept of learning implies that such readiness is rather nonspecific. But often, as in the case of the wasp, there is a readiness to learn very specific things. When such selective readiness is common to the species, the resulting behavior can hardly be distinguished from instinct or reflex.

We come, now, to a criticism of the tendency to ascribe all or most behavior to a few drives or instincts. During the past two years I have been observing the behavior of male-female pairings of late-adolescent chimpanzees. As youngsters these animals lived together, but well before puberty they were separated by sexes. Starting at least a year after the first menstruation, and at a higher chronological age for the males, these animals were put together for periods of observation at times when the female was in swelling, that is, during the periods of physiological receptivity. All possible pairings of five sexually naive males and a like number of females were made. The observations total over 100 in number. If I had used experienced, rather than inexperienced, chimpanzees under like conditions, a conservative estimate of the number of copulations which would have occurred is 200. In my observations there were no copulations.

However, except for what Carpenter has delicately called 'primary sex activity', the chimpanzees were very active during these hours of observation. These primates are notoriously inventive and varied in their behavior, and practically everything that a caged ape *can* do these animals *did* do in the course of my observations. The behaviors which occurred were both individual and social. The former included self-grooming, solo gymnastics such as somersaulting and doing cartwheels, sucking a thumb, or just sitting and thinking. Among the social interactions there were a few instances of serious aggression, many occurrences of bluffing or exhibitionistic behavior, a great deal of play-fighting, wrestling, playful slapping or boxing, tag or follow-the-leader, and mutual grooming. The point to be stressed is that, although there was no copulation, there was a great deal of social behavior, including most of the constituent acts which enter into the mating pattern.

The question now arises whether the observed behavior which did occur is properly and appropriately designated as sex behavior, as expression of the sex drive or instinct. The only excuse for doing so is *our* knowledge (*a*) that with other, experienced, male-female pairings the sex act would occur, and (*b*) that, with continuation of the prevailing conditions for a long enough time, the sex act most probably *will* occur, eventually, in each of these 25 pairings. But this is not adequate justification for ascribing these long sequences of variable behavior to the 'sex drive'. There was no consummatory act and no drive reduction; the reactions were not 'preparatory' (except in a far-fetched teleological sense) for mating.

What, then, did motivate the great variety of behavior which was observed? There are several theoretical possibilities. The old concept of youthful play as being the incomplete, nonserious expression of later biologically significant behavior patterns is particularly unsatisfactory here because, structurally and physiologically, these animals *are* ready for actual mating and its consequences. A second possibility is to postulate an independent drive, such as activity, exploration, play, or curiosity. The conceptualizations are too glib and facile – they 'explain' too much too easily, and give no 'handle' for experimental testing. Still another possibility is the idea of displacement reactions, as proposed by the German neonaturalists. They suggest that when the environment does not provide the stimuli or objects necessary for the development of the currently dominant instinct, reactions belonging to some other instinct will occur. This also is an *ad hoc* explanation which can be brought in as necessary to 'explain' almost anything.

Instead of starting with a dozen or so drives, instincts, or propensities, under one or another of which all behavior is ordered, we may, instead, postulate a multiplicity of self-motivated activities. What were conceived of as part-activities, all contributing towards some one definite end, are thought of, instead, as a series of independently motivated acts. Every postural adjustment, every approach to or avoidance of a given object, each episode of grooming, has its own, intrinsic motivation. To explain the vast number of movements and acts, extending over hours, and sometimes over weeks and months, as all being determined and guided by one drive, whose direct and identifiable expression can be seen only in a brief consummatory act, is pure anthropomorphism. The acrobatics, wrestling, and grooming seen in my male-female pairs of chimpanzees cover a longer period of time, and involve a greater variety of precise coordinations, than does the act of mating which takes less than a minute. But mating is all that may be strictly designated as sex behavior.

Mutual grooming by chimpanzees contains elements which, in human behavior, we call foreplay or petting and which we ascribe to the sex drive. Could it be suggested that petting is, sometimes, an end in itself, with no sinister motive towards a further ulterior goal? In chimpanzees, grooming occurs as frequently in preadolescent animals, who have had no sex experience, as it does in adults; it occurs in female-female pairs as much as in male-female pairs; and it occurs more often after mating than before. Looked at from the outside and as a whole, the goal-directedness of the behavior sequence is obvious, but that is the view seen by the human mind, not the view of the organism doing the behaving. To suppose that it is, is to endow the animal, anthropomorphically, with the foresight which characterizes the deliberate, devious, and planful behavior of man.

The behaviors legitimately and descriptively named sex, hunger, thirst, and so on, are relatively infrequent, isolated events in the flow of behavior; their motivation demands explanation no more, and no less, than do the many activities appearing in each of various sequences. To say that a given act is sometimes motivated by sex, another time by hunger, is to slur over the basic question of motivation. Differential sensitization, determining the probability of occurrence of various reactions, needs explanation. But more fundamental than the problem of frequency of elicitation is *why* grooming and wrestling and play-biting occur at all. Since they appear when there is no copulatory drive, and more often after reduction of the sex drive than before, they must be independently motivated.

The theme of the view which I am advocating might be summarized in the words of a once-popular song, whose title is, 'Every little movement has a meaning all its own'. I should perhaps restate this to read, 'Every little action has a motive all its own'. My point, of course, is not that sex has been overrated, but rather that it already has enough to account for, without our burdening it with more than its fair share of responsibility.

II Drive as the Activation of Response Mechanisms

The view of instinct theorists that there exists some driving
force that both initiates actions and provides the energy for
their execution was rejected by Woodworth. He argued that
the energizing factor, drive, merely sets certain neural
mechanisms in operation; it activates or initiates action, which
is then sustained by the energy inherent in the nerves and
muscles comprising the reaction system. Woodworth visualized
the immediate source of activation or stimulation of the
neural mechanisms corresponding to an activity to be the
spread of neural activity from some other neural structure.
Lashley, Hebb, and Morgan elaborated this idea, each in a
different way. The recent works of Andersson and his
collaborators and of Fisher provide examples of
experimental investigations of the neural mechanisms involved
in particular activities and the manner of stimulation of those
mechanisms.

7 R. S. Woodworth

Mechanisms and Drive

Excerpt from R. S. Woodworth, *Dynamic Psychology*, Columbia University Press, New York, 1918, Chapter II.

Once the point of view of a dynamic psychology is gained, two general problems come into sight, which may be named the problem of 'mechanism' and the problem of 'drive'. One is the problem, how we do a thing, and the other is the problem of what induces us to do it. Take the case of the pitcher in a baseball game. The problem of mechanism is the problem of how he aims, gauges distance and amount of curve, and coordinates his movements to produce the desired end. The problem of drive includes such questions as to why he is engaged in this exercise at all, why he pitches better on one day than on another, why he rouses himself more against one than against another batter, and many similar questions. It will be noticed that the mechanism questions are asked with 'How?' and the drive questions with 'Why?' Now science has come to regard the question 'Why?' with suspicion, and to substitute the question 'How?' since it has found that the answer to the question 'Why?' always calls for a further 'Why?' and that no stability or finality is reached in this direction, whereas the answer to the question 'How?' is always good as far as it is accurate, though, to be sure, it is seldom if ever complete. It may be true in our case, also, that the question of drive is reducible to a question of mechanism, but there is *prima facie* justification for making the distinction. Certainly the motives and springs of action of human life are of so much importance as to justify special attention to them.

This distinction between drive and mechanism may become clearer if we consider it in the case of a machine. The drive here is the power applied to make the mechanism go; the mechanism is made to go, and is relatively passive. Its passivity is, to be sure, only relative, since the material and structure of the mechanism determine the direction that shall be taken by the power applied. We might speak of the mechanism as reacting to the power applied and so producing the results. But the mechanism without the power is inactive, dead, lacking in disposable energy.

In some forms of mechanism, such as a loaded gun, stored energy is present, and the action of the drive is to liberate this stored energy, which then does the rest of the work. This sort of mechanism is rather similar to that of a living creature. The muscles contain stored energy, which is liberated by a stimulus reaching them, the stimulus that normally reaches them being the 'nerve impulse' coming along a motor nerve. The nerve drives the muscle. The nerve impulse coming out along a motor nerve originates in the discharge of stored energy in the nerve cells controlling this nerve; and these central cells are themselves excited to discharge by nerve impulses reaching them, perhaps from a sensory nerve. The sensory nerve drives the motor center, being itself driven by a stimulus reaching the sense organ from without. The whole reflex mechanism, consisting of sense organ, sensory nerve, center, motor nerve and muscle, can be thought of as a unit; and its drive is then the external stimulus.

If all behavior were of this simple reflex type, and consisted of direct responses to present stimuli, there would be no great significance in the distinction between drive and mechanism. The drive would simply be the external stimulus and the mechanism simply the whole organism. On the other hand, what we mean by a 'motive' is something internal, and the question thus arises whether we can work our way up from the drive as external stimulus to the drive as inner motive.

The first step is to notice the physiological facts of 'reinforcement' or 'facilitation' and of 'inhibition'. These mean, in neural terms, the coming together of different nerve impulses, with the result in some cases that one strengthens the other, and in some cases that one weakens or suppresses the other. Take the familiar 'knee-jerk' or 'patellar reflex' as an example. This involuntary movement of the lower leg, produced by some of the thigh muscles, can only be elicited by a blow on the tendon passing in front of the knee (or some equivalent, strictly local stimulus). But the force of the knee-jerk can be greatly altered by influences coming from other parts of the body. A sudden noise occurring an instant before the blow at the knee will decidedly reinforce the knee-jerk, while soft music may weaken it. Clenching the fist or gritting the teeth reinforces the knee-jerk. The drive operating the knee-jerk in such cases is not entirely the local stimulus, but other centers in the brain and spinal cord, being themselves aroused from outside, furnish drive for the center that is directly responsible for the movement. If one nerve center can thus furnish drive for another, there is some sense in speaking of drives.

Still, the conception of 'drive' would have little significance if the activity aroused in any center lasted only as long as the external stimulus acting upon it through a sensory nerve; for, taken as a whole, the organism would still be passive and simply responsive to the complex of external stimuli acting on it at any moment. It is therefore a very important fact, for our purpose, that a nerve center, aroused to activity, does not in all cases relapse into quiescence, after a momentary discharge. Its state of activity may outlast the stimulus that aroused it, and this residual activity in one center may act as drive to another center. Or, a center may be 'sub-excited' by an external stimulus that is not capable of arousing it to full discharge; and, while thus sub-excited, it may influence other centers, either by way of reinforcement or by way of inhibition. Thus, though the drive for nerve activity may be ultimately external, at any one moment there are internal sources of influence furnishing drive to other parts of the system.

This relationship between two mechanisms, such that one, being partially excited, becomes the drive of another, is specially significant in the case of what have been called 'preparatory and consummatory reactions' (Sherrington). A consummatory reaction is one of direct value to the animal – one directly bringing satisfaction – such as eating or escaping from danger. The objective mark of a consummatory reaction is that it terminates a series of acts, and is followed by rest or perhaps by a shift to some new series. Introspectively, we know such reactions by the satisfaction and sense of finality that they bring. The preparatory reactions are only mediately of benefit to the organism, their value lying in the fact that they lead to, and make possible, a consummatory reaction. Objectively, the mark of a preparatory reaction is that it occurs as a preliminary stage in a series of acts leading up to a consummatory reaction. Consciously, a preparatory reaction is marked by a state of tension.

Preparatory reactions are of two kinds. We have, first, such reactions as looking and listening, which are readily evoked when the animal is in a passive or resting condition, and which consist in a coming to attention and instituting a condition of readiness for a yet undetermined stimulus that may arouse further response.

The other kind consists of reactions which are not evoked except when the mechanism for a consummatory reaction has been aroused and is in activity. A typical series of events is the following: a sound or light strikes the sense organ and arouses the appropriate attentive reaction; this permits a stimulus of significance to the animal to take effect – for example, the sight of prey, which arouses a trend towards the consummatory reaction of devouring it. But this consummatory reaction cannot at once take place; what does take place is the preparatory reaction of stalking or pursuing the prey. The series of preparatory reactions may be very complicated, and it is evidently driven by the trend towards the consummatory reaction. That there is a persistent inner tendency towards the consummatory reaction is seen when, for instance, a hunting dog loses the trail; if he were simply carried along from one detail of the hunting process to another by a succession of stimuli calling out simple reflexes, he would cease hunting as soon as the trail ceased or follow it back again; whereas what he does is to explore about, seeking the trail, as we say. This seeking, not being evoked by any external stimulus (but rather by the absence of an external stimulus), must be driven by some internal force; and the circumstances make it clear that the inner drive is directed towards the capture of the prey.

The dog's behavior is to be interpreted as follows: the mechanism for a consummatory reaction, having been set into activity by a suitable stimulus, acts as a drive operating other mechanisms which give the preparatory reactions. Each preparatory reaction may be a response in part to some external stimulus, but it is facilitated by the drive towards the consummatory reaction. Not only are some reactions thus facilitated, but others which in other circumstances would be evoked by external stimuli are inhibited. The dog on the trail does not stop to pass the time of day with another dog met on the way; he is too busy. When an animal or man is too busy or too much in a hurry to respond to stimuli that usually get responses from him, he is being driven by some internal tendency.

'Drive' as we have thus been led to conceive of it in the simpler sort of case, is not essentially distinct from 'mechanism'. The drive is a mechanism already aroused and thus in a position to furnish stimulation to other mechanisms. Any mechanism might be a drive. But it is the mechanisms directed towards consummatory reactions – whether of the simpler sort seen in animals or of the more complex sort exemplified by human desires and motives – that are most likely to act as drives. Some mechanisms act at once and relapse into quiet, while others can only bring their action to completion by first arousing other mechanisms. But there is no absolute distinction, and it will be well to bear in mind the possibility that any mechanism may be under certain circumstances the source of stimulation that arouses other mechanisms to activity.

The inadequacy of either the consciousness or the behavior

psychology, in their narrower formulations at least, is that they fail to consider questions like these. Their advantage as against a dynamic psychology is that they are closer to observable phenomena. Behavior we can observe, consciousness we can observe with some difficulty, but the inner dynamics of the mental processes must be inferred rather than observed. Even so, psychology is in no worse case than the other sciences. They all seek to understand what goes on below the surface of things, to form conceptions of the inner workings of things that shall square with the known facts and make possible the prediction of what will occur under given conditions. A dynamic psychology must utilize the observations of consciousness and behavior as indications of the 'workings of the mind'; and that, in spite of formal definitions to the contrary, is what psychologists have been attempting to accomplish since the beginning.

Drive as Facilitation of Specific Neural Mechanisms

Excerpt from K. S. Lashley, 'Experimental analysis of instinctive behavior', *Psychological Review*, 1938, Vol. 45, pp. 445–71.

Most of the current theories concerning the nature of primitive drives have been derived by analogy with the hunger mechanism and assume some continued visceral activity, comparable to the contractions of the empty stomach, as the source of masses of excitation whose irradiation in the nervous system increases the general responsiveness of the animal. This analogy has certainly been overworked, especially as it is by no means assured that hunger motivation is itself synonymous with the hunger pangs. The work of Richter (1927) and Wada (1922) shows a correlation between rhythmic bodily activities and hunger contractions, but the activities of the animal under hunger motivation are not rhythmic. The rat in the maze does not, stop running between hunger pangs. Even for hunger motivation we must assume, I believe, some source of continued excitation which is no more than activated by the hunger contractions.

When the theories of motivation by somatic sensory facilitation were developed, there was little evidence that activity could be sustained within the central nervous system. The maintenance of tension or activity through some form of circular reflex was more in accord with the conception that all excitation must pass over immediately into motor response, as first formulated by Dewey (1896). The recent demonstration of recurrent nervous circuits, perhaps capable of indefinite reverberation, by the anatomic and physiologic studies of Lorente de Nò, relieves us from the necessity of finding a peripheral mechanism to account for the maintenance of activity or for the dynamic tensions which are implied by the phenomena of motivation. The studies of the sexual and maternal motivation strongly suggest a central nervous mechanism which is merely rendered excitable by hormone action. What this means is that the seeking activities or reactions to a deficit, such as are measured by the obstruction method, are not a reaction to a continuous peripheral stimulus, such as is assumed in the evacuation theory, but are the expression of some central nervous activity or state.

The relation between the reactions to deficit and the excitability of the specific patterns of behavior is obscure. It is generally stated that the drive is first aroused, as by endocrine action, and that this, in turn, causes the appearance of the instinctive sensorimotor reactions. An increase in the excitability of sexual reactions is accepted as evidence for intensification of the drive. But the phenomenon actually observed is only a more ready excitation of specific responses. There is no need to postulate an extraneous drive to account for the fluctuations in the threshold of such reactions. The mechanism is present and under the influence of the hormone or of excitation by an adequate stimulus its excitability is increased.

Only in cases of reaction to a deficit is there any justification for introducing the notion of a drive as a source of facilitation. An increase in general activity or in exploratory behavior indicates an increased responsiveness to stimuli not obviously related to the specific sensorimotor patterns of the instinctive behavior. There is also inhibition of reactions to other stimuli, as when the chick removed from companions refuses to eat. This is a selective facilitation of activity and the facilitation originates with the organism. Does it call for the postulation of some source of energy apart from that of the specific sensorimotor patterns? The evidence indicates that the facilitation is probably independent of somatic stimulation and is of central nervous origin. Stimulation of an instinctive pattern will increase the intensity of the apparent drive. Thus sexual excitement in the male rat is aroused only by the very specific pattern of the female in heat, but once the animal is so excited, he will respond to less definite patterns of stimulation. The waning retrieving activity of the female is intensified by supplying her with a younger litter. Motivation of the hungry animal in the maze is really effective only after the maze has been associated with the getting of food. In these cases the apparent motivation seems to derive from a specific sensorimotor mechanism.

I suspect that all cases of motivation will turn out to be of this character; not a general drive or libido, or disturbance of the organic equilibrium, but a partial excitation of a very specific sensorimotor mechanism irradiating to affect other systems of reaction. In his *Dynamic Psychology* Woodworth (1918) suggested that habits might acquire dynamic functions, that a mechanism might become a drive, as he expressed the matter. I should carry this notion a step further and suggest that physiologically all drives are no more than expressions of the activity of specific mechanisms.

References

Dewey, J. The reflex arc concept in psychology. *Psychol. Rev.*, 1896, 3, 357–370.

Richter, C. P. Animal behavior and internal drives. *Quart. Rev. Biol.*, 1927, 2, 307–343.

Wada, T. An experimental study of hunger in its relation to activity. *Arch. Psychol.*, 1922, No. 57.

Woodworth, R. S. *Dynamic Psychology.* New York: Columbia University Press, 1918. p. 210.

9 D. O. Hebb

Drives and the C.N.S. (Conceptual Nervous System)[1]

Reproduced in full from *Psychological Review*, 1955, Vol. 62, pp. 243–54.

The problem of motivation of course lies close to the heart of the general problem of understanding behavior, yet it sometimes seems the least realistically treated topic in the literature. In great part, the difficulty concerns that c.n.s., or 'conceptual nervous system', which Skinner disavowed and from whose influence he and others have tried to escape. But the conceptual nervous system of 1930 was evidently like the gin that was being drunk about the same time; it was homemade and none too good, as Skinner pointed out, but it was also habit-forming; and the effort to escape has not really been successful. Prohibition is long past. If we *must* drink we can now get better liquor; likewise, the conceptual nervous system of 1930 is out of date and – if we must neurologize – let us use the best brand of neurology we can find.

Though I personally favor both alcohol and neurologizing, in moderation, the point here does not assume that either is a good thing. The point is that psychology is intoxicating itself with a worse brand than it need use. Many psychologists do not think in terms of neural anatomy; but merely adhering to certain classical frameworks shows the limiting effect of earlier neurologizing. Bergmann (2) has recently said again that it is logically possible to escape the influence. This does not change the fact that, in practice, it has not been done.

Further, as I read Bergmann, I am not sure that he really thinks, deep down, that we should swear off neurologizing entirely, or at least that we should all do so. He has made a strong case for the functional similarity of intervening variable and hypothetical construct, implying that we are dealing more with differences of degree than of kind. The conclusion *I* draw is that both can properly appear in the same theory, using intervening variables to whatever extent is most profitable (as physics for example does), and conversely not being afraid to use some

1. Presidential address, Division 3, at American Psychological Association, New York, September, 1954. The paper incorporates ideas worked out in discussion with fellow students at McGill, especially Dalbir Bindra and Peter Milner, as well as with Leo Postman at California, and it is a pleasure to record my great indebtedness to them.

theoretical conception merely because it might become anatomically identifiable.

For many conceptions, at least, MacCorquodale and Meehl's (26) distinction is relative, not absolute; and it must also be observed that physiological psychology makes free use of 'dispositional concepts' as well as 'existential' ones. Logically, this leaves room for some of us to make more use of explicitly physiological constructs than others, and still lets us stay in communication with one another. It also shows how one's views concerning motivation, for example, might be more influenced than one thinks by earlier physiological notions, since it means that an explicitly physiological conception might be restated in words that have – apparently – no physiological reference.

What I propose, therefore, is to look at motivation as it relates to the c.n.s. – or conceptual nervous system – of three different periods: as it was before 1930, as it was say 10 years ago, and as it is today. I hope to persuade you that some of our current troubles with motivation are due to the c.n.s. of an earlier day, and ask that you look with an open mind at the implications of the current one. Today's physiology suggests new psychological ideas, and I would like to persuade you that they make psychological sense, no matter how they originated. They might even provide common ground – not necessarily agreement, but communication, something nearer to agreement – for people whose views at present may seem completely opposed. While writing this paper I found myself having to make a change in my own theoretical position, as you will see, and though you may not adopt the same position you may be willing to take another look at the evidence, and consider its theoretical import anew.

Before going on it is just as well to be explicit about the use of the terms motivation and drive. 'Motivation' refers here in a rather general sense to the energizing of behavior, and especially to the sources of energy in a particular set of responses that keep them temporarily dominant over others and account for continuity and direction in behavior. 'Drive' is regarded as a more specific conception about the way in which this occurs: a hypothesis of motivation, which makes the energy a function of a special process distinct from those S-R or cognitive functions that are energized. In some contexts, therefore, 'motivation' and 'drive' are interchangeable.

Motivation in the Classical (Pre-1930) C.N.S.

The main line of descent of psychological theory, as I have recently tried to show (20), is through associationism and the stimulus-response formulations. Characteristically, stimulus-response theory has treated the animal as more or less inactive unless subjected to special conditions of arousal. These conditions are first, hunger, pain, and sexual excitement; and secondly, stimulation that has become associated with one of these more primitive motivations.

Such views did not originate entirely in the early ideas of nervous function, but certainly were strengthened by them. Early studies of the nerve fiber seemed to show that the cell is inert until something happens to it from outside; therefore, the same would be true of the collection of cells making up the nervous system. From this came the explicit theory of drives. The organism is thought of as like a machine, such as the automobile, in which the steering mechanism – that is, stimulus-response connections – is separate from the power source, or drive. There is, however, this difference: the organism may be endowed with three or more different power plants. Once you start listing separate ones, it is hard to avoid five: hunger, thirst, pain, maternal, and sex drives. By some theorists, these may each be given a low-level steering function also, and indirectly the steering function of drives is much increased by the law of effect. According to the law, habits – steering functions – are acquired only in conjunction with the operation of drives.

Now it is evident that an animal is often active and often learns when there is little or no drive activity of the kinds listed. This fact has been dealt with in two ways. One is to postulate additional drives – activity, exploratory, manipulatory, and so forth. The other is to postulate acquired or learned drives, which obtain their energy, so to speak, from association with primary drives.

It is important to see the difficulties to be met by this kind of formulation, though it should be said at once that I do not have any decisive refutation of it, and other approaches have their difficulties, too.

First, we may overlook the rather large number of forms of behavior in which motivation cannot be reduced to biological drive plus learning. Such behavior is most evident in higher species, and may be forgotten by those who work only with the rat or with restricted segments of the behavior of dog or cat. (I do not suggest that we put human motivation on a different plane from that of animals (7); what I am saying is that certain peculiarities of motivation increase with phylogenesis, and though most evident in man can be clearly seen with other higher animals.) What is the drive that produces panic in the chimpanzee at the sight of a model of a human head; or fear in some animals, and vicious aggression in others, at the sight of the anesthetized body of a fellow chimpanzee? What about fear of snakes, or the young chimpanzee's terror at the sight of strangers? One can accept the idea that this is 'anxiety', but the anxiety, if so, is not based on a prior association of the stimulus object with pain. With the young chimpanzee reared in the nursery of the Yerkes Laboratories, after separation from the mother at birth, one can be certain that the infant has never seen a snake before, and certainly no one has told him about snakes; and one can be sure that a particular infant has never had the opportunity to associate a strange face with pain. Stimulus generalization does not explain fear of strangers, for other stimuli in the same class, namely, the regular attendants, are eagerly welcomed by the infant.

Again, what drive shall we postulate to account for the manifold forms of anger in the chimpanzee that do not derive from frustration objectively defined (22)? How account for the petting behavior of young adolescent chimpanzees, which Nissen (36) has shown is independent of primary sex activity? How deal with the behavior of the female who, bearing her first infant, is terrified at the sight of the baby as it drops from the birth canal, runs away, never sees it again after it has been taken to the nursery for rearing; and who yet, on the birth of a *second* infant, promptly picks it up and violently resists any effort to take it from her?

There is a great deal of behavior, in the higher animal especially, that is at the very best difficult to reduce to hunger, pain, sex, and maternal drives, plus learning. Even for the lower animal it has been clear for some time that we must add an exploratory drive (if we are to think in these terms at all), and presumably the motivational phenomena recently studied by Harlow and his colleagues (16, 17, 10) could also be comprised under such a drive by giving it a little broader specification. The curiosity drive of Berlyne (4) and Thompson and Solomon (46), for example, might be considered to cover both investigatory and manipulatory activities on the one hand, and exploratory on the other. It would also comprehend the 'problem-seeking' behavior recently studied by Mahut and Havelka at McGill (unpublished studies). They have shown that the rat which is offered a short, direct path to food, and a longer, variable and indirect pathway involving a search for food, will very frequently prefer the more difficult, but more 'interesting' route.

But even with the addition of a curiosity-investigatory-manipulatory drive, and even apart from the primates, there is still behavior that presents difficulties. There are the reinforcing effects of incomplete copulation (43) and of saccharin intake (42, 11), which do not reduce to secondary reward. We must not multiply drives beyond reason, and at this point one asks whether there is no alternative to the theory in this form. We come, then, to the conceptual nervous system of 1930 to 1950.

Motivation in the C.N.S. of 1930–1950

About 1930 it began to be evident that the nerve cell is not physiologically inert, does not have to be excited from outside in order to discharge (19, p. 8). The nervous system is alive, and living things by their nature are active. With the demonstration of spontaneous activity in c.n.s. it seemed to me that the conception of a drive system or systems was supererogation.

For reasons I shall come to later, this now appears to me to have been an oversimplification; but in 1945 the only problem of motivation, I thought, was to account for the *direction* taken by behavior. From this point of view, hunger or pain might be peculiarly effective in guiding or channeling activity but not needed for its arousal. It was not surprising, from this point of view, to see human beings liking intellectual work, nor to find evidence that an animal might learn something without pressure of pain or hunger.

The energy of response is not in the stimulus. It comes from the food, water, and oxygen ingested by the animal; and the violence of an epileptic convulsion, when brain cells for whatever reason decide to fire in synchrony, bears witness to what the nervous system can do when it likes. This is like a whole powder magazine exploding at once. Ordinary behavior can be thought of as produced by an organized series of much smaller explosions, and so a 'self-motivating' c.n.s. might still be a very powerfully motivated one. To me, then, it was astonishing that a critic could refer to mine as a 'motivationless' psychology. What I had said in short was that any organized process in the brain is a motivated process, inevitably, inescapably; that the human brain is built to be active, and that as long as it is supplied with adequate nutrition will continue to be active. Brain activity is what determines behavior, and so the only behavioral problem becomes that of accounting for *in*activity.

It was in this conceptual frame that the behavioral picture seemed to negate the notion of drive, as a separate energizer of behavior. A pedagogical experiment reported earlier (18) had been very impressive in its indication that the human liking for work is not a rare phenomenon, but general. All of the 600-odd pupils in a city school, ranging from 6 to 15 years of age, were suddenly informed that they need do no work whatever unless they wanted to, that the punishment for being noisy and interrupting others' work was to be sent to the playground to play, and that the reward for being good was to be allowed to do more work. In these circumstances, *all* of the pupils discovered within a day or two that, within limits, they preferred work to no work (and incidentally learned more arithmetic and so forth than in previous years).

The phenomenon of work for its own sake is familiar enough to all of us, when the timing is controlled by the worker himself, when 'work' is not defined as referring alone to activity imposed from without. Intellectual work may take the form of trying to understand what Robert Browning was trying to say (if anything), to discover what it is in Dali's paintings that can interest others, or to predict the outcome of a paperback mystery. We systematically underestimate the human need of intellectual activity, in one form or another, when we overlook the intellectual component in art and in games. Similarly with riddles, puzzles, and the puzzle-like games of strategy such as bridge, chess, and *go*; the frequency with which man has devised such problems for his own solution is a most significant fact concerning human motivation.

It is, however, not necessarily a fact that supports my earlier view, outlined above. It is hard to get these broader aspects of human behavior under laboratory study, and when we do we may expect to have our ideas about them significantly modified. For my views on the problem, this is what has happened with the experiment of Bexton, Heron, and Scott (5). Their work is a long step toward dealing with the realities of motivation in the well-fed, physically comfortable, adult human being, and its results raise a serious difficulty for my own theory. Their subjects were paid handsomely to do nothing, see nothing, hear or touch very little, for 24 hours a day. Primary needs were met, on the whole, very well. The subjects suffered no pain, and were fed on request. It is true that they could not copulate, but at the risk of impugning the virility of Canadian college students I point out that most of them would not have been copulating anyway and were quite used to such long stretches of three or four days without primary sexual satisfaction. The secondary reward, on the other hand, was high: $20 a day plus room and board is more than $7000 a year, far more than a student could earn by other means. The subjects then should be highly motivated to continue the experiment, cheerful and happy to be allowed to contribute to scientific knowledge so painlessly and profitably.

In fact, the subject was well motivated for perhaps four to eight hours, and then became increasingly unhappy. He developed a need for stimulation of almost any kind. In the first preliminary exploration, for example, he was allowed to listen to recorded material on request. Some subjects were given a talk for 6-year-old children on the dangers of alcohol. This might be requested, by a grown-up male college student, 15 to 20 times in a 30-hour period. Others were offered, and asked for repeatedly, a recording of an old stock-market report. The subjects looked forward to being tested, but paradoxically tended to find the tests fatiguing when they did arrive. It is hardly necessary to say that the whole situation was rather hard to take, and one subject, in spite of not being in a special state of primary drive arousal in the experiment but in real need of money outside it, gave up the secondary reward of $20 a day to take up a job at hard labor paying $7 or $8 a day.

This experiment is not cited primarily as a difficulty for drive theory, although three months ago that is how I saw it. It *will* make difficulty for such theory if exploratory drive is not recognized; but we have already seen the necessity, on other grounds, of including a sort of exploratory-curiosity-manipulatory drive, which essentially comes down to a tendency to seek varied stimulation. This would on the whole handle very well the motivational phenomena observed by Heron's group.

Instead, I cite their experiment as making essential trouble for my own treatment of motivation (19) as based on the conceptual nervous system of 1930 to 1945. If the thought process is internally organized and motivated, why should it break down in conditions of perceptual isolation, unless emotional disturbance intervenes? But it did break down when no serious emotional change was observed, with problem-solving and intelligence-test performance significantly impaired. Why should the subjects themselves report (a) after four or five hours in isolation that they could not follow a connected train of thought, and (b) that their motivation for study or the like was seriously disturbed for 24 hours or more after coming out of isolation? The subjects were reasonably well adjusted, happy, and able to think coherently for the first four or five hours of the experiment; why, according to my theory, should this not continue, and why should the organization of behavior not be promptly restored with restoration of a normal environment?

You will forgive me perhaps if I do not dilate further on my own theoretical difficulties, paralleling those of others, but turn now to the conceptual nervous system of 1954 to ask what psychological values we may extract from it for the theory of motivation. I shall not attempt any clear answer for the difficulties we have considered – the data do not seem yet to justify clear answers – but certain conceptions can be formulated in sufficiently definite form to be a background for new research, and the physiological data contain suggestions that may allow me to retain what was of value in my earlier proposals while bringing them closer to ideas such as Harlow's (16) on one hand and to reinforcement theory on the other.

Motivation and C.N.S. in 1954

For psychological purposes there are two major changes in recent ideas of nervous function. One concerns the single cell, the other an 'arousal' system in the brain stem. The first I shall pass over briefly; it is very significant, but does not bear quite as directly upon our present problem. Its essence is that there are two kinds of activity in the nerve cell: the spike potential, or actual firing, and the dendritic potential, which has very different properties. There is now clear evidence (12) that the dendrite has a 'slow-burning' activity which is not all-or-none, tends not to be transmitted, and lasts 15 to 30 milliseconds instead of the spike's one millisecond. It facilitates spike activity (23), but often occurs independently and may make up the greater part of the EEG record. It is still true that the brain is always active, but the activity is not always the transmitted kind that conduces to behavior. Finally, there is decisive evidence of primary inhibition in nerve function (25, 14) and of a true fatigue that may last for a matter of minutes instead of milliseconds (6, 9). These facts will have a great effect on the hypotheses of physiological psychology, and sooner or later on psychology in general.

Our more direct concern is with a development to which attention has already been drawn by Lindsley (24): the nonspecific or diffuse projection system of the brain stem, which was shown by Moruzzi and Magoun (34) to be an *arousal* system whose activity in effect makes organized cortical activity possible. Lindsley showed the relevance to the problem of emotion and motivation; what I shall attempt is to extend his treatment, giving more weight to cortical components in arousal. The point of view has also an evident relationship to Duffy's (13).

The arousal system can be thought of as representing a second major pathway by which all sensory excitations reach the cortex, as shown in the upper part of Fig. 1; but there is also feedback from the cortex and I shall urge that the *psychological* evidence further emphasizes the importance of this 'downstream' effect.

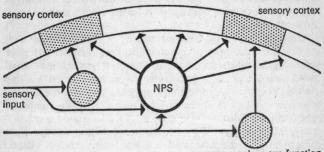

sensory cortex   sensory cortex

NPS

sensory input

sensory nucleus cue function

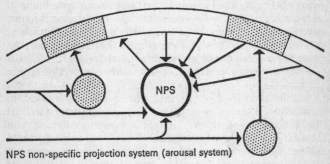

NPS

NPS non-specific projection system (arousal system)

Figure 1

In the classical conception of sensory function, input to the cortex was via the great projection systems only: from sensory nerve to sensory tract, thence to the corresponding sensory nucleus of the thalamus, and thence directly to one of the sensory projection areas of the cortex. These are still the direct sensory routes, the quick efficient transmitters of information. The second pathway is slow and inefficient; the excitation, as it were, trickles through a tangled thicket of fibers and synapses, there is a mixing up of messages, and the scrambled messages are delivered indiscriminately to wide cortical areas. In short, they are messages no longer. They serve, instead, to tone up the cortex, with a background supporting action that is completely necessary if the messages proper are to have their effect. Without the arousal system, the sensory impulses by the direct route reach the sensory cortex, but go no farther; the rest of the cortex is unaffected, and thus learned stimulus-response relations are lost. The waking center, which has long been known, is one part of this larger system; any extensive damage to it leaves a permanently inert, comatose animal.

Remember that in all this I am talking of the conceptual nervous system: making a working simplification, and abstracting for psychological purposes; and all these statements may need qualification, especially since research in this area is moving rapidly. There is reason to think, for example, that the arousal system may not be homogeneous, but may consist of a number of subsystems with distinctive functions (38). Olds and Milner's (37) study, reporting 'reward' by direct intracranial stimulation, is not easy to fit into the notion of a single, homogeneous system. Sharpless' (40) results also raise doubt on this point, and it may reasonably be anticipated that arousal will eventually be found to vary qualitatively as well as quantitatively. But in general terms, psychologically, we can now distinguish two quite different effects of a sensory event. One is the *cue function*, guiding behavior; the other, less obvious but no less important, is the *arousal* or *vigilance function*. Without a foundation of arousal, the cue function cannot exist.

And now I propose to you that, whatever you wish to call it, arousal in this sense is synonymous with a general drive state, and the conception of drive therefore assumes anatomical and physiological identity. Let me remind you of what we discussed earlier: the drive is an energizer, but not a guide; an engine but not a steering gear. These are precisely the specifications of activity in the arousal system. Also, learning is dependent on drive, according to drive theory, and this too is applicable in general terms – no arousal, no learning; and efficient learning is possible only in the waking, alert, responsive animal, in which the level of arousal is high.

Thus I find myself obliged to reverse my earlier views and accept the drive conception, not merely on physiological grounds but also on the grounds of some of our current psychological studies. The conception is somewhat modified, but the modifications may not be entirely unacceptable to others.

Consider the relation of the effectiveness of cue function, actual or potential, to the level of arousal (Fig. 2). Physiologically, we may assume that cortical synaptic function is facilitated by the diffuse bombardment of the arousal system. When this bombardment is at a low level an increase will tend to strengthen or maintain the concurrent cortical activity; when arousal or drive is at a low level, that is, a response that produces increased stimulation and greater arousal will tend to be repeated. This is represented by the rising curve at the left. But when arousal is at a high level, as at the right, the greater bombardment may interfere with the

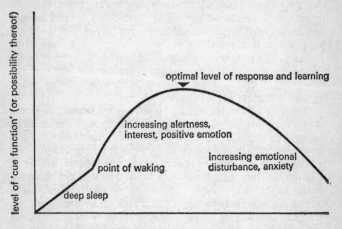

Figure 2

delicate adjustments involved in cue function, perhaps by facilitating irrelevant responses (a high D arouses conflicting $_SH_RS$?). Thus there will be an optimal level of arousal for effective behavior, as Schlosberg (39) has suggested. Set aside such physiologizing completely, and we have a significant behavioral conception left, namely, that the same stimulation in mild degree may attract (by prolonging the pattern of response that leads to this stimulation) and in strong degree repel (by disrupting the pattern and facilitating conflicting or alternative responses).

The significance of this relation is in a phenomenon of the greatest importance for understanding motivation in higher animals. This is the *positive attraction of risk taking*, or mild fear, *and of problem solving*, or mild frustration, which was referred to earlier. Whiting and Mowrer (49) and Berlyne (4) have noted a relation between fear and curiosity – that is, a tendency to seek stimulation from fear-provoking objects, though at a safe distance. Woodworth (50) and Valentine (48) reported this in children, and Woodworth and Marquis (51) have recently emphasized again its importance in adults. There is no doubt that it exists. There is no doubt, either, that problem-solving situations have some attraction for the rat, more for Harlow's (16) monkeys, and far more for man. When you stop to think of it, it is nothing short of extraordinary what trouble people will go to in order to get into more trouble at the bridge table, or on the golf course; and the fascination of the murder story, or thriller, and the newspaper accounts of real-life adventure or tragedy, is no less extraordinary. This taste for excitement *must* not be forgotten when we are dealing with human motivation. It appears that, up to a certain point, threat and puzzle have positive motivating value, beyond that point negative value.

I know this leaves problems. It is not *any* mild threat, *any* form of problem, that is rewarding; we still have to work out the rules for this formulation. Also, I do not mean that there are not secondary rewards of social prestige for risk taking and problem solving – or even primary reward when such behavior is part of lovemaking. But the animal data show that it is not always a matter of extrinsic reward; risk and puzzle can be attractive in themselves, especially for higher animals such as man. If we can accept this, it will no longer be necessary to work out tortuous and improbable ways to explain why human beings work for money, why school children should learn without pain, why a human being in isolation should dislike doing nothing.

One other point before leaving Fig. 2: the low level of the curve to the right. You may be skeptical about such an extreme loss of adaptation, or disturbance of cue function and S-R relations, with high levels of arousal. Emotion is persistently regarded as energizing and organizing (which it certainly is at the lower end of the scale, up to the optimal level). But the 'paralysis of terror' and related states do occur. As Brown and Jacobs (8, p. 753) have noted, 'the presence of fear may act as an energizer . . . and yet lead in certain instances to an increase in immobility.' Twice in the past eight months, while this address was being prepared, the Montreal newspapers reported the behavior of a human being who, suddenly finding himself in extreme danger but with time to escape, simply made no move whatever. One of the two was killed; the other was not, but only because a truck driver chose to wreck his truck and another car instead. Again, it is reported by Marshall (27), in a book that every student of human motivation should read carefully, that in the emotional pressure of battle no more than 15 to 25 per cent of men under attack even fire their rifles, let alone use them efficiently.

Tyhurst's (47) very significant study of behavior in emergency and disaster situations further documents the point. The adult who is told that his apartment house is on fire, or who is threatened by a flash flood, may or may not respond intelligently. In various situations, 12 to 25 per cent did so; an equal number show 'states of confusion, paralyzing anxiety, inability to move out of bed, "hysterical" crying or screaming, and so on.' Three-quarters or more show a clear impairment of intelligent behavior, often with aimless and irrelevant movements, rather than (as one might expect) panic reactions. There seems no doubt: the curve at the right must come down to a low level.

Now back to our main problem: If we tentatively identify a general state of drive with degree of arousal, where does this leave hunger, pain, and sex drives? These may still be anatomically separable, as Stellar (45) has argued, but we might consider instead the possibility that there is just one general drive state that can be aroused in different ways. Stellar's argument does not seem fully convincing. There are certainly regions in the hypothalamus that control eating, for example; but is this a *motivating* mechanism? The very essence of such a conception is that the mechanism in question should energize *other* mechanisms, and Miller, Bailey, and Stevenson (31) have shown that the opposite is true.

But this issue should not be pressed too far, with our present knowledge. I have tried to avoid dogmatism in this presentation in the hope that we might try, for once, to see what we have in common in our views on motivation. One virtue of identifying arousal with drive is that it relates differing views (as well as bringing into the focus of attention data that may otherwise be neglected). The important thing is a clear distinction between cue function and arousal function, and the fact that at low levels an increase of drive intensity may be rewarding, whereas at high levels it is a decrease that rewards. Given this point of view and our assumptions about arousal mechanisms, we see that what Harlow has emphasized is the exteroceptively aroused, but still low-level, drive, with cue function of course directly provided for. In the concept of anxiety, Spence and Brown emphasize the higher-level drive state, especially where there is no guiding cue function that would enable the animal to escape threat. The feedback from cortical functioning makes intelligible Mowrer's (35) equating anxiety aroused by threat of pain, and anxiety aroused in some way by cognitive processes related to ideas of the self. Solomon and Wynne's (44) results with sympathectomy are also relevant, since we must not neglect the arousal effects of interoceptor activity; and so is clinical anxiety due to metabolic and nutritional disorders, as well as that due to some conflict of cognitive processes.

Obviously these are not explanations that are being discussed, but possible lines of future research; and there is one problem in particular that I would urge should not be forgotten. This is the cortical feedback to the arousal system, in physiological terms: or in psychological terms, the *immediate drive value of cognitive processes*, without intermediary. This is psychologically demonstrable, and *has* been demonstrated repeatedly.

Anyone who is going to talk about acquired drives, or secondary motivation, should first read an old paper by Valentine (48). He showed that with a young child you can easily condition fear of a caterpillar or a furry animal, but cannot condition fear of opera glasses, or a bottle; in other words, the fear of some objects, that seems to be learned, was there, latent, all the time. Miller (29) has noted this possibility but he does not seem to have regarded it very seriously, though he cited a confirmatory experiment by Bergmann; for in the same passage he suggests that my own results with chimpanzee fears of certain objects, including strange people, may be dealt with by generalization. But this simply will not do, as Riesen and I noted (21). If you try to work this out, for the infant who is terrified on *first* contact with a stranger, an infant who has never shown such terror before, and who has always responded with eager affection to the only human beings he has made contact with up to this moment, you will find that this is a purely verbal solution.

Furthermore, as Valentine observed, you cannot postulate that the cause of such fear is simply the strange event, the thing that has never occurred before. For the chimpanzee reared in darkness, the first sight of a human being is of course a strange event, by definition; but fear of strangers does not occur until later, until the chimpanzee has had an opportunity to learn to recognize a few persons. The fear is not 'innate' but depends on some sort of cognitive or cortical conflict of learned responses. This is clearest when the baby chimpanzee, who knows and welcomes attendant

A and attendant *B*, is terrified when he sees *A* wearing *B*'s coat. The role of learning is inescapable in such a case.

The cognitive and learning element may be forgotten in other motivations, too. Even in the food drive, some sort of learning is fundamentally important: Ghent (15) has shown this, Sheffield and Campbell (41) seem in agreement, and so does the work of Miller and his associates (3, 32, 30) on the greater reinforcement value of food by mouth, compared to food by stomach tube. Beach (1) has shown the cortical-and-learning element in sex behavior. Melzack (28) has demonstrated recently that even pain responses involve learning. In Harlow's (16) results, of course, and Montgomery's (33), the cognitive element is obvious.

These cortical or cognitive components in motivation are clearest when we compare the behavior of higher and lower species. Application of a *genuine* comparative method is essential, in the field of motivation as well as of intellectual functions (22). Most disagreements between us have related to so-called 'higher' motivations. But the evidence I have discussed today need not be handled in such a way as to maintain the illusion of a complete separation between our various approaches to the problem. It *is* an illusion, I am convinced; we still have many points of disagreement as to relative emphasis, and as to which of several alternative lines to explore first, but this does not imply fundamental and final opposition. As theorists, we have been steadily coming together in respect of ideational (or representative, or mediating, or cognitive) processes; I believe that the same thing can happen, and is happening, in the field of motivation.

References
1. Beach, F. A. The neural basis at innate behavior. III. Comparison of learning ability and instinctive behavior in the rat. *J. comp. Psychol.*, 1939, 28, 225–262.
2. Bergmann, G. Theoretical psychology. *Annu. Rev. Psychol.*, 1953, 4, 435–458.
3. Berkun, M. M., Kessen, Marion L., & Miller, N. E. Hunger-reducing effects of food by stomach fistula versus food by mouth measured by a consummatory response. *J. comp. physiol. Psychol.*, 1952, 45, 550–554.
4. Berlyne, D. E. Novelty and curiosity as determinants of exploratory behavior. *Brit. J. Psychol.*, 1950, 41, 68–80.
5. Bexton, W. H., Heron, W., & Scott, T. H. Effects of decreased variation in the sensory environment. *Canad. J. Psychol.*, 1954, 8, 70–76.
6. Brink, F. Excitation and conduction in the neuron. In S. S. Stevens (Ed.), *Handbook of experimental psychology*. New York: Wiley, 1951. Pp. 50–93.

7. Brown, J. S. Problems presented by the concept of acquired drives. In *Current theory and research in motivation: a symposium.* Lincoln: Univer. of Nebraska Press, 1953. Pp. 1–21.

8. Brown, J. S., & Jacobs, A. The role of fear in the motivation and acquisition of responses. *J. exp. Psychol.*, 1949, 39, 747–759.

9. Burns, B. D. The mechanism of afterbursts in cerebral cortex. *J. Physiol.*, 1955, 127, 168–188.

10. Butler, R. A. Discrimination learning by rhesus monkeys to visual-exploration motivation. *J. comp. physiol. Psychol.*, 1953, 46, 95–98.

11. Carper, J. W., & Polliard, F. A. Comparison of the intake of glucose and saccharin solutions under conditions of caloric need. *Amer. J. Psychol.*, 1953, 66, 479–482.

12. Clare, M. H., & Bishop, G. H. Properties of dendrites; apical dendrites of the cat cortex. *EEG clin. Neurophysiol.*, 1955, 7, 85–98.

13. Duffy, Elizabeth. An explanation of 'emotional' phenomena without the use of the concept 'emotion'. *J. gen. Psychol.*, 1941, 25, 283–293.

14. Eccles, J. C. *The neurophysiological basis of mind.* London: Oxford Univer. Press, 1953.

15. Ghent, Lila. The relation of experience to the development of hunger. *Canad. J. Psychol.*, 1951, 5, 77–81.

16. Harlow, H. F. Mice, monkeys, men, and motives. *Psychol. Rev.*, 1953, 60, 23–32.

17. Harlow, H. F., Harlow, Margaret K., & Meyer, D. R. Learning motivated by a manipulation drive. *J. exp. Psychol.*, 1950, 40, 228–234.

18. Hebb, D. O. Elementary school methods. *Teach. Mag.* (Montreal), 1930, 12, 23–26.

19. Hebb, D. O. *Organization of behavior.* New York: Wiley, 1949.

20. Hebb, D. O. On human thought. *Canad. J. Psychol.*, 1953, 7, 99–110.

21. Hebb, D. O., & Riesen, A. H. The genesis of irrational fears. *Bull. Canad. Psychol. Ass.*, 1943, 3, 49–50.

22. Hebb, D. O., & Thompson, W. R. The social significance of animal studies. In G. Lindzey (Ed.), *Handbook of social psychology.* Cambridge, Mass.: Addison-Wesley, 1954. Pp. 532–561.

23. Li, Choh-Luh, & Jasper, H. Microelectrode studies of the cerebral cortex in the cat. *J. Physiol.*, 1953, 121, 117–140.

24. Lindsley, D. B. Emotion. In S. S. Stevens (Ed.), *Handbook of experimental psychology.* New York: Wiley, 1951. Pp. 473–516.

25. Lloyd, D. P. C. A direct central inhibitory action of dromically conducted impulses. *J. Neurophysiol.*, 1941, 4, 184–190.

26. MacCorquodale, K., & Meehl, P. E. A distinction between hypothetical constructs and intervening variables. *Psychol. Rev.*, 1948, 55, 95–107.

27. Marshall, S. L. A. *Men against fire.* New York: Morrow, 1947.

28. Melzack, R. The effects of early experience on the emotional responses to pain. Unpublished doctor's dissertation, McGill Univer., 1954.

29. Miller, N. E. Learnable drives and rewards. In S. S. Stevens (Ed.), *Handbook of experimental psychology.* New York: Wiley, 1951. Pp. 435–472.

30. Miller, N. E. Some studies of drive and drive reduction. Paper read at Amer. Psychol. Ass., Cleveland, September, 1953.

31. Miller, N. E., Bailey, C. J., & Stevenson, J. A. F. Decreased 'hunger' but increased food intake from hypothalamic lesions. *Science*, 1950, 112, 256–259.

32. Miller, N. E., & Kessen, Marion L. Reward effects of food via stomach fistula compared with those via mouth. *J. comp. physiol. Psychol.*, 1952, 45, 555–564.

33. Montgomery, K. C. The effect of activity deprivation upon exploratory behavior. *J. comp. physiol. Psychol.*, 1953, 46, 438–441.

34. Moruzzi, G., & Magoun, H. W. Brain stem reticular formation and activation of the EEG. *EEG clin. Neurophysiol.*, 1949, 1, 455–473.

35. Mowrer, O. H. Motivation. *Annu. Rev. Psychol.*, 1952, 3, 419–438.

36. Nissen, H. W. Instinct as seen by a psychologist. *Psychol. Rev.*, 1953, 60, 291–294.

37. Olds, J., & Milner, P. Positive reinforcement produced by electrical stimulation of septal area and other regions of rat brain. *J. comp. physiol. Psychol.*, 1954, 47, 419–427.

38. Olszewski, J. The cytoarchitecture of the human reticular formation. In E. D. Adrian, F. Bremer, & H. H. Jasper (Eds.), *Brain mechanisms and consciousness*. Oxford: Blackwell, 1954.

39. Schlosberg, H. Three dimensions of emotion. *Psychol. Rev.*, 1954, 61, 81–88.

40. Sharpless, S. K. Role of the reticular formation in habituation. Unpublished doctor's dissertation, McGill Univer., 1954.

41. Sheffield, F. D., & Campbell, B. A. The role of experience in the 'spontaneous' activity of hungry rats. *J. comp. physiol. Psychol.*, 1954, 47, 97–100.

42. Sheffield, F. D., & Roby, T. B. Reward value of a non-nutritive sweet taste. *J. comp. physiol. Psychol.*, 1950, 43, 471–481.

43. Sheffield, F. D., Wulff, J. J., & Backer, R. Reward value of copulation without sex drive reduction. *J. comp. physiol. Psychol.*, 1951, 44, 3–8.

44. Solomon, R. L., & Wynne, L. C. Avoidance conditioning in normal dogs and in dogs deprived of normal autonomic functioning. *Amer. Psychologist*, 1950, 5, 264. (Abstract.)

45. Stellar, E. The physiology of motivation. *Psychol. Rev.*, 1954, 61, 5–22.

46. Thompson, W. R., & Solomon, L. M. Spontaneous pattern discrimination in the rat. *J. comp. physiol. Psychol.*, 1954, 47, 104–107.

47. Tyhurst, J. S. Individual reactions to community disaster: the natural history of psychiatric phenomena. *Amer. J. Psychiat.*, 1951, 107, 764–769.

48. Valentine, C. W. The innate bases of fear. *J. genet. Psychol.*, 1930, 37, 394–419.

49. Whiting, J. W. M., & Mowrer, O. H. Habit progression and regression – a laboratory study of some factors relevant to human socialization. *J. comp. psychol.*, 1943, 36, 229–253.

50. Woodworth, R. S. *Psychology*. New York: Holt, 1921.

51. Woodworth, R. S., & Marquis, D. G. *Psychology*. (5th Ed.) New York: Holt, 1947.

The Central Motive State

Excerpts from C. T. Morgan, 'Physiological mechanisms of
motivation'. In M. R. Jones (Ed.), *Nebraska Symposium on
Motivation*, University of Nebraska Press, Lincoln, 1957, pp. 1–35.

Theory of the Central Motive State

The theory as first presented considered three stages in the motivational process: (1) the arousal of motivated behavior, (2) the
maintenance of such behavior by 'central motive states' within
the nervous system, and (3) the satiation or termination of such
behavior. Taking these three stages in order, I shall briefly restate the theory, making slight changes in terminology. Then, in
later sections, the theory will be evaluated, modified, and extended on the basis of the experimental evidence accumulating
in recent years.

Arousal

Drives are sometimes aroused by stimuli, applied either to
exteroceptors or to receptors within the body. Stomach contractions, headaches, dry throats, pain, heat, and cold, all *can* be
motivating. In some simpler cases, it is permissible to think of
stimuli as constituting the drive if motivated behavior appears
and disappears with the waxing and waning of the stimulus. However, it is more often the case that a stimulus initiates activity in
the nervous system that outlasts the stimulus or persists even
during lapses in stimulation. This activity is motivating in the
sense that it imparts an impetus to behavior. The more general
case, therefore is of a motive state intervening between the
stimulus and the motivated behavior – a state whose properties
depend only in part on the stimulus that aroused it. Hence, it is
simpler and more correct to regard all drives as central states
that may in some instances be aroused or facilitated by receptor-
mediated stimuli.

Chemical and hormonal conditions in the blood may also
arouse motive states. In the ordinary course of affairs, they probably account for the arousal of considerably more motivational
activity than do peripheral stimuli. These chemical and hormonal
conditions, which I earlier referred to as the humoral motive

factor (h.m.f.), may affect the brain in one or more of three possible ways: (1) by directly stimulating centers and systems of the brain concerned in motivated behavior; (2) by stimulating internal receptors; and (3) by producing changes in effectors, which in turn excite receptors. We shall examine below the case that can be made for these modes of arousal of drives.

Properties of the motive state

The theory goes on to present four characteristics of a central motive state (c.m.s.): (1) Once initiated, a c.m.s. tends to persist without outside support from sensory inputs or excitants. That is not to say that it would go on forever without such supports but merely that it tends to 'coast' on its own. It perseverates. (2) General activity accompanies a central motive state and is an integral part of its expression. (3) A c.m.s. may 'emit' certain patterns of behavior characteristic of the state without specific receptor stimulation. (4) A c.m.s. predisposes the organism to react in certain ways to particular stimuli and not to react to others. In other words, a c.m.s. selectively sets or primes certain responses to stimuli.

Satisfaction

The theory includes, finally, a statement of four possible ways in which a motive state, once aroused, may be terminated: (1) by elimination of the stimulus or h.m.f. which originally gave rise to it; (2) by the liberation of some humoral messengers different from those arousing drive but capable of directly reducing the c.m.s.; (3) by the stimulation of receptors in the course of behavior emitted by c.m.s.; and (4) by the behavior per se resulting from c.m.s.

Classification of Drives

Psychologists have made many attempts to devise a useful classification of drives and motives. The task has not been easy, nor do I think it will ever be. Without considering the so-called derived motives, we find at the physiological level alone almost as many drives as there are components of the diet or things an organism can do in a given environment. It is easily possible to compile a long list of drives – too long to be very manageable or useful for theory-building purposes, as Hebb (1955), Nissen (1953), and others have pointed out.

One of the difficulties, it would seem, is that the physiological mechanisms of drive are not so organized as to be mutually exclusive of one another. When we attempt to manipulate hunger, we also include thirst, and vice versa. Activity seems to be a drive of its own, yet varies with thirst, hunger, and sex drives. All these drives, and emotional drives as well, depend in part on 'activating' functions of sensory stimuli and on the reticular system. Conditions within the internal environment that arouse drives interact with one another, and the neural centers and pathways concerned in physiological drives interconnect and overlap each other. For these reasons, there is little hope of concocting a classification that provides for independent, mutually exclusive physiological drives.

Since nature has not seen fit to meet our demands for nicely compartmentalized drives, I see no alternative but to admit that any classification we choose to make must be arbitrarily devised to suit the practical or theoretical purposes of the moment. If our aim is to understand regulatory mechanisms in food acceptance, we may have to assume a dozen or more hunger drives. If we are concerned with more molar problems of personality dynamics, we may find it best to devise a very general classification of physiological drives. There would seem then to be no one classification of drives that can accommodate the various purposes to which psychologists may wish to put it.

Recent research, however, would seem to justify some additions to our classical list of physiological drives. I refer particularly to the work on exploratory, curiosity, and manipulative drives. The evidence that such drives exist as innate physiological drives is now becoming quite impressive. These drives are sufficient to motivate animals to learn many of the same tasks for which hunger motivation was previously used. Work has not proceeded far enough to tell us how the drives are related to each other or how they may be analyzed. We may, however, find it justifiable to distinguish between 'somatic' and 'perceptual' components of these drives.

There is already evidence for a relatively independent 'somatic' activity drive, released by external stimuli but reduced by the activity itself. We might consider some components of the exploratory and manipulative drives to be simply special cases of an activity drive, with the particular type of activity that is manifested being a question only of the structural make-up of the individual or of the stimulating conditions of the environment. On the other hand, the 'perceptual' component might prove to be a 'drive for stimulation', a sort of stimulus hunger for novelty. Thompson and Solomon (1954) seem to have some evidence for such a component. These investigators were able to demonstrate 'interest' in visual stimuli and, in fact, the formation of a visual discrimination merely by changing patterns in the visual environment while opportunities for somatic activity were held constant.

They find, moreover, in this type of experiment and in experiments restricting the visual environment during infancy that 'curiosity' or 'perceptual drive' seems to be reduced by becoming familiar with a particular stimulus situation. If one considers the amount of time domestic and laboratory animals are engaged in investigating their environment, the hours people spend at television sets, and the billions of dollars tourists spend 'looking' at things, it would seem that the 'perceptual drive', as I prefer to call it, is one of considerable significance in human and animal behavior. We may find that it supplies a missing link in understanding personality dynamics, as well as the intellectual activities of some of our more creative individuals.

So far little is known about the physiological mechanisms of 'perceptual' drive. There is one report of diminished curiosity in a monkey after lesions of the temporal lobe (Butler and Harlow 1954). Perhaps more research will be forthcoming in the future, especially as conditions for experimenting with somatic and perceptual drives are more clearly delimited. There would seem to be no reason, though, why they should not yield to the same sort of physiological analysis that has been made for the other physiological drives.

References

Butler, R. A., & Harlow, H. F. Persistence of visual exploration in monkeys. *J. comp. physiol. Psychol.*, 1954, 47, 258–263.

Hebb, D. O. Drives and the c.n.s. *Psychol. Rev.*, 1955, 62, 243–254.

Nissen, H. W. Instinct as seen by a psychologist. In Allee, W. C., Nissen, H. W., & Nimkoff, M. F. A re-examination of the concept of instinct. *Psychol. Rev.*, 1953, 60, 287–297.

Thompson, W. R., & Solomon, L. M. Spontaneous pattern discrimination in the rat. *J. comp. physiol. Psychol.*, 1954, 47, 104–107.

11 B. Andersson and S. M. McCann

Search for Neural Mechanisms Controlling Drinking

An abridged version of B. Andersson and S. M. McCann, 'A further study of polydipsia evoked by hypothalamic stimulation in the goat', *Acta Physiologica Scandanavia*, P. A. Norstedt & Soner, Stockholm, 1955, Vol. 33, pp. 333–46.

It has been reported earlier that hypertonic sodium chloride solutions could produce primary polydipsia when injected into a certain region of the hypothalamus of the goat (Andersson 1952, 1953). The injection of about 0·1 ml of a 1·5 to 2% sodium chloride solution into the medial hypothalamus induced the animals to drink large volumes of water in many cases. In order if possible to obtain a more precise localization of the portion of the hypothalamus concerned with this response, microinjections, as reported in the following, were performed. Since it has been impossible to determine the effective spread of these injections and the effect obtained often has been difficult to repeat, the study has also been extended to include electrical stimulation.

Methods

Full grown, female goats were used for the experiments. Microinjections into the hypothalamus were performed according to a method described elsewhere (Andersson and Larsson 1955). For electrical stimulation, Hess' technique (1932, 1949), somewhat modified for use in goats (Andersson 1951) was used. Three electrodes could be stimulated, either simultaneously or individually, at a given depth in the hypothalamus with this technique.

Histological technique

After killing the goats by decapitation, the heads were perfused with Bouin's fixative. After fixation in Bouin's and paraffin imbedding, the hypothalamus with attached pituitary was serially sectioned and stained by Gomori's chrom alum hematoxylin method (Gomori 1941) as described by Bargmann (1950). The localization of the effective points of stimulation was in most cases facilitated by the injection of minute amounts of 1% osmium acid or by electrocoagulation just prior to killing the animals.

Results

Microinjections into the hypothalamus

Injections of 0.003 to 0.01 ml of 2 to 3% sodium chloride solutions into different parts of the hypothalamus were made in 16 experiments. The injection technique made it possible to inject the solutions at several locations in each experiment. The area of the hypothalamus where injections of this kind had an obvious polydipsic effect was more restricted than that found when using larger amounts of hypertonic saline (Andersson 1953). Micro-injections into other regions of the hypothalamus failed to produce polydipsia; however, no systematic exploration has been made of the region just dorsal to that which induced drinking.

Positive results were obtained from one or more points of stimulation in 8 of these experiments. The volume of water drunk as a consequence of such injections varied between 2 to 8 liters. The time of onset of drinking varied between 30 to 60 seconds after the injection, and the goats drank more or less continuously for two to five minutes thereafter. The effect was, however, not always repeatable on renewed injection. It could be obtained three times at the most. Other effects such as increased food intake, licking, etc., were also seen in some cases following the injections, but in many cases there were no observable effects other than drinking.

The most obvious polydipsia was obtained in two experiments. These two goats drank 6 and 8 liters of water, respectively, as a result of the injections.

Electrical stimulation of the hypothalamus

This type of stimulation was carried out in 7 experiments on 6 goats with the aim to study the water intake. In each experiment, many points in the hypothalamus were stimulated. Polydipsia was obtained from 5 different points of stimulation. These points were found to lie within a strictly limited area between Columna fornicis descendens and Tractus Vicq d'Azyr, at the horizontal level of the middle of the hypothalamus. The most striking polydipsic effects were obtained in two goats. The points of stimulation in these two cases were immediately adjacent to each other.

The following abbreviated protocols of these two experiments document more fully the remarkable reproducibility of the phenomenon.

I. Times: Dec. 3, 1954 Goat 'G'. Weight: 39 kg.

11.45   Operation completed, animal in good condition.

12.00–15.00 Stimulations 1 to 2 mm from the point which later gave the most pronounced drinking induced drinking of approximately 3 liters of water. Since stimulation was not always effective, the electrodes were then moved slightly.

15.03–15.25 The animal drank during each of 6 consecutive stimulations by the most rostral of the three electrodes (stimulus strength 0.5–1.0 Volt, 50 cycles/sec.). The time of latency before the onset of drinking varied between 9 and 25 seconds. The stimulations were continued for 10 to 20 seconds after drinking had started. The goat stopped drinking 2 to 3 seconds after cessation of stimulation. Five liters of water were consumed during the 6 stimulations.

15.27 After 2 more effective stimulations, the stimulus was repeated as above, but the animal was now offered a mixture of urine and water. She started to drink after 10 seconds and continued to drink steadily during the 8 seconds the stimulation was continued and for 2 seconds thereafter. By this time the animal had drunk an additional 2 liters of water.

15.45 After another positive stimulation at this point, she was again stimulated for 4 minutes in an attempt to produce extreme overhydration. During this period she drank with occasional short interruptions another 4.5 liters.

16.40 After two brief effective stimulations by the rostral electrode, a slight effect was obtained by the middle electrode, whereas stimulation by the caudal electrode at the same strength was completely ineffective. The animal now looked sick and exhibited rapid, shallow breathing. The goat had now drunk 16 liters during the whole course of this experiment. Her rumen was quite hard and distended by water. Large volumes of dilute urine were voided containing considerable hemoglobin.

16.53 Electrocoagulation was performed at the effective point of stimulation. The electrodes were then removed, and the animal was left overnight with free access to food and water.

Discussion

Several hypotheses have been proposed to explain the sensation of thirst. Much evidence indicates that Cannon's theory (1918) that the sensation arises from the mouth inadequately explains the feeling of thirst (Bellows and Van Wagenen 1939, Steggerda 1939). According to another widely held theory, the sensation is closely correlated with cellular dehydration (Gilman 1937). Wolf (1950) on the basis of his osmometric analysis of thirst has even postulated that 'osmoreceptors' such as those which probably govern the secretion of antidiuretic hormone (Verney 1947) might also regulate water intake.

Evidence for the view that the hypothalamus might play a role in the regulation of water intake was provided by the observation that primary polydipsia could be evoked by injections of hypertonic saline solutions into the hypothalamus of the goat (Andersson 1952, 1953). The choice of a ruminant animal such as the goat for experiments of this type appears to offer several advantages. The voluminous rumen can function as a fluid reservoir (Andersson 1955), which permits consumption of large volumes of water before significant inhibitory influences from the distension of the digestive tract seem to suppress the thirst mechanism. Furthermore, the placid goat is very well suited for hypothalamic stimulation in the conscious state.

The microinjections reported here have more closely localized the region of the hypothalamus where stimulation of this kind can evoke drinking. As, however, other effects were sometimes seen in association with polydipsia from the injections, conclusive proof has not been obtained for the view that the osmotic stimulus was the adequate stimulus to the tissue producing the drinking response. But that the osmotic stimuli may preferentially excite the 'thirst mechanism' is indicated by the fact that electrical stimulation of the regions adjacent to the most effective area usually gave more side effects than similarly placed injections.

Insufficient reproducibility and the failure to obtain a more exact localisation appeared to constitute the principal disadvantages of this type of stimulation. Both of these disadvantages have been circumvented by electrical stimulation of the hypothalamus. When stimulating electrically, it was possible to repeat the effect very frequently and without fail. The fact that during this type of stimulation the animal drank a urine water mixture indicates that the urge to drink was very strong. Furthermore, the short time of latency before the onset of drinking and the short period of drinking after the cessation of stimulation clearly relates the polydipsia to the applied stimulus. The fact that stimulation continued over longer periods, when the animals where already considerably hydrated, could produce an enormous overhydration shows that any inhibitory mechanism in these cases was insufficient to overcome the experimentally induced drinking. This taken together with the marked hemodilution found here clearly proves the primacy of the polydipsia from these hypothalamic stimulations.

The active region of the hypothalamus determined by microinjections and electrical stimulation is included within the somewhat larger area which was previously found using larger volumes of hypertonic saline (Andersson 1953). The portion of the middle hypothalamus which appears to be concerned with water intake is included in the area where Hess in his stimulations, compiled by Brügger (1943), found bulimia in cats. In some of these experiments, the cats showed a preference for milk as contrasted to meat, suggesting that they might also have drunk water if it had been offered to them. The polydipsia seen in the experiments reported here has been completely separated from hyperphagia, which would be consistent with the idea that the region governing food intake may lie more laterally (Anand and Brobeck 1951, Larsson 1954).

References

Anand, B. K. and J. R. Brobeck, Proc. Soc. Exp. Biol. Med. 1951. 77. 323.
Andersson, B., Acta Physiol. Scand. 1951. 23. 8.
Andersson, B., Experientia. 1952. VIII/4. 157.
Andersson, B., Acta Physiol. Scand. 1953. 28. 188.
Andersson, B., Ibidem. 1955. 33. 50.
Andersson, B. and S. Larsson, Experientia. 1955, XI/3. 116.
Bargmann, W., Mikroskopie (Wien) 1950. 5. 289.
Bellows, R. T. and W. P. Van Wagenen, Amer. J. Physiol. 1939. 126. 13.
Brügger, M., Helv. Physiol. Acta 1943. 1. 183.
Cannon, W. B., Proc. Roy. Soc., B. 1918. 90. 283.
Gilman, A., Amer. J. Physiol. 1937. 120. 323.
Gomori, G., Amer. J. Path. 1941. 17. 395.
Hess, W. R., Beiträge zur Physiologie des Hirnstammes I. Georg Thieme, Leipzig 1932.
Hess, W. R., Das Zwischenhirn. Benno Schwabe & Co, Basel 1949.
Larsson, S., Acta Physiol. Scand. 1954. 32. Suppl. 115.
Steggerda, F. R., Amer. J. Physiol. 1939. 126. 635.
Verney, E. B., Proc. Roy. Soc., B. 1947, 135, 25.
Wolf, A. V., Ibidem 1950. 161. 75.

Maternal and Sexual Behavior Induced by Intracranial Chemical Stimulation

Reproduced in full from *Science*, 1956, Vol. 124, pp. 228–29.

A technique permitting chemical or electric stimulation, or both, of restricted brain areas in unanesthetized rats, and electro-encephalographic (EEG) recording from these areas, has been developed and found to be of value (1).

Implants are prepared as follows. Two Tygon-insulated copper or silver wires (0·1 mm in diameter) are baked along the outside of No. 22 hypodermic tubing extending from 2 to 9 mm below the base of a plastic holder (2). The wires lead from contact points on the holder and terminate at opposite sides of the end of the shaft as a bipolar stimulating-and-recording electrode. The implant shaft is permanently inserted in the brain while the anesthetized rat is held in a stereotaxic instrument. Four holes in the base of the holder permit rigid attachment to the skull with jeweler's screws.

Two or more days later, rats are placed in 3- by 3- by 2·5-ft boxes for stimulation testing. A small clip connects the implant to light overhead leads from a 0- to 12-v, 60 cy/sec stimulator, or to an EEG machine. The clip also contains a No. 30 metal cannula that penetrates the implant shaft to the depth of the electrode tips or lower. Seven feet of PE 10 polyethylene tubing (0·024 in. in diameter) leads from the cannula to a micro-syringe which can release a minimum of 0·0001 cm³ of solution into the brain. All overhead leads are intertwined and spring-mounted, permitting repeated, controlled stimulation of a freely moving animal. Behavioral tests with a series of external stimulus objects are given before, during, and after chemical stimulation, and placebo solutions and nonhormonal neural excitants are used for control brain injections during initial tests or retests.

The technique is first being used to test whether there are 'primary drive centers' under hormonal influence or control (3). Thus far, maternal and sexual behavior have been elicited from separate brain loci in a series of males during stimulation with sodium testosterone sulfate in 0·09-percent saline, and, subject to verification, a mixture of a pure salt of estrone and a suspension of progesterone has induced heat behavior in two females (4). Maternal behavior elicited during chemical stimulation includes nest building and a persistent retrieving and grooming of litters of young. All aspects of mating behavior have been induced or accentuated. Attendant high-drive states are suggested by an exaggerated speed, compulsiveness, and frequency of all overt responses during positive test periods.

Although individual animals respond positively for up to 4 test days, duplication of effect from animal to animal has imposed difficult problems. Of 130 male operates tested with the testosterone salt, five have shown complete maternal response, 14 have shown nesting behavior only, and six have shown exaggerated sexual response. Histological data suggest that locus of immediate action is a critical factor, with slight variation in placement leading to incomplete, confounded, or diffuse drive states, or negative results. Initial findings tentatively implicate the medial preoptic area in maternal behavior and the lateral preoptic area in sexual behavior.

A variety of effects have been noted during testosterone stimulation at adjacent loci. Those seen in five or more cases include respiratory changes, diffuse hyperactivation, long-lasting exploratory-like behavior, repetitive localized muscular response, digging, leaping, and seizures.

The following list includes other significant points of departure from chemical or electric-stimulation data reported in the literature. Since positive test responses completely transcend control behavioral data, two single cases of possible theoretical significance are also briefly described.

1) Elicited behavior, whether specific or diffuse, commonly continues without decrement for more than 90 minutes following chemical stimulation.

2) An entire hierarchy of related responses can be brought to the threshold of activation, with adequate stimulus objects insuring integrated behavior.

3) A segment of a response hierarchy may occur alone. Excessive nest-building is often seen, and one aspect of the nesting pattern, 'pick up paper and push under body', continued rapidly for more than 1 hour in three cases.

4) Specific behavior has occurred in the absence of appropriate external stimuli. One male continuously 'retrieved' his tail when stimulated with testosterone and then repeatedly retrieved a female in heat. When pups and paper were supplied, however,

the male built a nest and retrieved and groomed the young, neglecting the objects to which he previously reacted.

5) In one case, maternal and sexual drives were activated simultaneously. The testosterone-treated male reacted to stimuli related to each drive and to a degree never shown in control tests. Double activation was most convincingly illustrated when a female (not in heat) and newborn rat pups were presented. The male attempted copulation twice while a pup he was retrieving to a nest was still in his mouth. Shaft placement was adjacent to both areas previously implicated in sexual and maternal response.

All effects have followed injection of minute amounts of solution, containing from 0·003 to 0·05 mg of the testosterone salt. In this connection, it must be emphasized that the possibility remains that causative factors other than hormonal properties may be operating. Thus far, however, control testing with neural excitants, physiological saline, and electric stimulation has failed to produce or perpetuate these complex behavior patterns.

Initial EEG data are promising. Records from six testosterone-treated 'maternal' or 'nesting' males have shown single spiking lawfully spaced in a normal record rather than the general spiking seen after picrotoxin or metrazol injection. Selective chemical action seems probable. Also, testosterone-induced spiking occurs before, not during, elicited overt behavior. Correlation of EEG changes with brain stimulation and with elicited response presents technical problems but could become a powerful tool.

The early data suggest other implications and further applications.

1) A neurophysiological definition of drive seems within reach. The role of hormones in eliciting behavior should be clarified as well as the organization of neural circuits that mediate or integrate primary drives. Present data favor a 'neural center' theory, but control studies are needed.

2) Responses analogous to symptoms of mental dysfunction often occur during chemical stimulation. These include 'obsessive-compulsive acts,' tics, diffuse excitation, and states of hypo- and hypersensitivity to sensory stimuli. Further work may establish tie-ins between shifts in chemical balance in the central nervous system and certain forms of mental dysfunction.

3) Males having no adult contact with females, young, or paper have responded to chemical stimulation with integrated maternal behavior on the first trial. The data are pertinent to the

problem of whether innate, centrally organized sensory-motor connections exist for complex response systems.

4) Testosterone has ostensibly elicited both sexual and maternal patterns. The findings may reflect multiple properties for the hormone. Limited progesterone-like activity has been proposed for the androgens by Selye, and progesterone has been linked to maternal response.

5) Chemical stimulation has elicited long-lasting, integrated behavior that was free of lapse or interference. The data strongly suggest selective chemical action within the central nervous system. Further work may demonstrate that differential sensitivity to specific physiological change by functionally organized areas of the nervous system is a basic principle of neural function.

In summary, integrated, long-lasting drive states have been induced by direct chemical stimulation of brain loci. Further work with techniques of this type could well lead to breakthroughs in the study of pharmaceutical action, brain organization and function, and the dynamics of behavior.

References and Notes

1. I initiated the work as a public health post-doctoral fellow at McGill University with D. O. Hebb as sponsor. Work continues at the University of Wisconsin during the second fellowship year with H. F. Harlow as sponsor.
2. The Lucite holder is identical with that described by J. Olds and P. Milner, *J. Comp. Physiol. and Psychol.* 47, 419 (1954).
3. For example, F. A. Beach, *Psychosomat. Med.* 4, 173 (1942).
4. Hormone salts supplied by Ayerst, McKenna, and Harrison, Ltd., Montreal, Canada.

III Drive as a Theoretical Construct

While speculations about the neural processes that constitute drive were in progress, Hull introduced 'drive' as an intervening variable in his formal behaviour theory. He was concerned with explaining two types of effects of experimental 'drive manipulations' (e.g., varying hours of food deprivation): (1) drive manipulations usually produce a change in the overall activity or excitement level of the animal, and (2) they produce a change in the tendency to make certain specific responses (e.g., eating or running). Correspondingly, Hull postulated two hypothetical factors. He suggested that experimental drive manipulations alter the degree of *general drive* (D), as well as the degree of prevalence of cues associated with particular responses, *drive stimuli* (S_D). As a construct, related in theoretical postulates either to certain antecedent, independent variables (e.g., hours of deprivation, intensity of electric shock) or to dependent, response variables (e.g., speed of response, rate of lever pressing), *drive* has been found useful in various fields of research. Examples of this are found in the works of Mowrer, Miller, and Amsel.

Drive as an Intervening Variable in a
Formal Behavior System

Excerpts from C. L. Hull, *Principles of Behavior*,
Appleton-Century-Crofts, New York, 1943, Chapters 5 and 14.

Drives are Typical Intervening Variables

It is important to note in this connection that the general concept
of drive (D) tends strongly to have the systematic status of an
intervening variable, never directly observable. The need of food,
ordinarily called hunger, produces a typical primary drive. Like
all satisfactory intervening variables, the presence and the amount
of the hunger drive are susceptible of a double determination on
the basis of correlated events which are themselves directly
observable. Specifically, the amount of the food need clearly increases with the number of hours elapsed since the last intake of
food; here the amount of hunger drive (D) is a function of observable *antecedent* conditions, i.e., of the need which is measured by the number of hours of food privation. On the other
hand, the amount of energy which will be expended by the
organism in the securing of food varies largely with the intensity
of hunger drive existent at the time; here the amount of 'hunger'
is a function of observable events which are its *consequence*. As
usual with unobservables, the determination of the exact quantitative functional relationship of the intervening variable to both
the antecedent and the consequent conditions presents serious
practical difficulties. This probably explains the paradox that
despite the almost universal use of the concepts of need and drive,
this characteristic functional relationship is not yet determined
for any need.

Primary Motivational Concepts

At the outset it will be necessary to introduce two notions not
previously discussed. These new concepts are analogous to that
of habit strength ($_SH_R$) which, it will be recalled, is a logical
construct conceived in the quantitative framework of a centigrade
system.

The first of the two concepts is *strength of primary drive*; this
is represented by the symbol D. The strength-of-drive scale is

conceived to extend from a zero amount of primary motivation (complete satiation) to the maximum possible to a standard organism of a given species. In accordance with the centigrade principle this range of primary drive is divided into 100 equal parts or units. For convenience and ease of recall, this unit will be called the *mote*, a contraction of the word *motivation* with an added *e* to preserve normal pronunciation.

Because of the practical exigencies of exposition the second of the new concepts has already been utilized occasionally in the last few pages, where it has been referred to as the 'reaction tendency', a term in fairly general use though lacking in precision of meaning. For this informal expression we now substitute the more precise equivalent, *reaction-evocation potentiality*; or, more briefly, *reaction potential*. This will be represented by the symbol $_sE_R$. Like habit ($_sH_R$) and drive (D), reaction-evocation potential is also designed to be measured on a 100-point scale extending from a zero reaction tendency up to the physiological limit possible to a standard organism. The unit of reaction potentiality will be called the *wat*, a contraction of the name *Watson*.

It should be evident from the preceding paragraphs that D and $_sE_R$ are symbolic constructs in exactly the same sense as $_sH_R$, and that they share both the advantages and disadvantages of this status. The drive concept, for example, is proposed as a common denominator of all primary motivations, whether due to food privation, water privation, thermal deviations from the optimum, tissue injury, the action of sex hormones, or other causes. This means, of course, that drive will be a different function of the objective conditions associated with each primary motivation. For example, in the case of hunger the strength of the primary drive will probably be mainly a function of the number of hours of food privation, say; in the case of sex it will probably be mainly a function of the concentration of a particular sex hormone in the animal's blood; and so on. Stated formally,

$$D = f(h)$$
$$D = f(c)$$
$$D = \text{etc.},$$

where h represents the number of hours of food privation of the organism since satiation, and c represents the concentration of a particular hormone in the blood of the organism.

Turning now to the concept of reaction-evocation potentiality, we find, thanks to Perin's investigation (1942) that we are able at once to define $_sE_R$ as the product of a function of habit strength

$(_sH_R)$ multiplied by a function of the relevant drive (D). This multiplicative relationship is one of the greatest importance, because it is upon $_sE_R$ that the amount of action in its various forms presumably depends. It is clear, for example, that it is quite impossible to predict the vigor or persistence of a given type of action from a knowledge of either habit strength or drive strength alone; this can be predicted only from a knowledge of the product of the particular functions of $_sH_R$ and D respectively; in fact, this product constitutes the value which we are representing by the symbol $_sE_R$.

Summary and Preliminary Physiological Interpretation of Empirical Findings

Having the more important concepts of the systematic approach of primary motivation before us, we proceed to the formulation of some empirical findings as related to motivation.

Most, if not all, primary needs appear to generate and throw into the blood stream more or less characteristic chemical substances, or else to withdraw a characteristic substance. These substances (or their absence) have a selective physiological effect on more or less restricted and characteristic portions of the body (e.g., the so-called 'hunger' contractions of the digestive tract) which serves to activate resident receptors. This receptor activation constitutes the drive stimulus, S_D. In the case of tissue injury this sequence seems to be reversed; here the energy producing the injury is the drive stimulus, and its action causes the release into the blood of adrenal secretion which appears to be the physiological motivating substance.

It seems likely, on the basis of various analogies, that, other things equal, the intensity of the drive stimulus would be some form of negatively accelerated increasing function of the concentration of the drive substance in the blood. However, for the sake of expository simplicity we shall assume in the present preliminary analysis that it is an increasing linear function.

The afferent discharges arising from the drive stimulus (S_D) become conditioned to reactions just the same as any other elements in stimulus compounds, except that they may be somewhat more potent in acquiring habit loadings than most stimulus elements or aggregates. Thus the drive stimulus may play a rôle in a conditioned stimulus compound substantially the same as that of any other stimulus element or aggregate. As a stimulus, S_D naturally manifests both qualitative and intensity primary stimulus generalization in common with other stimulus elements or aggregates in conditioned stimulus compounds.

It appears probable that when blood which contains certain chemical substances thrown into it as the result of states of need, or which lacks certain substances as the result of other states of need, bathes the neural structures which constitute the anatomical bases of habit ($_sH_R$), the conductivity of these structures is augmented through lowered resistance either in the central neural tissue or at the effector end of the connection, or both. The latter type of action is equivalent, of course, to a lowering of the reaction threshold and would presumably facilitate reaction to neural impulses reaching the effector from any source whatever. As Beach (1942) suggests, it is likely that the selective action of drives on particular effector organs in non-learned forms of behavior acts mainly in this manner. It must be noted at once, however, that sensitizing a habit structure does not mean that this alone is sufficient to evoke the reaction, any more than that caffeine or benzedrine alone will evoke reaction. Sensitization merely gives the relevant neural tissue, upon the occurrence of an adequate set of receptor discharges, an augmented facility in routing these impulses to the reactions previously conditioned to them or connected by native (inherited) growth processes. This implies to a certain extent the undifferentiated nature of drive in general, contained in Freud's concept of the 'libido'. However, it definitely does not presuppose the special dominance of any one drive, such as sex, over the other drives.

While all drives seem to be alike in their powers of sensitizing *acquired* receptor-effector connections, their capacity to call forth within the body of the organism characteristic and presumably distinctive drive stimuli gives each a considerable measure of distinctiveness and specificity in the determination of action which, in case of necessity, may be sharpened by the process of patterning to almost any extent that the reaction situation requires for adequate and consistent reinforcement. In this respect, the action of drive substances differs sharply from that of a pseudo-drive substance such as caffeine, which appears to produce nothing corresponding to a drive stimulus.

Postulate 5

The effective habit strength $S\overline{H}R$ is jointly (1) a negative growth function of the strength of the habit at the point of reinforcement (S) and (2) of the magnitude of the difference (d) on the continuum of that stimulus between the afferent impulses of s and s

in units of discrimination thresholds (j.n.d.'s); where d represents a qualitative difference, the slope of the gradient of the negative growth function is steeper than where it represents a quantitative difference.

Postulate 6

Associated with every drive (D) is a characteristic drive stimulus (S_D) whose intensity is an increasing monotonic function of the drive in question.

Postulate 7

Any effective habit strength ($_s\overline{H}_R$) is sensitized into reaction potentiality ($_sE_R$) by all primary drives active within an organism at a given time, the magnitude of this potentiality being a product obtained by multiplying an increasing function of $_sH_R$ by an increasing function of D.

From Postulates 5, 6, and 7 there may be derived the following corollary:

Major Corollary

The amount of reaction potentiality ($_sE_R$) in any given primary motivational situation is the product of (1) the effective habit strength ($s_1 + s_D\overline{H}_R$) under the existing conditions of primary drive multiplied by (2) the quotient obtained from dividing the sum of the dominant value of the primary drive (D) plus the aggregate strength of all the non-dominant primary drives ($\dot{D}$) active at the time, by the sum of the same non-dominant drives plus the physiological drive maximum (M_D).

References

Beach, F. A. Arousal, maintenance, and manifestation of sexual excitement in male animals. *Psychosomatic Medicine*, 1942, 4, 173–198.
Perin, C. T. Behavior potentiality as a joint function of the amount of training and the degree of hunger at the time of extinction. *J. Exper. Psychol.*, 1942, 30, 93–113.

Fear as an Intervening Variable

Excerpt from O. H. Mowrer and R. R. Lamoreaux, Fear as an
intervening variable in avoidance conditioning, *Journal of
Comparative Psychology*, 1946, Vol. 39, pp. 29–50.

If conditioning were the simple process of stimulus substitution,
or associative learning, it is sometimes said to be, a conditioned
response should be an exact replica of the reaction made to the
so-called unconditioned stimulus. Sometimes, during the early
stages of conditioning, this is indeed the case; but more commonly the CR differs from the UnCR both quantitatively and
qualitatively. Hilgard and Marquis (1940), after surveying the
literature on this problem, conclude that the reaction to a conditioned stimulus can take any of four forms: (a) it may be a more
or less perfect reproduction, or 'redintegration', of the unconditioned response; (b) it may be a 'fractional component' of the
unconditioned response; (c) it may serve as a preparation, or
'set', for the unconditioned stimulus; or (d) it may be a response
which is due, not to conditioning proper, but to the 'sensitization'
produced by the unconditioned stimulus alone (hence the term
'pseudo-conditioning'). Much of the mystery concerning the non-
correspondence which is thus evidenced between conditioned
responses and their putative unconditioned prototypes can, we
believe, be removed by introducing the concept of fear as an
intervening variable in all conditioning experiments in which the
unconditioned stimulus is a noxious one.

In the study already cited (Mowrer and Lamoreaux, 1942), the
present writers have shown that an avoidance CR is acquired
much more quickly in rats if the CS, or 'danger signal,' terminates
the instant the CR occurs, instead of a few seconds before or a
few seconds afterwards. From this and related findings (Mowrer,
1939; Mowrer, 1940), it appears that, once the CS has become
capable of arousing fear, termination of the CS and the attendant
reduction in fear constitute a rewarding state of affairs which
powerfully reinforces the connection between the fear and whatever behavior immediately precedes (i.e., ordinarily 'causes') the
fear-reduction.

In a situation involving a traumatic (unconditioned) stimulus
and a warning (conditioned) stimulus, there are thus *two* types of

problems to be solved. Once the traumatic stimulus impinges upon the organism, the organism will engage in whatever type of behavior is best calculated to eliminate that stimulus; but when the warning signal occurs alone, the organism will be motivated only by fear and will engage in whatever type of behavior is best calculated to eliminate this painful emotion.

If the same response that eliminates the traumatic stimulus will also, when made anticipatorily, eliminate the premonitory warning and the attendant fear, then the so-called conditioned and unconditioned responses will be more or less identical. Or, in other words, if the same action provides the solution to the problem occasioned by the secondary drive as well as to the one occasioned by the primary one, then one and the same response will become habitual to both types of drive. But if the situation is such that the response required to eliminate the warning signal and the attendant fear is *different* from the response which must be made when the trauma itself occurs, then the so-called conditioned and the unconditioned response can be expected to differ accordingly. Obviously such responses may differ slightly or quite radically, but this non-correspondence, whatever its magnitude, need occasion no perplexity if the two responses are seen as the solutions to two different problem situations.

Whether an anticipatory response which reduces fear but is radically different from the response which reduces the traumatic stimulus of which the fear is premonitory should be called a 'conditioned response' is perhaps debatable; but it is certainly legitimate to say that it is produced by the conditioned stimulus, provided we do not lose sight of the fact that the occurrence of fear is an essential intermediate step. Strictly speaking, the CS produces the fear which then elicits the fear-reducing response – a response which, as we have seen, may be either the same as or markedly different from the response which has been found most appropriate to the unconditioned stimulus.

References

Hilgard, E. R., and Marquis, D. G. *Conditioning and learning.* New York: D. Appleton-Century, 1940.

Mowrer, O. H. A stimulus-response analysis of anxiety and its role as a reinforcing agent. *Psychol. Rev.*, 1939, 46, 553–565.

Mowrer, O. H. Anxiety-reduction and learning. *J. Exper. Psychol.*, 1940, 27, 497–516.

Mowrer, O. H., and Lamoreaux, R. R. Avoidance conditioning and signal duration – A study of secondary motivation and reward. *Psychol. Monogr.*, 1942, 54, No. 5, 34 pp.

Fear as an Acquirable Drive

An abridged version of N. E. Miller, Studies of fear as an acquirable drive: 1: Fear as motivation and fear-reduction as reinforcement in the learning of new responses, *Journal of Experimental Psychology*, 1948, Vol. 38, pp. 89–101.

An important role in human behavior is played by drives, such as fears, or desires for money, approval, or status, which appear to be learned during the socialization of the individual (1, 9, 11, 12, 13). While some studies have indicated that drives can be learned (2, 7, 10), the systematic experimental investigation of acquired drives has been scarcely begun. A great deal more work has been done on the innate, or primary drives such as hunger, thirst, and sex.

Fear is one of the most important of the acquirable drives because it can be acquired so readily and can become so strong. The great strength which fear can possess has been experimentally demonstrated in studies of conflict behavior. In one of these studies (3) it was found that albino rats, trained to run down an alley to secure food at a distinctive place and motivated by 46-hour hunger, would pull with a force of 50 gm. if they were restrained near the food. Other animals, that had learned to run away from the end of the same alley to escape electric shock, pulled with a force of 200 gm. when they were restrained near that place on trials during which they were not shocked and presumably were motivated only by fear. Furthermore, animals, that were first trained to run to the end of the alley to secure food and then given a moderately strong electric shock there, remained well away from the end of the alley, demonstrating that the habits motivated by fear were prepotent over those motivated by 46-hour hunger (8). This experimental evidence is paralleled by many clinical observations which indicate that fear (or anxiety as it is called when its source is vague or obscured by repression) plays a leading role in the production of neurotic behavior (4, 5).

The purpose of the present experiment was to determine whether or not once fear is established as a new response to a given situation, it will exhibit the following functional properties characteristic of primary drives, such as hunger: (a) when present motivate so-called random behavior and (b) when suddenly reduced serve as a reinforcement to produce learning of the immediately preceding response.

Apparatus and Procedure

The apparatus used in this experiment is illustrated in Fig. 1. It consisted of two compartments: one white with a grid as a floor and the other black with a smooth solid floor. Both of these had a glass front

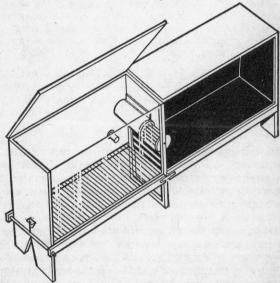

Figure 1 Acquired drive apparatus. The left compartment is painted white, the right one black. A shock may be administered through the grid which is the floor of the white compartment. When the animal is placed on the grid which is pivoted at the inside end, it moves down slightly making a contact that starts an electric timer. When the animal performs the correct response, turning the wheel or pressing the bar as the case may be, he stops the clock and actuates a solenoid which allows the door, painted with horizontal black and white stripes, to drop. The E can also cause the door to drop by pressing a button. The dimensions of each compartment are $18 \times 6 \times 8\frac{1}{2}$ in.

to enable the experimenter to observe the animal's behavior. The two compartments were separated by a door which was painted with horizontal black and white stripes. This door was held up by a catch operated by a solenoid and could be caused to drop in any one of three different ways: (a) by the E pushing a button, (b) by the rat moving a little cylindrical wheel made of horizontal rods stretched between

Bakelite disks and exposed above the right hand half of the door, (c) by a bar projecting $1\frac{1}{4}$ in. from the side of the apparatus in front of the upper left hand corner of the door.

The support of the grid was pivoted at the end near the door and held slightly above a contact by a little spring at the far end. Placing the rat into the apparatus caused the grid to move down a fraction of an inch and close the contact. This started an electric clock. When the animal caused the door to drop by rotating the wheel a fraction of a turn or pressing the bar (depending upon the way the apparatus was set), he stopped the clock which timed his response. The wheel was attached to a ratchet in such a way that the part of it facing the rat could only be moved downward. A brush riding on a segment of the wheel which projected through the back of the apparatus was arranged in such a way that each quarter of a revolution was recorded on an electric counter.

The animals used in this experiment were male albino rats approximately six months old. They had been tamed by handling but had not been used in any other experiment. They were allowed plenty of food and water in their home cages at all times.

Results

Before training, the animals showed no marked preference for either compartment. Then they were placed in the white compartment, received an electric shock from the grid, and escaped into the black compartment through the open door. After a number of such trials, the animals would run out of the white compartment even if no shock was on the grid.

To demonstrate that an acquired drive (fear or anxiety) had been established, the animals were taught a *new* habit *without further shocks*. The door (previously always open) was closed. The only way that the door could be opened was by rotating a little wheel, which was above the door, a fraction of a turn. Under these conditions, the animals exhibited trial-and-error behavior and gradually learned to escape from the white compartment by rotating the wheel.

If conditions were changed so that only pressing a bar would open the door, wheel turning extinguished, and a second new habit (bar pressing) was learned.

Control experiments demonstrated that the learning of the new habits was dependent upon having received moderately strong electric shocks during the first stages of training.

Discussion

The general pattern of the fear response and its capacity to produce a strong stimulus is determined by the innate structure of the animal. The connection between the pain and the fear is also presumably innate. But the connection between the cues in the white compartment and the fear was learned. Therefore the fear of the white compartment may be called an acquired drive. Because fear can be learned, it may be called acquirable; because it can motivate new learning, it may be called a drive.

Running through the door and into the black compartment removed the animal from the cues in the white compartment which were eliciting the fear and thus produced a reduction in the strength of the fear response and the stimuli which it produced. This reduction in the strength of the intense fear stimuli is presumably what gave the black compartment its acquired reinforcing value.

If the reduction in fear produced by running from the white into the black was the reinforcement for learning the new habit of wheel turning, we would expect this habit to show experimental extinction when that reinforcement was removed. This is exactly what happened. During the first trial on which turning the wheel no longer dropped the door, the animals gradually stopped performing this response and began to exhibit other responses. As would be expected, the one of these responses, pressing the bar, which caused the door to drop and allowed the animal to remove himself from the fear-producing cues in the white compartment, was gradually learned in a series of trials during which the wheel turning was progressively crowded out. Thus, it can be seen that the escape from the white compartment, which presumably produced a reduction in the strength of the fear, played a crucial role, similar to that of a primary reward, in the learning and maintenance of the new habits.

Some of the implications of the principles which this experiment has demonstrated should be mentioned briefly. It can be seen that being able to learn a response (fear of the white compartment) which in turn is able to motivate the learning and performance of a whole category of new responses (turning the wheel, pressing the bar, and any other means of escape from the white compartment) greatly increases the flexibility of learned behavior as a means of adapting to a changing environment.

The present experiment has demonstrated the drive function of fear as a response which presumably produces a strong stimulus. But if fear is a strong response-produced stimulus, it will be expected to function, not only as a drive, but also as a cue mediating secondary generalization. Thus, when fear is learned as a new response to a given situation, all of the habits which have been learned elsewhere in response to fear, as well as the innate responses to fear, should tend to be transferred to that new situation. Evidence supporting this deduction has been secured in a recent experiment by May (6).

It seems possible that the potentialities of response-produced stimuli as mediators of secondary generalization and sources of acquirable drive may account in stimulus-response, law-of-effect terms for the type of behavior which has been described as 'expectancy' and considered to be an exception to this type of explanation. If it should turn out that all of the phenomena of expectancy can be explained on the basis of the drive and cue functions of response-produced stimuli, expectancy will of course not vanish; it will be established as a secondary principle derivable from more primary ones.

The mechanism of acquired drives allows behavior to be more adaptive in complex variable situations. It also allows behavior to appear more baffling and apparently lawless to any investigator who has not had the opportunity to observe the conditions under which the acquired drive was established. In the present experiment the learning and performance of the responses of turning the wheel and pressing the bar are readily understandable. An E dealing with many rats, a few of which without his knowledge had been shocked in the white compartment, might be puzzled by the fact that these few rats became so preoccupied with turning the wheel or pressing the bar. In the present experiment, the white and black compartments are very obvious features of the animal's environment. If more obscure external cues or internal ones had been involved, the habits of turning the wheel and pressing the bar might seem to be completely bizarre and maladaptive. One hypothesis is that neurotic symptoms, such as compulsions, are habits which are motivated by fear (or anxiety as it is called when its source is vague or obscured by repression) and reinforced by a reduction in fear.

References

1. Allport, G. W. *Personality*. New York: Henry Holt, 1937.
2. Anderson, E. E. The externalization of drive: III. Maze learning by non-rewarded and by satiated rats. *J. genet. Psychol.*, 1941, 59, 397–426.
3. Brown, J. S. Generalized approach and avoidance responses in relation to conflict behavior. New Haven: Dissertation, Yale Univ., 1940.
4. Freud, S. *New introductory lectures on psychoanalysis.* New York: Norton, 1933.

5. Freud, S. *The problem of anxiety*. New York: Norton, 1936.
6. May, M. A. Experimentally acquired drives. *J. exp. Psychol.*, 1948, 38, 66–77.
7. Miller, N. E. An experimental investigation of acquired drives. *Psychol. Bull.*, 1941, 38, 534–535.
8. Miller, N. E. Experimental studies of conflict behavior. In: *Personality and the behavior disorders* (Ed. J. McV. Hunt), New York: Ronald Press, 1944, 431–465.
9. Miller, N. E., & Dollard, J. *Social learning and imitation*. New Haven: Yale Univ. Press, 1941.
10. Mowrer, O. H., & Lamoreaux, R. R. Fear as an intervening variable in avoidance conditioning. *J. comp. Psychol.*, 1946, 39, 29–50.
11. Shaffer, L. F. *The psychology of adjustment*. Boston: Houghton Mifflin, 1936.
12. Watson, J. B. *Psychology from the standpoint of a behaviorist*. Philadelphia: Lippincott, 1924.
13. Woodworth, R. S. *Dynamic psychology*. New York: Columbia Univ. Press, 1918.

16   A. Amsel and J. Roussel

Motivational Properties of Frustration

Reproduced in full from Motivational properties of frustration: I.
'Effect on a running response of the addition of frustration to the
motivational complex', *Journal of Experimental Psychology*, Vol. 43,
1952, pp. 363–68.

This paper reports an attempt to test two hypotheses derived
from assumptions relative to frustration. The assumptions are:
(*a*) that frustration is a motivational condition, and (*b*) that
strength of frustration varies with time in the frustrating situation. In this experiment, frustration is defined as a state which
results from the nonreinforcement of an instrumental response
which previously was *consistently* reinforced. Saying that frustration can be produced in this way does not, of course, exclude
other possibilities, such as blocking of a strongly learned instrumental sequence by a physical barrier.

In a recently reported study, Rohrer (7) employed the term
frustration drive to account for the reduction in strength of a bar-
pressing response. He showed that when two groups of rats are
conditioned equally strongly to bar-pressing, and each is subsequently extinguished twice under a particular degree of massing
of trials, the more highly massed group takes fewer trials to the
second extinction. It is our opinion that such findings do not
require the introduction of the notion of a motivational frustration state to explain them. They can be handled by existing inhibition theory (3). Rohrer's results are not in our opinion a test of
the motivational characteristics of frustration, nor were they
probably intended to be. In order to show that frustration is a
motivating condition it would seem necessary to demonstrate
that its presence increases some aspect of behavior. It is not
sufficient simply to show a decrease in strength of the response
leading to frustration.

If frustration is to be conceived of as a need state, it would,
then, seem reasonable to demonstrate, at the outset, that this
state has the accepted properties of need states. Thus, Hull's
treatment of motivation (3) would demand that adding frustration to a motivational complex increases the strength of some ongoing response through increase in generalized drive strength,

1. Supported by a grant from the Tulane University Council on Research.

provided that the frustration drive stimulus has not become connected to a response which is antagonistic to the criterion response (1).

This experiment was designed to test the following specific hypotheses stemming from the earlier assumptions: (*a*) when a running response has been maximally elicited under hunger motivation, the addition of frustration to the motivational complex will result in the establishment of a new and higher maximum running speed; (*b*) the facilitating effect of frustration on running speed will vary with variation in the amount of time spent in the frustrating situation just preceding that running.

Method

Subjects and apparatus

Eighteen male albino rats of Wistar strain were *S*s in this experiment. Their ages were between 100–120 days at the beginning of preliminary training.

The apparatus was a modified simple straightaway consisting of a starting compartment, two runways and two goal boxes. They were arranged in a straight line in the following order: starting box, Runway A, Goal box 1, Runway B, Goal box 2. The entire apparatus, except for Goal box 2, was 2.5 in. wide and 4 in. high (inside dimensions). The starting box was 9 in. long; Runway A was 3.5 ft. long; Goal box 1, 1 ft. long; and Runway B, 10 ft. long. Goal box 2 was $11 \times 7 \times 10$ in. Guillotine doors separated the starting compartment from Runway A, and Goal box 1 from Runway B. At the entrance to Goal boxes 1 and 2 were swing doors designed to be manipulable by *S*. The entire apparatus, with the exception of Goal box 2, was painted flat black. Goal box 2 was unpainted pine. The apparatus was covered with $\frac{1}{4}$-in. hardware cloth mesh. A small metal food cup was flush with the floor of Goal box 1. The food cup in Goal box 2 was a clear glass coaster.

The measurements of performance were made in Goal box 1 and Runway B. A running time measure was taken by the use of a Standard Electric Timer (.001 min.) and a microswitch arrangement. The switches were placed under hinged segments of the floor of Runway B so that the weight of the animal would trip them. The first switch was placed 1 ft. beyond Goal box 1, the second switch 1 ft. from Goal box 2. The running time was, then, the time to traverse the middle 8-ft. portion of Runway B. The latency measure was taken with a 1/10-sec. stopwatch. This was, on each of the test trials, the elapsed time between the raising of the door of Goal box 1, and the activation of the first microswitch in the running-time circuit.

A separate swing-door and goal-box arrangement was employed during preliminary training to acquaint each *S* with the door-pushing response. This was of similar construction to the experimental apparatus, but was 4 in. wide and 12 in. long, and was painted gray.

Experimental procedure
The entire experimental sequence required 52 days. This period was divided into three sections.

Preliminary training. – This was a period of 12 days designed to adapt Ss to handling by E and to the apparatus. All Ss, beginning at this stage, were maintained on a 22-hr. hunger schedule. Their daily food ration was 9 gm. of Purina dog chow checkers. On each of the first seven days the Ss were handled by E. On Day 8, Ss were put into the apparatus in pairs with all doors raised, for 10 min. per pair. On Day 9 each S explored the apparatus individually for 7 min. Days 10, 11, and 12 were spent in training each S to manipulate a swing door such as those at the entrance to the goal boxes. Each S was given six trials on each of these three days. A pellet of food was given after each entrance into the goal box. After these trials none of the 18 Ss had any difficulty manipulating the door.

Measurement of maximum running speed under 22-hr. food deprivation. – For the next 28 days, Days 13 to 40, each S was run three times per day in the apparatus under the strong hunger drive. During these trials food was in both goal boxes. The details of procedure on an individual trial are as follows: (*a*) S put into starting box; (*b*) after 3 sec., door raised; (*c*) S traverses Runway A, enters Goal box 1, eats one puppy pellet of chow; (*d*) after 30 sec. in Goal box 1, door is raised; (*e*) S traverses Runway B into Goal box 2, time to run this alley is measured; (*f*) S consumes food pellet in Goal box 2, and is returned to individual carrying cage.

The Ss were run in rotation, nine at a time, so that each of the three runs on a single day for any S was separated from the others by about 20 min.

After these 84 trials on 28 days the running speed of the Ss seemed to have reached a stable maximum.

Measurement of latency and running speed under 22-hr. hunger with and without frustration. – During this 12-day period each S was run three times a day, a total of 36 trials. Of these, 18 trials were *frustration* trials and 18 were *reward* trials. The reward trials were identical with those in the previous period. The frustration trials differed from the reward trials in that S found Goal box 1 empty (no food or food cup), after traversing Runway A. Each S, therefore, served as its own control to test the effect of frustration on the level of the performance which immediately followed the frustrating event.

To test the second hypothesis, Ss were split into three subgroups, matched on the basis of mean running time in the preliminary running trials. These will be termed Group 5, Group 10, and Group 30. They are differentiated by the amount of time spent in Goal box 1, during these 12 test days, *on frustration trials*. Group 5 remained in the frustrating situation for 5 sec.; Groups 10 and 30 were in the frustrating situation for 10 and 30 sec., respectively. All Ss continued to remain for 30 sec. in Goal box 1 on reward trials.

During this test period, two performance measures were employed on every trial. The running time measure (time to traverse the 8-ft. segment of Runway B) was taken as before. In addition, a latency measure was obtained. This was the time interval separating the raising of the door of Goal box 1 (after 5, 10, or 30 sec.) and the activation of the first microswitch. The E raised the door of Goal box 1 only when S was oriented in that direction. This meant that on some trials, the 5-, 10-, or 30-sec. interval in Goal box 1 was slightly exceeded.

In running equal numbers of frustration and reward trials in this test period the following arrangement of daily trials was employed to control for any possible effect of order of presentation: FRF RFR FFR RRF FRR RFF. These symbols represent the order of frustration and reward trials for six days (18 trials). On the next six test days, this sequence was repeated.

Results and Discussion

Test of two hypotheses

Both means and medians were calculated. In all cases the general nature of the results is the same for both, except that means are higher and more variable than medians.

To evaluate the results of the test period, mean and median running time and latency scores were computed for each S under reward (R) and frustration (F) conditions. Each of these scores is an average of 18 test-trial measurements. Comparison of the R and F scores showed that for each of the 18 Ss, median running time and latency measures are lower on frustration trials than on reward trials. The means show similar results with the frustration trials producing faster subsequent running than the reward trials for 16 of 18 Ss. Seventeen of 18 Ss had shorter mean latencies on F trials than on R trials. The median of individual S median reward running times was 0·048 min.; the corresponding frustration median was 0·041. The over-all means were 0·054 and 0·044 min. The over-all median R and F latencies were 1·65 and 0·65 sec.; the mean latencies were 4·86 and 1·69 sec. Since the raw data cannot be presented here, it should be indicated that for any given S the distribution of 18 frustration measurements overlapped very little, when at all, with the 18 reward scores. The first hypothesis – an increase in strength of performance with the addition of frustration to a motivational complex – is strongly supported.

Table 1

Running Time and Latency Averages
on Reward and Frustration Test Trials

| Group | Running Time (Minutes) | | | | Latency (Seconds) | | | |
| | Median | | Mean | | Median | | Mean | |
	R	F	R	F	R	F	R	F
5	·053	·042	·056	·045	1·35	0·65	4·13	1·87
10	·048	·036	·052	·041	1·30	0·45	4·25	1·33
30	·046	·041	·053	·046	3·75[1]	1·25	6·19[1]	1·90

1. Since running times, but not latencies, were measured during the preliminary period, the groups could be equated only for running times. For this reason, it is not surprising that Group 30 deviates so greatly from the other groups in Median and Mean latency on reward test trials.

In order to test the second hypothesis, the test performance of the Ss must be considered according to whether they were in the 5-, 10-, or 30-sec. group. Table 1 shows running time and latency medians and means for each of the three groups under reward and frustration conditions. A simple analysis of variance was performed with the individual R–F scores to test whether the three conditions of time in the frustrating situation resulted in different frustration effects on running time and latency. The F ratio for running time was 3·06; the latency F ratio was 1·12. With 2 and 15 df, the 5 % level of confidence requires an F ratio of 3·68. We cannot, therefore, say that time in the frustrating situation was a relevant variable in this experiment, although the average vigor of response of the Group 10 Ss on frustration trials is consistently greater than that of the other groups.

Possibly, the range from 5 to 30 sec. *in a frustrating situation* is one which produces relatively little change in the frustration effect. The performance of the Ss under 22-hr. food privation may already have been so strong as to obscure differences in frustration which may have been present in three groups. Certainly, our groups were small for this test. It would seem reasonable, on the basis of common sense and on the basis of the typical characteristics of labile states, to expect a very rapid building up of the frustration state (perhaps almost complete by

5 sec.) followed by a gradual falling off of its intensity. This falling off would have a faster rate outside of the frustrating situation than in it.[2] Since, in this experiment, there was no significant difference between 5, 10, and 30 sec. in the frustrating situation, we offer the speculation that the period from 5 to 30 sec. is a period of relative stability of frustration before the dissipation of the state begins.

Comparison of reward and frustration test trials with preliminary reward trials

Figure 1 shows the median running time data for reward conditions on the initial pretest days, and for the R and F conditions during the test trials. It should be noted that the two test-trial curves represent the median running times of the same Ss under both reward and frustration conditions, so that the first F trial was the first test trial, whereas the first R trial was the second test trial, and so on in random arrangement of F and R. For this reason, at any point on the abscissa of the test-trial graph the probability of the F curve being lower than the R curve would be 0.5, if there were no frustration effect. Actually, the F curve is lower than the R curve at 17 of the 18 points, and at most of these points it is very much lower. Taking the appropriate term in a binomial expansion, we find that the probability of such a chance occurrence is less than 0.0001. This is further confirmation of our first hypothesis.

The F curve approaches an asymptote which appears to be about 0.010 min. lower than that of the initial R curve, and that of the test-trial R curve. This is quite striking when one considers the great stability of the initial running time curve before the introduction of the test trials. The test reward curve remains at about the same level as the pretest curve. The greater apparent variability in the test trial data than in the initial data can be attributed to the fact that the test curves were plotted from medians of individual trials while the initial curve was plotted from medians of each day's performance, and there were three trials on each of these days for each S.

2. A pertinent experiment of Miller and Stevenson (5) reports an increase in agitated behavior of rats immediately following non-rewarded trials. This increased agitation was observed in the alley leading to the goal box where S had 10 sec. previously been frustrated (non-reward following consistent reward). In the Miller and Stevenson study, this frustration-motivated response was found to decrease in vigor when intervals longer than 10 sec. separated a frustration occurrence from the next run of S. By 2 min., the agitated behavior was no longer apparent. Here, time between non-reward and observation of agitated behavior was spent by S outside of the frustrating situation.

Since there is, on the first four test trials, very little difference between the R and F curves, and since the difference which becomes evident by Trial 5 is due mainly to a decrease in running time on F trials, there might be some basis for arguing that the frustration effect is learned, and not simply the result of a sudden increase in motivational strength. There is however an explanation of this part of the data which would not involve adopting this position. Early in the test period, frustration due to non-giving of food in the first goal box is minimized because of the strong secondary-reinforcing properties of that region built up during the initial trials; later, when the secondary-reinforcing power of this goal box extinguishes, the frustration effect is increased.

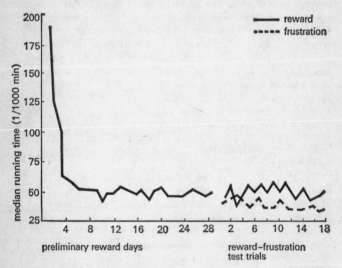

Figure 1 Comparison of test-trial performance under reward and frustration conditions

Another interpretation. – There is an interpretation of the present results which does not involve the introduction of frustration as an explanatory concept, i.e., it does not apparently necessitate attributing special properties to nonreinforcement.[1] This would hold that the running times in Runway B during the initial trials were actually depressed because of hunger reduction in Goal box 1 preceding those trials; and that from the beginning, the running time in Runway B would have been faster, and the final limit of performance would have been lower, if there were no eating just preceding the performance in

1. Suggested by Dr I. E. Farber in a personal communication.

the second runway. According to this interpretation, the increased vigor of performance which follows failure to reward a previously-rewarded response is due not to the presence of a new additional motivational component (frustration), but to the absence of a reduction in hunger tension which had consistently depressed performance before.

Actually, failure to reward Goal box 1 changes the stimulus to running in Runway B on frustration trials, and should also, therefore, tend to *reduce* running speed on those trials. Also, there is evidence that introducing food immediately before a hunger-motivated response may actually increase the level of performance, presumably by increasing incentive motivation.[2] Both of these factors, if operating, would have an opposite effect to that suggested.

It is possible that all the factors mentioned are operating in this experimental situation, and that frustration-produced motivation is also operating. If special emergent properties are to be attributed to non-reinforcement, it remains to show, by other experiments, that the frustration effect operates independently of, and in addition to, other effects which have already been conceptualized.

Summary

This experiment was designed to test the assumptions that frustration is a motivational state, and that its strength is related to time in the frustrating situation.

Eighteen male albino rats were trained under hunger drive to run down an alley into a goal box, then leave that goal box and run down a second alley into a second goal box distinctively different from the first one. Their time to traverse the alley between Goal box 1 and Goal box 2 was measured during a preliminary period. When this time had reached a stable minimum, their running time and latency in leaving Goal box 1 were measured during test trials. In half of these trials they were frustrated in Goal box 1; in the other half, they were not. During this test period *S*s were split into sub-groups differentiated according to time spent in Goal box 1 on the frustration trials (5-, 10-, and 30-sec. groups).

An implication of the first assumption – that strength of performance on frustration test trials should be greater than that during the preliminary trials or that on reward test trials – was strongly supported by the data. There was, however, no statistically significant empirical support for the hypothesis of variation

2. Some support for this statement can be derived from certain of the early speed of locomotion experiments (2, 6). The whole question of the effect on vigor of performance of giving a small amount of reward immediately before a trial has recently been treated by Maltzman (4).

in strength of frustration when the time in the frustrating situation was varied between 5, 10, and 30 sec.

References

1. Amsel, A. The effect upon level of consummatory response of the addition of anxiety to a motivational complex. *J. exp. Psychol.*, 1950, 40, 709–715.
2. Bruce, R. H. An experimental investigation of the thirst drive in rats with especial reference to the goal-gradient hypothesis. *J. gen. Psychol.*, 1937, 17, 49–60.
3. Hull, C. L. *Principles of behavior*. New York: D. Appleton-Century, 1943.
4. Maltzman, I. The process need. *Psychol. Rev.*, 1952, 59, 40–48.
5. Miller, N. E., & Stevenson, S. S. Agitated behavior of rats during experimental extinction and a curve of spontaneous recovery. *J. comp. Psychol.*, 1936, 21, 205–231.
6. Morgan, C. T., & Fields, P. E. The effect of variable preliminary feeding upon the rat's speed of locomotion. *J. comp. Psychol.*, 1938, 26, 331–348.
7. Rohrer, J. H. A motivational state resulting from non-reward. *J. comp. physiol. Psychol.*, 1949, 42, 476–485.

IV Extension and Evaluation of the Drive Construct

Hull had suggested that a factor that might contribute to response occurrence is incentive motivation (K). He visualized this as some kind of a learned drive arising from the association of stimulus cues to a reward. Spence clarified and extended the concept of *incentive motivation*, and made it a corner stone of his own learning theory. Brown has examined the concept of *secondary drive* and advised against its extravagant use as an explanatory concept. Estes has argued that the specific cue factor, S_D of Hull, is all that is required to explain the observed effect of drive manipulations; the generalized drive construct (D) is superfluous. And Skinner, considering the circumstances under which psychologists resort to the drive construct, questions its explanatory value altogether.

17 K. W. Spence

Incentive Motivation

Excerpt from K. W. Spence, *Behavior Theory and Conditioning*. New Haven: Yale University Press, 1956. Chapter 5.

The implication of Hull's theory with regard to reduction of incentive magnitude was never worked out in detail in the *Principles*. Hull merely stated that reduction of incentive size would be expected to lead on successive trials to a progressive lowering of performance level. Strictly speaking, Hull's hypothesis that the magnitude of H is a function of the magnitude of the reward, taken in conjunction with his assumption that habit (H) was a relatively permanent condition left by reinforcement within the nervous system, implied, as far as the value of H itself is concerned, that a shift to a smaller reward should not lead to a decrement in performance. However, the well-known fact that reduction to zero reward (experimental extinction) results in response decrement apparently led Hull to believe that any reduction in reward size less than to zero was related in some manner to experimental extinction and thus would result in some response decrement. Apparently he intended to return to this topic in the later chapter on experimental extinction, but he did not do so.

Incentive Motivational Interpretations of the Effects of Reward Magnitude

In subsequent formulations of his theoretical system Hull (1950, 1951, 1952) abandoned this hypothesis that habit strength varied with the magnitude of the reward and instead conceived of variations in this experimental variable as affecting the strength of an incentive motivational factor which he designated by the symbol K. Like the motivational factor, D, this K factor was assumed to multiply habit strength to determine the excitatory potential (E). In this modification of his theory Hull was anticipated by Crespi (1944), who on the basis of his experimental findings rejected Hull's differential habit interpretation and proposed in its stead an emotional drive or, as he anthropomorphically described it, an eagerness theory. According to this notion the basis of the differential drive strength was a variation in the amount of anticipatory tension or excitement that developed with different amounts of reward.

My own approach to these experimental phenomena has also always been a motivational one. Indeed, at the time that Hull was writing the chapter on magnitude of reinforcement for his *Principles of Behavior* our correspondence reveals a vigorous disagreement over his learning (habit) interpretation. The basis of my disagreement, in part, was the finding of Nissen and Elder (1935) and Cowles and Nissen (1937) with respect to variation of the magnitude of the goal object in delayed-response experiments with chimpanzees. After showing that the level of performance in this situation was a function of the magnitude of the incentive, these investigators further demonstrated that, after attaining a certain level of response with a given size of food, a drop in level of performance occurred if a smaller piece of food was used. Similarly, a shift to a larger piece of food was shown to lead to improvement in performance. These shifts up and down seemed to me to suggest changes in a motivational rather than a habit factor, and it is interesting to note that Cowles and Nissen interpreted their findings in terms of a mechanism which they described as reward expectancy.

My preference for a motivational interpretation was also greatly influenced, as I have already indicated, by our theorizing concerning the role of the fractional anticipatory goal response in our latent learning experiments with the simple T maze (Spence, Bergmann, and Lippitt, 1950). This theory assumed, it will be recalled, that stimulus cues in the goal box and from the alley just preceding the goal box become conditioned to the goal response, R_g. Through generalization the stimulus cues at earlier points in the runway are also assumed to acquire the capacity to elicit R_g, or at least noncompetitional components of R_g that can occur without the actual presence of the food (e.g., salivating and chewing movements). As a result this fractional conditioned response, which we shall designate as r_g, moves forward to the beginning of the instrumental sequence. Furthermore, the interoceptive stimulus cue (s_g) produced by this response also becomes a part of the stimulus complex in the alley and thus should become conditioned to the instrumental locomotor responses. But more important, in addition to this associative function we have assumed that this r_g–s_g mechanism also has motivational properties that vary with the magnitude or vigor with which it occurs.

A number of different conceptions of the manner in which the r_g–s_g mechanism may operate to affect motivational level have been suggested. One that was mentioned in my chapter on theories of learning in Stevens' *Handbook of Experimental Psychology* (Spence, 1951) was that the occurrence of these fractional goal responses results in a certain amount of conflict and hence in heightened tension or excitement. This heightened tension, it was assumed, might contribute to an increase in the existing state of general drive level, D. This conception, it will be seen, is very similar to that of Crespi. Another possibility is that variation of the intensity of s_g provides an internal stimulus dynamism akin to Hull's notion of stimulus dynamism (V) resulting from different intensities of external stimulation. However, my preference is merely to introduce an intervening variable, K, which is regarded as representing, quantitatively, the motivational property of the conditioned r_g–s_g mechanism and which is defined in terms of the experimental variables that determine the vigor of the latter.

From our assumption that the basic mechanism underlying this incentive motivational factor, K, is the classical conditioned r_g, we are necessarily committed to a number of assumptions as to the variables that determine its strength. Thus, being itself a conditioned response, r_g will vary with the number of conditioning trials given in the goal box. Secondly we must assume that its intensity or vigor will be a negatively accelerated, exponential function of the number of these conditioning trials. Furthermore, on the basis of experimental studies of generalization of conditioning we will need to assume that its strength at any point in the alley distant from the goal box will be a function of the similarity of the environmental cues at that point and those in the goal box. If internal proprioceptive cues from the running response play an important role, the differences in these cues at different distances from the goal box will have to be considered. Unfortunately we know very little, as yet, concerning either of these variables. Finally, any property of the goal object that produces unconditioned consummatory responses of different intensity or vigor will presumably determine the value of K, for there is some evidence to support the notion that the intensity or vigor of the response may be conditioned *as such* (Hull, 1943).

The diagram shown in Figure 1 attempts to summarize these various assumptions relating K on the one hand to the experimental variables of which it is a function and on the other to the intervening variables and behavior. Actually, as will become apparent, considerable more research needs to be done before we can specify in a systematic and precise manner the experimental variables that affect K. The listing in the diagram is in terms of the

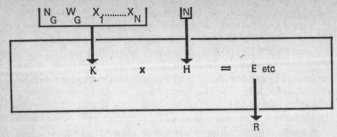

Figure 1 Diagram summarizing some of the assumptions of incentive motivation theory. Some of the experimental variables which are assumed to contribute to the level of incentive motivation (K) are shown above the rectangle on the left. The multiplicative assumption of K and H combination is shown inside the rectangle. For definition of symbols and further explanation see text.

specific experimental operations that different investigators have so far employed. Thus N_G refers to the number of classical conditioning trials, which has typically been designated as the number of times the subject enters the goal box and responds to (consumes or sees) the goal object. W_G refers to the amount, e.g., the number, weight, or volume, of the goal objects consumed, while $X_1 \ldots X_n$ refers to a number of known and as yet unknown variables that presumably determine the vigor of the consummatory response, e.g., the sweetness of the object, the amount of sucking effort required to obtain the object in the case of liquids, possibly the hardness of the reward object, and so on. Again, as we shall see, these variables are not entirely independent of one another. The tentative hypothesis being proposed here is that these different experimental variations of reinforcing agents will determine K, either through the habit strength of r_g or through the particular r_g, i.e., the particular vigor of r_g being conditioned.

Having defined K in terms of these experimental variables, we must next relate it to our other intervening variables and thus eventually to the response variables. Being conceived of as a motivational factor, K is assumed to multiply the habit strength of the instrumental response to determine its excitatory strength. Thus, with D held constant E equals $K \times H$. This is not, of course, a complete picture of our current theorizing concerning K.

References

Cowles, J. T., & Nissen, H. W. Reward-expectancy in delayed responses of chimpanzees. *J. comp. Psychol.*, 24, 345–58. 1937.

Crespi, L. P. Amount of reinforcement and level of performance. *Psychol. Rev.*, 51, 341–57. 1944.

Hull, C. L. *Principles of behavior.* New York: Appleton-Century-Crofts, 1943.

Hull, C. L. Behavior postulates and corollaries – 1949. *Psychol. Rev.,* 57, 173–80. 1950.

Hull, C. L. *Essentials of behavior.* New Haven: Yale University Press, 1951.

Hull, C. L. *A behavior system.* New Haven: Yale University Press, 1952.

Nissen, H. W., & Elder, J. H. The influence of amount of incentive on delayed response performances of chimpanzees. *J. Genet. Psychol.,* 47, 49–72. 1935.

Spence, K. W., Bergmann, G., & Lippitt, R. A study of simple learning under irrelevant motivational-reward conditions. *J. exp. Psychol.,* 40, 539–51. 1950.

Spence, K. W. Theoretical interpretations of learning. In Stevens, S.S., Ed. *Handbook of experimental psychology.* New York: Wiley, 1951.

Problems Presented by the Concept of Acquired Drives

Reproduced in full from *Current Theory and Research in Motivation: A Symposium*. University of Nebraska Press, Lincoln, 1953, pp. 1–21.

It is perhaps safe to assert that in every serious attempt to account for the behavior of living organisms, the concept of motivation, in one guise or another, has played a major explanatory role. But it is not safe to assert that students of behavior have reached appreciable agreement as to how drives can be most meaningfully defined, what mechanisms are involved in each case, how many drives there are, or precisely how drives function as behavior determinants.

It is in the area of the biogenic or physiological drives that the major research efforts of experimental psychologists have been concentrated during the past several decades; and it is not surprising, therefore, that level of achievement and amount of agreement is highest there. Considerable progress has certainly been made, notably in the case of the hunger, thirst, and sex drives as they are revealed in animal behavior.

But there is a substantial group of psychologists, who, though they might applaud progress in the understanding of biogenic drives, minimize vociferously the importance of those drives for the interpretation of adult human behavior. Part of the motivation behind this attitude may stem from a desire to elevate man to a unique, emergent position on the phylogenetic scale. Biological drives are regarded as too crass for an organism as noble as man. But a more important reason for this attitude, and probably a more defensible one, is that in a well-fed culture like ours, intense degrees of such drives as hunger and thirst are aroused too infrequently to bear a heavy explanatory burden. And to this may be added the fact that doctrines which hold instinctive sources of motivation to be of significance for human behavior have all but vanished from the psychological scene. These and other influences have led many to the belief that the important human motives are produced by learning during the processes of socialization and acculturation.

But to say that human motives are learned contributes little to our understanding until the details of the learning process have been clearly outlined in each instance. We must be able to specify precisely what has been learned, what conditions affect the acquisition and retention of the learned reactions, and how such motives operate as determinants of behavior. With the exception of recent work on fear, few details of this sort have been filled in for the acquired drives. Many writers speak glibly of acquired drives for money, for food, for specific liquids, for prestige; but they fail completely to specify the variables and processes involved in the acquisition of such motives. As a consequence, almost no two writers agree on answers to the questions of whether habits can become drives, whether learned drives can become functionally autonomous, whether incentives arouse drives, or which learning paradigms can be most meaningfully applied to motives.

An examination of contemporary discussions of motivation suggests that one of the major sources of misunderstanding is the failure of most writers to distinguish clearly between drives or motives, on the one hand, and habits or reaction tendencies on the other. When psychologists first became concerned with drives, they dealt almost exclusively with the unlearned, biogenic drives; and since the gap between such drives and learned reactions was large, little confusion resulted. But when they began to speak of *acquired* drives, which embody the characteristics of both a learned reaction and a motive, precision of expression faded and the concepts of drives and habits lost their individualities.

For a psychology that seeks to discover lawful relations between environmental events and reactions, whenever an organism learns something, that something attains the systematic status of a response. Moreover, the process of learning is described as the formation of a new association between the designated response and some particular environmental event. On this view, if an organism can acquire a drive, then whatever is acquired qualifies as a response. But the response must be more than a response if it is also to be classified as a drive. Thus to have an acquired drive, is to learn a response possessing the characteristics of other responses and, in addition, the capacity to act as a drive. Since the higher organisms normally learn a great many responses, it is imperative that reactions having the added function of drives be clearly distinguished from those that do not. If drive is an important concept in its own right, and if it is indeed different from learned reaction tendencies, then this kind of classification should be both possible and desirable. But if drive is not a different concept, then there is clearly no need for employing two different terms.

Functional Properties of Drives

Apparently, then, it is especially easy, when dealing with learned motives, to confuse the processes of learning and of motivation; and because of this, it is especially important that an effort be made to keep them distinct. In order to do so, however, one needs a reasonably clear conception of the several ways in which a drive, whether biogenic or acquired, functions as a determinant of behavior. As an aid to the organization of our thinking let us consider at this point several functional properties of drives that seem to be of major importance.[1]

1. *Drives function in combination with existing reaction tendencies to produce overt behavior.* – This property is usually termed the *energizing* or *activating* property of drives. It refers to the fact that if an organism has a learned (or unlearned) potentiality for behaving in a specific way in the presence of given cues it will be more likely to exhibit such behavior when a drive is present than when it is not. Moreover it implies that mere reaction tendencies (associative predispositions, habits, cognitions) can never, in the absence of drive, culminate in overt behavior. As this property is usually described it includes no reference to a capacity to direct or steer behavior.

The tendency to attribute this nondirecting, energizing function to drives has grown naturally out of observations of a number of behavioral phenomena. Of particular importance, is the frequent observation of a *marked disproportionality between the energy content of a stimulus and the energy expended in the response*. A whispered warning at a time of danger may be followed by intensely effortful escape reactions; the faint creaking of a stair in a haunted house may lead to exceedingly vigorous action. Such behavioral relations have many physical analogies. For example, the disproportionality between the minute energy required to press the trigger of a gun and the tremendous energy released thereby from the cartridge. In all such instances some concept of a driving or moving force seems to be demanded; and in none of them is the energizing agent endowed with directing or steering functions.

The psychologist's 'drive' to speak of the energizing function of

---

1. Although this discussion of the functional properties of drives and the reasons for their introduction by psychologists contains no explicit references to the work of others, no pretense of originality is made by the present writer. An attempt has been made simply to rephrase and regroup certain ideas long prevalent in the literature on motivation and learning.

drive is also aroused by observing that a single organism will, in exactly the same stimulus situation, behave differently on different occasions, and by observing that supposedly identical organisms also will react differently to identical conditions. A rat may eat slowly on one day, rapidly on another, and not at all on still another. If on the basis of independent evidence, we can be confident the rat 'knows how' to eat, and if this 'know how' can be assumed to remain constant from time to time, we cannot attribute the variations in its behavior to fluctuations in its cognitions or reaction tendencies. As a consequence, *we may find it useful to invoke different degrees of hunger to explain the observed variability*. Of course, not all instances of the occurrence or nonoccurrence of a given response *must* be explained by the introduction of drive even though the environmental conditions yield nothing in the way of significantly related stimulus variations. In many cases it might be more sensible to appeal to structural anomalies, inhibitory states, competing reactions, or inherited capacities.

To complete the picture, it may be noted that sometimes an energizing drive is introduced to explain *response constancy in the face of normally effective variations in environmental conditions*. Let us imagine that three different foods are fed to three different rats, one food to each, and that all eat at the same rate. Suppose further that on previous occasions the three foods had always been eaten at different rates. These results, if genuine, might be explained by introducing individual hunger drives of sufficient strengths to compensate for the expected differential effects of the three foods. Less-preferred foods would be eaten at the same rate as more-preferred ones if hunger were greater when eating the less preferred ones.

It is important to point out that the drive property under discussion here has been phrased in such a manner that the drive can always activate reaction tendencies and yet lead in some instances to a decrease rather than an increase in overt activity. As a case in point, it is well known that rats when placed in an open field situation often show marked signs of fear such as excessive defecation and urination. Their overt skeletal activity, however, may be markedly reduced, the animals sometimes becoming completely immobile. Thus the strong drive of fear seems to lead to inaction rather than action. We would disagree, therefore, with the frequently expressed view that drives always lead to more vigorous overt activity. What they *do*, is to act in concert with reaction tendencies to produce whatever behavior is called for by the tendencies in conjunction with the specific environmental situation. If the dominant habit tendency is to freeze or to feign death, then this is intensified or energized. But if a tendency to escape, or do something else, is dominant, then this will be activated by the drive.

2. *A reduction in drive following a response will function under special conditions to increase the probability that the response will occur again in the same situation.* – Since this is simply the familiar functional property of reinforcement, it seems unnecessary to comment upon it at length. It should be noted, however, that there is nothing in the above statement to indicate that *all* responses are learned because of drive reduction or that a given response is *always* learned if followed by drive reduction. The qualifying phrase 'under special conditions' is included to take care of possible exceptions. Thus if a rat upon first traversing a maze is allowed to eat to satiation in the goal box, it may show no improvement in performance if re-introduced immediately into the starting box. It may go to sleep. Improvement can only be shown by a 'special condition' such as providing a day's delay between the first and second trials. Other special conditions include such variables as the time between the response and the reduction in drive, the emotional state of the organism at the moment, amount of drive reduction, and rapidity of drive reduction.

3. *An abrupt increase in drive following a response will function under special conditions to reduce the probability that the response will occur again at the same situation.* – This is the typical picture presented by punishment, and the range of conditions under which the property can be demonstrated is even more restricted than in the case of the preceding drive-reduction property. Thus, although abrupt increases in pain can be brought about following a response by the use of almost any intense stimulus, comparably quick increases in the hunger or thirst drives cannot be realized. We need not, at this time, concern ourselves with the mechanisms responsible for, or involved in, the realization of this functional property. The older view that punishment or pain as such weakens S–R bonds has few advocates at present. But it is still empirically true that a response followed by pain tends to be abandoned. This may be attributed to the elicitation of an incompatible response by the punishment and the reinforcing of that new response by the cessation of punishment. In so far as this interpretation is applicable, this third property of drives becomes identical with the second. The same phenomenon might also be explained

by assuming that fear becomes conditioned to cues antedating the noxious stimulus. Subsequently, responses of avoiding or withdrawing from those cues would tend to be strengthened by the consequent reduction of fear.

Some Aspects of the Drive-Habit Confusion[2]

In the preceding discussion, the desirability of making a clear distinction between drives and habits has been emphasized and three functional properties of drives have been suggested as an aid to the making of such a distinction. This point of view, however, can scarcely be said to be generally characteristic of present-day psychology. The majority of writers in the field of motivation, though they use the two terms, not only seldom stress their separate functional properties, but often speak of drives as if they have the same guiding and directing functions usually attributed to habits. Allport (1), Leeper (14), McClelland (16), Krech (12), and Young (25), to mention but a few, all maintain that drives or motives function to direct and organize behavior as well as to impel it.

By way of contrast, the position defended here is simply that *every case of directed behavior is to be ascribed, not to drives or motives, but to the capacities of stimulus cues, whether innate or acquired, to elicit reactions.* The property of directing or guiding behavior was deliberately omitted from the group of drive properties that has just been considered.

The confabulation of drive, habits, and rewards, is especially evident in interpretations of token-reward studies. This becomes apparent initially when one notes that many general treatments of learning and of learnable drives discuss the well-known studies of Wolfe (24) and of Cowles (5) under the heading of *acquired drives*. Some authors who do this seem to recognize the attendant difficulties and attempt to sidestep the issue of whether such studies demonstrate acquired drives or simply habits. Thus Miller (18) in his chapter on 'Learnable drives and rewards' in the *Handbook of Experimental Psychology* presents the results of 21 studies of secondary rewards in a section entitled 'Learned rewards and drives based on food and hunger'. But in his tabular summary of the principles demonstrated by these studies, not a single study is cited as providing evidence for an acquired drive.

2. The word *confusion* is used here to mean simply a blending or mixing leading to indistinctness. It is not intended to carry connotations of an approbrious nature. The term *habit* is employed in a rather loose, general sense to cover any associate predisposition whether learned or unlearned.

Deese, however, who also treats the token-reward studies as examples of learned drives says, in reference to Wolfe's studies that '... the chimpanzees showed that they had developed a secondary drive for poker chips.' (6, p. 95.) But on the following page he speaks of 'The *token-reward habit* in Wolfe's experiment...' (Italics by the present writer). Clearly there is indecision here since the same bit of behavior is described as a *secondary drive* on one page and as a *token-reward habit* on the next. From the present point of view, it is necessary to conclude that although tokens or other stimulus objects can serve as reinforcements for the learning of new responses, this fact alone does not constitute adequate grounds for introducing a new acquired drive for tokens. Such behavior can perhaps be explained by recourse to learned reaction tendencies, on the further assumption that the tokens acquired their secondary reinforcing power through their previous association with food. The pressure to introduce a 'token drive' would obviously be much greater had the chimpanzees demonstrated a willingness to work for the chips when not hungry and when the chips were not exchangeable for food.

The temptation to endow drives with response-steering functions is especially difficult to resist when the steering stimuli are internal and when, in addition, there is reason to suppose they have resulted from the same operations that produced the drives. Perhaps, therefore, a major reason for the common tendency to amalgamate drives and habits is that antecedent conditions leading to drive states may also lead to internal events exhibiting the functional (steering) properties of stimuli.

The assumption that functionally effective internal stimuli may accompany drives is of course a common one and its heuristic worth as an explanatory mechanism is, in some circles, well recognized. It seems worth while, therefore, at this point to digress briefly in order to list a few of the behavioral phenomena that have been interpreted by reference to these internal drive-accompanying stimuli. These are all, in a sense, manifestations of a single functional property of *drive stimuli*, viz., the capacity to lead to specific, directed reactions.

In the first place, conditions which are believed to bring about the arousal of a drive seem, on occasion, to lead also to the appearance of novel, relatively specific responses. And often, in such cases, no environmental stimuli can be found to which the new reactions can be traced. When this occurs in the apparent absence of adequate opportunities for learning, it may be assumed that the drive-arousing conditions have generated internal stimuli to which the novel responses are innately attached. Thus drive stimuli have been assigned a significant role in the production of new, perhaps highly patterned, responses (10, 18, 4).

Secondly, it has been assumed that any learnable reaction can become attached to whatever stimuli attend a given drive, and that different responses can also become associated with the stimuli of *different* drives (10, 11, 22). The first of these potential capacities is said to underlie the ability of an organism to make responses appropriate to a given drive. An adult organism, when hungry, probably seldom ingests large quantities of water by mistake if food is available. And because it does approach and ingest food, one may be tempted to endow it with a drive *for* food. What appears to be a preferable interpretation is this. The drive of the hungry organism is not a drive *for* food; the drive *qua* drive is here assumed to have only the three nondirective functions mentioned above. Not drives, but *drive stimuli*, in combination with external events, are assigned the property of eliciting responses directed towards objects capable of reducing drives. In the case of the newborn infant, the period between birth and the first feeding presumably leads to hunger and to hunger stimuli. But until food has actually been ingested, it appears unwise to assume, with higher level organisms at least, that the drive stimuli have any marked capacity to elicit directed behavior. In this sense, the infant does not have a hunger for food, or for milk, or for any special kind of food. As it matures, however, it learns to make specific responses when hungry and these can become attached to stimuli attending hunger. It is these reaction-eliciting tendencies of drive stimuli that provide the directional characteristics often attributed to the drive.

The second of the above capacities, the association of different drive stimuli with different reactions, is exemplified by the classical studies of Hull (9) and of Leeper (13) in which rats were taught, in the absence of differential external cues, to make one response when hungry and another when thirsty.

A third explanatory role that can be assumed by drive stimuli, one originally proposed by Hull in his paper on *Knowledge and purpose as habit mechanisms* (8), is that of serving as an integrative mechanism. On this view, the presence of any persisting internal stimulus could function, through a kind of redintegrative action, to bring about the chaining of otherwise quite unrelated acts. All that would be required would be for each of the diverse reactions to become conditioned to the same internal stimulus.

A fourth example of the explanatory utility of internal drive stimuli is to be found in those instances where drives do not lead to more vigorous overt behavior or to performance facilitation. Here the drive-stimulus-elicited reactions are said to be incompatible with the responses typically evoked in a given situation (3). Their presence, as the result of an increase in drive, and an attendant intensification of the drive stimuli, could lead, therefore, to performance decrement rather than facilitation.

Finally, drive stimuli might be utilized in interpreting the apparent effects of drives upon the perception of external stimulus complexes. To take a hypothetical experiment, let us suppose that both hungry and satiated subjects are presented with near-threshold exposures of pictures of both edible and non-edible objects. From the results of recent studies of motivation and perception we might expect that the hungry subjects would be 'perceptually sensitized' to the food pictures, and would consequently be more successful in identifying them correctly. Such results might be explained within the present framework as due primarily to the drive stimuli accompanying hunger. For obvious reasons, foods of various kinds are more likely to be seen when one is hungry than when one is not. And at such times considerable practice is obtained in learning to make appropriate verbal (naming) responses to the visual patterns provided by the foods. Consequently, the naming responses should come to be associated with a pattern of stimuli composed of both internal hunger cues and external visual ones. Were this the case, it would not be surprising if the hungry Ss, who possess both the internal hunger cues and the impoverished visual cues, should do better than the nonhungry Ss, who possess only the visual cues. On the present view, the hungry group might also be superior to the nonhungry group on nonfood pictures, though their superiority should be less than in the case of the food pictures. Facilitation of performance on nonfood pictures would be attributed to the energizing effects of drive *per se*, not to the presence of hunger stimuli. Perhaps some such mechanism as this, appropriately elaborated, would yield an adequate explanation of some instances of the sensitizing effects of motivation upon the response tendencies defining perceptions.

Returning now to the drive-habit confusion, a final point must be made. This concerns the role of verbal behavior in the tendency to postulate a different drive for each and every goal toward which directed reactions are exhibited. Human subjects are prolific in their use of phrases like 'I *want* that object' or 'I *desire* this' or 'I *need* those.' Since the subject *says* he has a multitude of needs, and since he did not say so at birth, the unwary psychologist, especially if he pays too much attention to similar statements of his own, is likely to conclude that each such statement demands the postulation of a corresponding acquired motive. The mistake lies in the failure to realize that *these verbal phrases may indicate the presence and strength of reaction tendencies* rather than, or in addition to, the presence and strength of drives.

It is instructive, in this connection, to observe that the inclination to introduce a multitude of acquired drives for sought-after goals is minimal in reports of research on non-verbal animals. For example, if a rat has been repeatedly rewarded for turning left in a simple T maze it will exhibit a strong tendency to approach the left alley. Typically this behavior is explained by saying that the response of approaching has become strongly connected to the cues of the left alley. The habit tendency is said to be strong, or the cognition, perhaps, is said to be very clear. But what is apparently seldom said is that the rat has a strong *left-alley-seeking drive*. Such a statement would probably be made, however, if the rat could talk, since it might, while in the starting box, exclaim, 'I have a strong desire to get into that left alley!' Perhaps the 'rat psychologist' has been spared some confusion because of the rat's inability to use words which can indicate the presence of either habits or drives, or both.

But let us take still another example. Nearly all will agree, perhaps, that the cessation of a fear-arousing stimulus, though it is an event, rather than an object like money, is empirically reinforcing. Certainly the accumulated data on animal experiments (20, 17, 15, 2) are convincing in showing that such a cessation, if it is sufficiently great, sufficiently abrupt, and sufficiently near in time to a preceding response, results in an increase in the probability that the response will occur on later occasions. Here, however, even though the event of stimulus-cessation might be described as a kind of goal, no one asserts that the fearful animal has a drive for stimulus cessation. To do so would be tantamount to postulating a *drive* for *drive-cessation*.

Up to this point, an attempt has been made to clarify our understanding of acquired drives, primarily by insisting that the nondirective properties of drives be sharply separated from the directive functions of external and of internal stimuli. It is imperative, therefore, that we now examine some specific examples of supposed acquired drives in an effort to determine the possible utility of the distinctions that have been made.

The So-Called Acquired Drives for Money, Praise, Prestige, etc.

It has already been noted that although many discussions of motivation assert the presence and importance of learned drives for such objects or goals as money, companionship, and eminence, no convincing and theoretically integrated accounts of the processes by which such drives are acquired and maintained have been presented. The acquired drive of fear stands alone as one for which the theoretical steps in the process of its acquisition and maintenance have been carefully worked out.

According to the formulations of Mowrer (19) and of Miller (17) the process of fear-acquisition is adequately described by the paradigm of classical conditioning. Thus if an originally neutral cue is repeatedly associated with a pain-arousing stimulus, the former will acquire the capacity to evoke an anticipatory form of the pain reaction. This premonitory response is termed fear or anxiety, and the functional properties of primary drives are assumed to accompany its arousal. It is also hypothesized that fear may carry with it distinctive stimuli to which new reactions as well as innate ones may be connected (15, 18). At one and the same time, therefore, fear is learned, it is internal, it appears to possess at least two of the nondirective properties of unlearned drives, and it has the capacity to generate response-steering stimuli.

This formulation appears to work rather well for fear; but in the case of the supposed drives for specific goal objects such as money, a similar paradigm is almost impossible to apply. What, for example, is the originally adequate (unconditioned) stimulus capable of arousing a money-seeking drive (or response) so that it can become conditioned to a neutral stimulus? Obviously, the operation of deprivation will not work, since removing a person's money before he has learned of its value cannot arouse a drive for money. If it did, we would be put in the position of maintaining that deprivation of something one doesn't want leads to a drive for that something. It seems likely, therefore, that the difficulties involved in attempting to apply the classical conditioning paradigm to any of the supposed drives for specific goal objects or situations stem from our inability to denote appropriate unconditioned stimuli for the to-be-learned drives or responses.

It would be foolish to maintain, of course, that the paradigm for the learning of the so-called drive for money must be that of classical conditioning. Certain of the learning principles of the perceptual-cognitive variety might better serve to satisfy our need for an integrative schemata. Unfortunately, experts in the manipulation of such concepts have not, for the most part, been interested in acquired drives and have made no serious attempts to clarify these obscurities.

It is the writer's belief, however, that the problem of which brand of learning concepts to use is relatively unimportant and that the real roots of the difficulty lie deeper. Perhaps the greatest hindrance to progress lies in assuming the existence of drives where no such assumption need to be made. We might advance more rapidly if we were to start afresh and deny at the outset that each and every object or situation for which an organism has learned to strive must be accompanied by a characteristic acquired drive for that object. To do so, of course, is simply to deny that acquired drives, when functioning as drives, have behavior-directing properties.

Suppose then, that people, in spite of what they say, do not acquire drives for any specific goal object whatsoever. What they can and do acquire are multitudinous sets of habits or modes of responding to complex stimulus situations composed of both external and internal elements. And those reactions are reinforced repeatedly by objects or situations or events possessing acquired rewarding power.

Conceivably one might be able to account for all of the apparent instances of complex acquired drives by appealing solely to these habit phenomena. But most conceptions of behavior demand the presence of some kind of motivation if habits are to eventuate in acts. Let us consider, therefore, whether some source of *acquired* motivation can be uncovered to which we can sensibly attribute the general functional properties of drives.

One possible solution to our problem is to assume that the *important motivating component of many of the supposed acquired drives for specific goal objects is actually a learned tendency to be discontented or distressed or anxious in the absence of those goal objects.* On this view, stimulus cues signifying a lack of affection, a lack of prestige, insufficient money, etc., would be said to acquire, through learning, the capacity to arouse an anxiety reaction having drive properties. This learned anxiety would then function to energize whatever behavior is directed toward goal objects by stimuli, and its reduction, following the achievement of those goals, would be powerfully reinforcing.

Should such a proposal prove fruitful, it would lead to a substantial reduction in the number of acquired drives commonly deemed necessary. Moreover, it would satisfy our specification that drives must be nondirectional, while at the same time leaving room for the presence of internal behavior-steering stimuli. It might also simplify the task of detailing the steps in the acquisition process. For illustrative purposes, let us attempt to outline the principal elements of the process by which the anxiety underlying the so-called drive for money might be acquired.

During the first few years of a child's life there are innumerable occasions upon which the child experiences genuine pain. Its fingers get cut, burned, or mashed, it falls from chairs and tables, it catches childhood diseases, *ad infinitum*. And on nearly all of these occasions, normally solicitous parents behave in a worried, anxious manner. The frequent combination of pain with the cues provided by the sight of the worried parents could result in the acquisition by those cues of the capacity to elicit anxiety reactions in the child. If such an associative connection were very strongly established, the stimuli attending the behavior of anxious parents could then serve as the functional equivalent of an anxiety-arousing unconditioned stimulus in other situations.

Now if at the time anxiety is evoked by the parents' worried looks, they were to complain of being worried by a lack of money, the words, 'we have no money,' could become a higher-order conditioned stimulus with power to arouse the child's anxiety on subsequent occasions. Through the frequent repetition of the same or similar combinations of stimulating events the anxiety could become strongly connected to a multitude of phrases or conditions all having in common the meaning 'lack of money'. (We need not at this point, concern ourselves with whether mere contiguity is adequate for the formation of such associations, as Mowrer (21) would maintain, or whether some other factor such as drive-reduction is also necessary.) After such learning has taken place the child will tend to become anxious whenever it hears phrases like 'that costs too much' or 'we can't afford it this month' or 'we haven't the money for that'. Each of these cue phrases might be individually conditioned to anxiety, though some might evoke the reaction via stimulus generalization or mediated generalization. By this mechanism any verbally announced phrase carrying the meaning for the child of 'lack of money' or any equivalent stimulus, such as an empty purse, could become the exact counterpart of the fear-arousing conditioned stimulus in animal studies.

But if this is true, then the actual presence of money is the specific condition for producing the *cessation* of the anxiety-arousing cues. Having money in one's possession is equivalent to escaping from the white-box cues into the black-box cues in Miller's (17) classical experiment on fear. If not having money is the cue for anxiety, then having money is the principal means, though probably not the only one, for removing or obliterating the anxiety-arousing cues.

Following this line of reasoning further, it can now be asserted that any response, if it occurs during a period of anxiety resulting from insufficient money, is likely to be reinforced by the drop in anxiety attending the receipt of money. Money thus functions as a reward or reinforcement. Here, however, it is especially important to note that money has become a reinforcer, not because of any previous association with the reduction of a primary drive such as hunger, but simply because anxiety has become connected to cues of not having money, and because having money eliminates such cues.

It also seems likely that a variety of other events than money could also serve to reduce the anxiety aroused by cues denoting insufficient money. Any activity such as getting drunk, making love, eating, or whatever, that successfully directs the individual's attention away from the disquieting cues and thereby leads to a diminution of anxiety would tend to be reinforced. Moreover, such behavior would also tend to become connected to both the anxiety-precipitating cues and to the anxiety-generated cues. With sufficient repetition it might well become a habitual, though unrealistic, adjustment to lack of money. By this reasoning, it might be possible to explain a number of instances where activities or objects that have never been associated with the reduction of primary drives seem nevertheless to have gained the power of reinforcement.

The essentials of the foregoing interpretation may be summarized as follows. In many instances, if not all, where adult human behavior has been strongly marked by money-seeking responses there appears to be little need for postulating the operation of a learned money-seeking drive. One does not learn to have a drive for money. Instead, one learns to become anxious in the presence of a variety of cues signifying the absence of money. The obtaining of money automatically terminates or drastically alters such cues, and in so doing, produces a decrease in anxiety. Money-seeking responses, or other reactions, appearing during the arousal of anxiety are strongly reinforced by the decline of anxiety attending the receipt of money.

It seems worth while at this point to observe that the proposed method of dealing with some of the acquired drives is not at all novel, at least in its general structure. Tolman, for example, has outlined a somewhat similar mechanism in the case of what he calls the drive of gregariousness. Thus, he writes, 'In *gregariousness* the individual, when separated from the flock or herd or group, seeks to get back into it in order to prevent an internal sufferance which in gregarious species seems to result directly from lack of surrounding animals.' (23, p. 21.) Although Tolman regards this as an example of a biological, not a learned, drive, it is evident that his 'internal sufferance' is the functional equivalent of anxiety, and that it is aroused by cues indicating a deficit of a special kind. Dollard and Miller (7) have followed a similar line of reasoning in describing the anxiety of a child separated from its mother. According to them, the child responds to cues of being separated from the mother with the drive of fear, and its reactions of approaching the mother are rewarded by the fear relief attending her actual presence. Although these authors suggest that this mode of analysis might be extended to other acquired drives, only a single paragraph is specifically devoted to the possibility that fear or anxiety might be an important component of many socially learned motives. Moreover, they do not attempt to make the sharp distinction between drives and habits which is here regarded as essential to the further clarification of acquired-drive problems.

One aspect of this interpretation of the so-called 'drive for money', upon which we have not yet touched, concerns the role that might be played by internal stimuli accompanying anxiety. In an earlier section of this paper the potential importance of stimuli accompanying unlearned drives was outlined in some detail. If discriminable internal stimuli also attend the inception of anxiety, and if conditions conducive to learning are operative, a wide diversity of behavior patterns could become attached to those stimuli. And predominant among those patterns would be various responses of seeking money. Because anxiety might thereby lead, through the response-eliciting agency of its characteristic stimuli, to money-seeking behavior, it would be easy to confuse its driving and response-eliciting function, and to assert that people have a 'drive for money'. From the present viewpoint, the observation of directed behavior at a time of anxiety arousal should not be ascribed to a new drive for the object which reduces the insecurity. Rather, it should be explained by appeal to the cue stimuli attending anxiety and to the drive property of anxiety in activating the latent reaction tendencies attached to those cues.

Although the foregoing analysis has dealt principally with behavior of seeking or working for money, a similar interpretation might be made of the so-called drives for prestige, for affection, for eminence, etc. That is, it might be useful in these and other cases to deny that a unique drive must be postulated in each instance, and to assume instead a single drive of uneasiness or insecurity or anxiety common to all. Thus, cues signifying 'lack of affection', 'lack of achievement', or 'lack of prestige', could acquire, through the process of learning, the power to serve as anxiety arousers. The attainment of affection or eminence would thereupon function to eliminate the anxiety-arousing cues, and consequently, anxiety.

By way of qualification, it should be observed that the proposed analysis does not apply necessarily to the behavior of animals in token-reward studies. The chimpanzee subjects in Cowles' and Wolfe's experiments can hardly be said to have been anxious in the absence of poker chips. Nor does it seem likely that the chips were rewarding because of their capacity to reduce anxiety. But if we deny the existence of both a specific drive for chips and an anxiety drive, to what can we appeal? Hunger appears to be the most likely candidate in this situation. In support of this selection, it may be recalled that the animals would not work for chips when satiated for food. This could mean either that they had no drive for chips, or, as Deese suggests, that the chip-drive was somehow specifically attached to hunger. Since the second of these possibilities requires the postulation of two drives, it seems less preferable than the first. If hunger is assumed to be the only functioning motive, we would not expect the habits of operating the test devices to be activated by the mere sight of poker chips under conditions of satiation. But such habits should be activated if hunger were present, and should continue in effective strength for some time even when the immediate reward was not food, but chips. The capacity of the chips to function as rewards can be readily interpreted as an instance of secondary reinforcement. Brass tokens, not exchangeable for food, acquired no such rewarding power, and the regular poker chips lost that power when their insertion into the 'chimpomat' failed to produce food. Thus it could be maintained that the behavior of the chimpanzees was not attributable to a poker-chip-getting drive, but to a hunger drive, and that new responses were learned because of the secondary reinforcing power of the chips and not because of their effectiveness in reducing a learned drive for chips.

It is quite likely that an identical interpretation is applicable to many cases of money-reinforced behavior in humans. Not all money-seeking behavior need be motivated by anxiety. It could be motivated by other drives such as hunger, or thirst, with the ultimately obtained money acting as a reward because of its close and frequent association with the receipt of food or water. This is probably the most common interpretation to be found in the literature, and both this mechanism and the proposed anxiety mechanism could well operate jointly in all instances of the supposed drive for money.

One final point with respect to the incentive problem. A number of writers in discussing the functions of incentives in behavior have been puzzled by the capacity of a lure – say, a banana seen at a short distance by a chimpanzee – apparently to serve as both a drive-arouser and, when actually eaten, as a drive-reducer. According to the position held here, this seeming paradox would be resolved by denying that the sight of a goal object can arouse a drive for that object. As we have repeatedly insisted, neither learned nor unlearned drives *per se* can be said to be directed toward, or for that matter, away from, any object. The supposed driving function of incentives would therefore be interpretable as an associative phenomenon, not as a motivational phenomenon. Such an interpretation would stress the fact that the goal stimuli, the incentives, have been repeatedly present, along with other stimuli when the organism has made approaching responses. These responses have been suitably rewarded, and hence the sight of the object becomes a part of the complex of stimuli eliciting approach strivings. Considered as such, the goal object is basically the same as any other stimulus that has acquired strong approach-response-evoking tendencies. The only difference lies in the tremendous amount of previous overlearning that may have taken place in the case of goal objects such as food. When the food is actually in the mouth, it can no longer serve as a stimulus for approach. For one thing, the organism cannot see it any more. It therefore loses its activity-arousing properties and becomes, instead, a stimulus that elicits eating and, perhaps, relaxation.

Summary

Many contemporary students of motivation hold to the view that the most significant of the human drives are not biological; rather, they are learned during the normal course of socialization and development. Unfortunately, the ardor with which this view is defended and the degree of confidence placed in its soundness far exceed the precision with which the details of the underlying mechanisms have been specified. In most instances, not even tentative paradigms for the learning of the supposed motives have been outlined in reasonably acceptable form.

Broadly viewed, this lack of adequate conceptualization may be ascribed to a failure to differentiate between drives as determinants of behavior and specific tendencies to react to particular stimulus situations. Of more direct significance, however, is the widespread failure to distinguish carefully between the characteristics of learned motives and the characteristics of other learned reaction tendencies.

In an effort to bring these difficult problems into sharper focus it has been suggested that the principal functional properties of drives, whether innate or acquired, are: (1) to activate or energize latent reaction (associative) tendencies; (2) to reinforce responses whose elicitation is followed by a reduction in drive; (3) to function as a punishment whenever abrupt increases in drive occur following a response. Any capacity to elicit *directed* behavior is specifically denied to drives *qua* drives. Only those events, whether external or internal, that have the properties of stimuli are alleged to provide the occasions for directed reactions.

The popular contemporary inclination to ascribe response-steering properties to drives is believed to stem from (1) the possibility that conditions leading to drive arousal may also produce internal stimuli capable of directing behavior; and from (2) the fact that human subjects use verbal phrases whose manifest reference is to motives, but which, with equal reason, can be interpreted as reflecting the strength of habits.

In exploring the implications of these distinctions, certain of the so-called acquired drives for goals like affection, money, and eminence, have been discussed. Because drives, as such, are regarded as incapable of steering or directing behavior, it is necessary to deny that individuals can acquire drives for any specific goal object or situation whatsoever. What individuals do acquire are numerous habits or modes of reacting to complex situations made up of both external and internal stimulus components. In some instances, biological drives alone may be adequate to activate these reaction tendencies. But in others, it may be necessary to appeal to activating motivations that are themselves acquired.

As a tentative solution to this problem, it is proposed that the significant motivational component underlying many of the supposed acquired drives for particular goal objects may be a learned tendency to be anxious (discontented, insecure) in the absence of those objects. On this hypothesis, stimulus cues signifying a lack of affection, a lack of prestige, insufficient money, and the like, are said to acquire, through learning, a potentiality for arousing a state of uneasiness or anxiety having the functional properties of a drive. Thus this learned uneasiness would function to energize whatever behavior is directed toward the securing of affection, prestige, or money; and its reduction, subsequent to the achieving of those goals, would be reinforcing.

In order to provide a concrete illustration of this view, an attempt has been made to work out the details of the learning process by which the anxiety underlying the so-called drive for money might be acquired. The suggested mechanism is coordinate with the paradigm of conditioning and with current conceptions of the acquisition of fear.

The writer is grateful to his colleagues in the Department of Psychology and in the Iowa Child Welfare Research Station for their stimulating and critical comments on the material presented in this paper. Additional thanks are due to Dr I. E. Farber for a careful reading of the manuscript and to Dr Julia S. Brown for several positive contributions to the final sections.

References

1. Allport, G. W. *Personality: A psychological interpretation.* New York: Holt, 1937.
2. Brown, J. S. and Jacobs, A. The role of fear in the motivation and acquisition of responses. *J. exp. Psychol.*, 1949, 39, 747–759.
3. Brown, J. S., Kalish, H. I., and Farber, I. E. Conditioned fear as revealed by magnitude of startle response to an auditory stimulus. *J. exp. Psychol.*, 1951, 41, 317–328.
4. Brown, J. S. and Farber, I. E. Emotions conceptualized as intervening variables – with suggestions toward a theory of frustration. *Psychol. Bull.*, 1951, 48, 465–495.
5. Cowles, J. T. Food tokens as incentives for learning by chimpanzees. *Comp. Psychol. Monogr.*, 1937, 14, No. 5.
6. Deese, J. *The psychology of learning.* New York: McGraw-Hill, 1952.
7. Dollard, J. and Miller, N. E. *Personality and psychotherapy.* New York: McGraw-Hill, 1950.
8. Hull, C. L. Knowledge and purpose as habit mechanisms. *Psychol. Rev.*, 1930, 37, 511–525.
9. Hull, C. L. Differential habituation to internal stimuli in the albino rat. *J. comp. Psychol.*, 1933, 16, 255–273.
10. Hull, C. L. *Principles of behavior.* New York: Appleton-Century-Crofts, 1943.
11. Kendler, H. H. An experimental examination of the non-selective principle of association of drive-stimuli. *Amer. J. Psychol.*, 1949, 62, 382–391.

12. Krech, D. Cognition and motivation in psychological theory. In *Current trends in psychological theory*. Pittsburgh: Univ. Pittsburgh Press, 1951.
13. Leeper, R. W. The role of motivation in learning: a study of the phenomenon of differential motivational control of the utilization of habits. *J. genet. Psychol.*, 1935, 46, 3–40.
14. Leeper, R. Current trends in theories of personality. In *Current trends in psychological theory*. Pittsburgh: Univ. Pittsburgh Press, 1951.
15. May, M. A. Experimentally acquired drives. *J. exp. Psychol.*, 1948, 38, 66–77.
16. McClelland, D. C. *Personality*. New York: Sloane, 1951.
17. Miller, N. E. Studies of fear as an acquirable drive: I. Fear as motivation and fear-reduction as reinforcement in the learning of new responses. *J. exp. Psychol.*, 1948, 38, 89–101.
18. Miller, N. E. Learnable drives and rewards. In S. S. Stevens (Ed.) *Handbook of experimental psychology*. New York: Wiley, 1951.
19. Mowrer, O. H. A stimulus-response analysis of anxiety and its role as a reinforcing agent. *Psychol. Rev.*, 1939, 46, 553–566.
20. Mowrer, O. H. and Lamoreaux, R. R. Avoidance conditioning and signal duration – a study of secondary motivation and reward. *Psychol. Monogr.*, 1942, 54, No. 5.
21. Mowrer, O. H. On the dual nature of learning – a reinterpretation of 'conditioning' and 'problem solving'. *Harv. educ. Rev.*, 1947, 17, 102–148.
22. Spence, K. W. Theoretical interpretations of learning. In C. P. Stone (Ed.) *Comparative psychology*. New York: Prentice-Hall, 1951.
23. Tolman, E. C. *Drives toward war*. New York: Appleton-Century, 1942.
24. Wolfe, J. B. Effectiveness of token rewards for chimpanzees. *Comp. Psychol. Monogr.*, 1936, 12, No. 60.
25. Young, P. T. Emotion as disorganized response – a reply to Professor Leeper. *Psychol. Rev.*, 1949, 56, 184–191.

Stimulus Elements as a Substitute for the Drive Concept

Excerpts from W. K. Estes, 'Stimulus-response theory of drive'. In M. R. Jones (Ed.), *Nebraska Symposium on Motivation*, University of Nebraska Press, Lincoln, 1958, pp. 35–69.

Since the publication of Hull's *Principles of Behavior* (9) in 1943, his two-factor theory of drive has moved into a steadily more dominant role in the literature of behavior theory. For a number of years, a principal motif was that of testing the two-factor conception. More recently, and especially in Spence's *Behavior Theory and Conditioning* (14), we find the validity of this conception no longer treated as a live issue. Attention is turned instead to such matters of detail as determining the arithmetical rule by which habit and drive interact.

Reasons for the hegemony of Hull's conception are not hard to find. Preceding formulations, insofar as they were specific at all, had viewed drive either as a particular type of stimulus (Guthrie [7]) or as a vaguely defined energizing function (16, 19, Ch. 2, 4, 5). By combining both stimulus and energizing factors into a single theory, Hull automatically enabled himself to explain far more phenomena than his nearest competitor. At the same time, Hull departed from custom even more radically by making his concepts reasonably definite and specific. This latter feature of Hull's formulation led directly to the parametric studies (1, 6, 8, 10, 11, 12, 15, 17, 18) which have done much to bring some semblance of order and structure out of a diffuse and amorphous research area.

In the literature, both experimental and theoretical, the almost universal tendency has been to account for as many relationships as possible in terms of drive as an energizer, holding the notion of drive stimulus in reserve. The latter is brought into the picture only when absolutely necessary to handle some otherwise refractory phenomenon. But of the two factors, that of drive stimulus is the one most nearly forced upon us by experimental facts. Why, then, would it not be reasonable to try reversing the coin – to account for as many relationships as possible in terms of the apparently indispensable concept of drive stimulus, leaving the notion of a general energizing factor to be brought in only if it really turns out to be necessary?

One's immediate thought may be that 'this has been tried before'. But has it? Guthrie (7) has long been identified with a stimulus conception of drive, but Guthrie's views have never been developed in sufficient detail to be tested against specific experimental data. Even in Hull's formulation, drive stimulus has been the stepchild, employed only at a qualitative level while the D factor received the benefits of provisional quantification and formal incorporation into the equations defining excitatory potential.

Theory of Drive-Stimuli

The remainder of this paper will be devoted to evening up the score. My objective shall be to do as thorough a job of developing the concept of drive stimulus as Hull and Spence have done for the energizing factor.

Assumptions

1. First of all, I assume that drive stimuli are simply stimuli, with no special properties whatsoever. Thus I shall be applying to a particular class of experiments the general stimulus theory developed in preceding papers by myself, Burke, and others (2, 3, 4, 5, 13). I shall not recapitulate previous papers here, but I shall review methods and assumptions as occasion arises to apply them in particular contexts. From this viewpoint, the essential characteristic differentiating experiments on drive from other classes of experiments is that in the former some of the important sources of stimulation are not directly observable. In order to reduce a very large task to conceivably manageable proportions, I shall deal almost exclusively with experiments upon hunger and thirst as determiners of instrumental response strength (in mammals), and within this still large class of experiments primarily with the parametric studies that have demonstrated reasonably clearcut functional relationships between response measures and degree of food or water deprivation.

2. In order to apply general stimulus theory to experiments on drive, we require explicit assumptions concerning the different sources of stimulation operative in an experimental situation. The four sources I shall distinguish are illustrated schematically in Fig. 1. The four columns in the figure represent an experimental situation at four deprivation times. The row labelled *CS* represents experimentally controlled signals, discriminative cues, or the like, and other apparatus cues whose sampling probabilities can be assumed constant from trial to trial. The row labelled *Extr.*

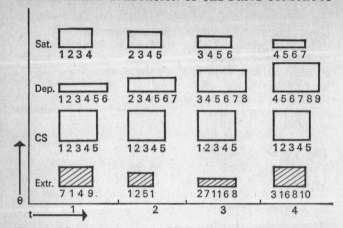

Figure 1 Schematic representation of the four classes of stimuli assumed to be operative in any experimental situation. The classification is based on the relationship between deprivation time (t) and stimulus sampling probabilities (θ)

represents extraneous stimuli; these are randomized with respect to both time and experimental treatments by standard experimental designs. The row labelled *Sat.* represents cues, including for example those produced by distention of the stomach, whose probabilities of occurrence decrease with deprivation time. Finally, the row labelled *Dep.* represents cues whose probabilities of occurrence increase with deprivation time.

The horizontal dimension of each rectangle in Fig. 1 represents the number of cues (stimulus elements) in the set, while the vertical dimension represents the average sampling probability of the elements. The area of the rectangle represents what we shall term the *weight* of the stimulus set; the weight is a parameter which can be evaluated experimentally and which may be taken to signify the relative importance of the given stimulus set in determining behavior.

3. Our only general assumptions concerning weights of the various stimulus sets are as follows. (*a*) The weight of the CS set is constant over deprivation time. (*b*) The weight of the Extraneous set varies randomly, but the average weight is constant over deprivation time. (*c*) The weight of the Satiation set decreases with deprivation time; for simplicity in calculations, I shall take the function to be linear, as shown in the figure. (*d*) The weight of the Deprivation set increases with deprivation time; again for

simplicity I have taken the function to be linear. (*e*) The combined weight of Satiation and Deprivation sets together increases with deprivation time.

4. The numerals under the various rectangles in Fig. 1 signify individual cues and are intended to illustrate my assumptions concerning overlap of the sets available for sampling at different deprivation times. In the case of the CS, exactly the same set of elements is assumed available at all deprivation times. The subsets of Extraneous cues represent random samples from a population large enough so that particular individual cues will rarely recur on different trials or periods of an experiment. For Satiation cues, and similarly for Deprivation cues, we assume a sequence of partially overlapping sets, the proportion of overlap between any two sets in either sequence decreasing linearly with the time difference as illustrated in the figure. Thus as time passes following a period of eating or drinking, some of the Satiation cues produced by the consummatory activity drop out and are replaced by others, the latter being a consequence of digestion and other bodily activities that follow food or water intake with some delay; similarly the detailed makeup of the set of effective Deprivation cues is assumed to change progressively with time. The psychological significance of these assumptions is that of the cues which become conditioned to a response during training at a particular deprivation time, progressively more will be replaced by unconditioned cues as we test at deprivation times further from the training value.

5. Probability of any response is assumed to be determined by all cues present at the time of testing. More specifically, probability is assumed equal to the weight of all cues connected (i.e., conditioned, associated) to the given response divided by the weight of all cues present. In Fig. 1, and others to follow, I have indicated cues connected to the reference response by white areas and cues connected to competing responses by crosshatched areas. This figure might be taken to represent an experiment in which the reference response has received extensive training at all deprivation times. Thus all of the CS, Satiation, and Deprivation sets are represented by white areas. Presumably some Extraneous cues would also have become conditioned to the response, but since these rarely recur, the Extraneous sets are nevertheless represented by crosshatched areas. Now the probability of the reference response at any one deprivation time would be given by the area of the CS, Sat., and Dep. rectangles divided by the total area of all four rectangles.

General implications of the theory

It will be apparent from Fig. 1 that in any one training situation, the effect of drive stimuli upon the asymptotic level of performance can be regarded as an amplification of the effects of the CS. In standard simple learning situations, conditions of reinforcement are such that drive cues and CS cues will become conditioned to the same responses; under these circumstances, the CS-plus-drive cues will more heavily outweigh any unconditioned extraneous cues present than would the CS alone, thus yielding a higher response probability. The magnitude of this amplifying effect will depend upon a number of conditions. Some measures of performance are more vulnerable than others to the effects of extraneous cues. When rate measures are taken, as in a Skinner box, or response time measures, as in a runway, competing responses evoked by extraneous cues must almost invariably depress the measure of performance; but when relative frequency measures are taken, extraneous cues may have little effect. When, for example, a rat in a T maze stops to scratch its head or explore a vagrant odor, the running time for the trial will necessarily be increased, but the choice of left *vs.* right alley will probably be affected, if at all, only upon trials when an extraneous cue disturbs the animal precisely at the choice point. Thus asymptotic rate of bar-pressing in a Skinner box and asymptotic running time in a runway or maze should be expected to depend strongly upon level of deprivation over a considerable range of deprivation times, while an asymptotic frequency measure in a two-choice situation should depend only weakly upon level of deprivation.

If training in an instrumental situation were given at several different levels of deprivation, then one would expect, on grounds either of intuition or of general experience, that asymptotic performance would be an increasing function of deprivation time. Considering the successive columns in Fig. 1, we can readily see that this outcome is predicted by the theory; for the total white area increases as we go from left to right while the crosshatched area fluctuates around a constant value. However, we also note that if extraneous cues could be completely eliminated, the theory would no longer predict an increase in asymptotic response probability with deprivation time. The white area would still increase, but since there would be no crosshatched area to be outweighed, response probability would be constant from column to column.

It is probably impossible to eliminate all extraneous cues,

partly because some of them are internal in origin (e.g., itches, sneezes, coughs). However, Cotton, in a doctoral research done at Indiana University a few years ago, has done the next best thing by demonstrating the effects of removing from a set of runway data all trials on which behavioral evidence indicated the presence of appreciable extraneous stimulation. Cotton trained rats on his runway at each of a series of deprivation times and then tested asymptotic running times at all deprivations. He first

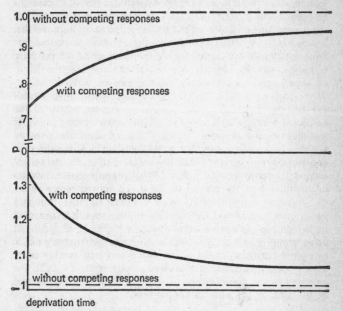

Figure 2 Theoretical curves for Cotton's experiment

plotted raw mean response times, then he eliminated from the protocols all trials on which observable competing responses (face-washing, exploring cracks, etc.) occurred and replotted mean response time for the remaining trials, presumably relatively free of the effects of extraneous cues. Predictions computed from the present theory for this experiment are illustrated in Fig. 2. In the upper panel are shown theoretical response probabilities for the two conditions, and in the lower panel theoretical response times. Those who have read Cotton's paper (1) or who have seen his empirical functions reproduced in Spence's book will recognize the close correspondence between our predictions and Cotton's findings.

Apparently one important basis for Hull's assumption of an energizing factor was the positive correlation normally observed between deprivation time and such measures of activity as operant level in a Skinner-type situation, activation of a running wheel or tambour cage when no obvious source of reinforcement is associated with responding, and asymptotic response rates or response times in instrumental learning situations. According to the present theory, however, there is no universal or unmodifiable relation between activity and deprivation time. To the extent that behaviors which are tapped by a given measure of activity have become conditioned to drive stimuli, either during or previous to an experiment, a positive correlation between activity and deprivation is predictable by the reasoning sketched in the preceding section. Even in these cases, the detailed nature of the predicted relationship differs for the two kinds of theory. On the assumption of a D factor, a high degree of deprivation should generate a greater excitatory potential than a low degree of deprivation, and for any particular measure of excitatory potential the difference between high and low deprivation groups should be constant over the period during which activity is measured. (A constant proportionality should obtain if habit strength varies over the period.) According to the stimulus theory, a higher degree of deprivation produces a higher total weight of drive stimuli which in turn tends to eliminate interruptions of the measured performance; at a low deprivation, pauses are more likely, because extraneous cues have greater relative weight, but between pauses the measure of response rate or speed should be the same as for a higher deprivation.

References
1. Cotton, J. W. Running time as a function of amount of food deprivation. *J. exp. Psychol.*, 1953, 46, 188–198.
2. Estes, W. K. Toward a statistical theory of learning. *Psychol. Rev.*, 1950, 57, 94–107.
3. Estes, W. K. Statistical theory of spontaneous recovery and regression. *Psychol. Rev.*, 1955, 62, 145–154.
4. Estes, W. K., and Burke, C. J. A theory of stimulus variability in learning. *Psychol. Rev.*, 1953, 60, 276–286.
5. Estes, W. K., and Lauer, D. W. Conditions of invariance and modifiability in simple reversal learning. *J. comp. physiol. Psychol.*, 1957, 50, 199–206.
6. Finan, J. L. Quantitative studies in motivation. I. Strength of

conditioning in rats under varying degrees of hunger. *J. comp. Psychol.*, 1940, 29, 119–134.

7. Guthrie, E. R. *The psychology of learning* (Rev. Ed.). New York: Harpers, 1952.
8. Horenstein, Betty R. Performance of conditioned responses as a function of strength of hunger drive. *J. comp. physiol. Psychol.*, 1951, 44, 210–224.
9. Hull, C. L. *Principles of behavior*. New York: Appleton-Century-Crofts, 1943.
10. Kimble, G. A. Behavior strength as a function of the intensity of the hunger drive. *J. exp. Psychol.*, 1951, 41, 341–348.
11. Perin, C. T. Behavior potentiality as a joint function of the amount of training and the degree of hunger at the time of extinction. *J. exp. Psychol.*, 1942, 30, 93–113.
12. Saltzman, I., and Koch, S. The effect of low intensities of hunger on the behavior mediated by a habit of maximum strength. *J. exp. Psychol.*, 1948, 38, 347–370.
13. Schoeffler, M. S. Probability of response to compounds of discriminated stimuli. *J. exp. Psychol.*, 1954, 48, 323–329.
14. Spence, K. W. *Behavior theory and conditioning*. New Haven: Yale Univer. Press, 1956.
15. Williams, S. B. Resistance to extinction as a function of the number of reinforcements. *J. exp. Psychol.*, 1938, 23, 506–522.
16. Woodworth, R. S. *Dynamic psychology*. New York: Columbia Univer. Press, 1918.
17. Yamaguchi, H. G. Drive (D) as a function of hunger (h). *J. exp. Psychol.*, 1951, 42, 108–117.
18. Yamaguchi, H. G. Gradients of drive stimulus (S_D) intensity generalization. *J. exp. Psychol.*, 1952, 43, 298–304.
19. Young, P. T. *Motivation of behavior*. New York: Wiley, 1936. Chapters 2, 4, 5.

Drive, Reinforcement, and Control of Behavior

Excerpts from B. F. Skinner, *Science and Human Behavior*, Macmillan, New York, 1953, Chapter 9.

In traditional terms an organism drinks because it *needs* water, goes for a walk because it *needs* exercise, breathes more rapidly and deeply because it *wants* air, and eats ravenously because of the promptings of *hunger*. Needs, wants, and hungers. They are said to have various dimensions. Needs and wants are likely to be thought of as psychic or mental, while hungers are more readily conceived of as physiological. But the terms are freely used when nothing with these dimensions has been observed. Sometimes the inner operation is inferred from the operation responsible for the strength of the behavior – as when we say that someone who has had nothing to drink for several days 'must be thirsty' and probably will drink. On the other hand, it is sometimes inferred from the behavior itself – as when we observe someone drinking large quantities of water and assert without hesitation that he possesses a great thirst. In the first case, we infer the inner event from a prior independent variable and predict the dependent variable which is to follow. In the second case, we infer the inner event from the event which follows, and attribute it to a preceding history of deprivation. So long as the inner event is inferred, it is in no sense an explanation of the behavior and adds nothing to a functional account.

Needs and wants are convenient terms in casual discourse, and many students of behavior have been interested in setting up similar hypothetical intervening states as legitimate scientific concepts. A need or want could simply be redefined as a condition resulting from deprivation and characterized by a special probability of response. Since it is difficult to lay the ghosts which hover about these older terms, there is a certain advantage in using a term which has fewer connotations. 'Drive' is sometimes used. A drive need not be thought of as mental or physiological. The term is simply a convenient way of referring to the effects of deprivation and satiation and of other operations which alter the probability of behavior in more or less the same way. It is convenient because it enables us to deal with many cases at once. There are many ways of changing the probability that an organism will eat; at the same time, a single kind of deprivation strengthens many kinds of behavior. The concept of hunger as a drive brings these various relations together in a single term.

The simplicity of the concept of drive is only apparent. This is true as well of need and want. No concept can eliminate an actual diversity of data. *A drive is a verbal device with which we account for a state of strength, and it cannot answer experimental questions.* We cannot control the behavior of an organism by directly changing its hunger, its thirst, or its sex drive. In order to change these states indirectly, we must deal with the relevant variables of deprivation and satiation and must face all the complexity of these operations.

Satiation and deprivation are obviously related to operant reinforcement. To a hungry organism food is both reinforcing and satiating. It is necessary, although sometimes difficult, to distinguish between these effects. In reinforcement the presentation of food is contingent upon a response; we can satiate without consistently reinforcing if we avoid this contingency. We can also reinforce without substantial satiation or at least before satiation has taken place. But there is an inevitable connection between the two processes: the effect of operant reinforcement will not be observed if the organism has not been appropriately deprived. The net result of reinforcement is not simply to strengthen behavior but to strengthen it *in a given state of deprivation.* Reinforcement thus brings behavior under the control of an appropriate deprivation. After we have conditioned a pigeon to stretch its neck by reinforcing with food, the variable which controls neck-stretching is food deprivation. The response of stretching the neck has merely joined that group of responses which vary with this operation. We can describe the effect of reinforcement in no simpler way.

By conditioning and extinguishing a response under different degrees of deprivation, it is possible to see the effect of deprivation in detail. If we reinforce a response in a group of organisms at the same level of deprivation and extinguish it in subgroups at different levels, we find that the number of responses in the extinction curve is a function of deprivation. The hungrier the organism, the more responses it will emit during extinction. If, on the other hand, we condition at different levels of deprivation and extinguish at the same level, we find, surprisingly enough, that the two extinction curves contain approximately the same number of responses. The effect of deprivation is felt during extinction, not during conditioning.

Behavior which has been strengthened by a conditioned reinforcer varies with the deprivation appropriate to the primary reinforcer. The behavior of going to a restaurant is composed of a sequence of responses, early members of which (for example, going along a certain street) are reinforced by the appearance of discriminative stimuli which control later responses (the appearance of the restaurant, which we then enter). The whole sequence is ultimately reinforced by food, and the probability varies with food deprivation. We increase the chances that someone will go to a restaurant, or even walk along a particular street, by making him hungry. We do not say that there are special drives associated with the early responses in the sequence, because there are no parallel operations of deprivation. Such traditional terms as 'needs', 'wants', and so on recognize these subsidiary steps. For example, we might say that a man first *wants* a taxi, that he then *wants* the driver to take him to Fifty-sixth Street, that he then *wants* to find a particular restaurant, that he then *wants* to open the door, that he then *wants* a table, a menu, and the roast beef. But since there are no processes of satiation and deprivation appropriate to the behavior which is involved here, except for the last item, we have no reason to set up corresponding drives. A man does not need a taxi in the sense of not having had a taxi for a long time. Certain behavior which requires a taxi for its execution is strong and occurs as soon as a taxi is available. The appearance of the taxi reinforces any behavior which brings it about. It is also an enabling event which makes a later response possible and hence brings the earlier behavior to an end. It would only confuse the issue, however, to say that the appearance of the taxi had satiated the behavior of hailing taxis. The practical use of the relation reveals its essentials. If for some reason we want to induce a man to hail a taxi, we strengthen any behavior requiring a taxi; we do not deprive him of taxis. He will not hail a taxi if he already has one because other behavior then intervenes.

Generalized reinforcers raise this issue in a more acute form. They are important precisely because they are effective under a number of deprivations, some of which are likely to be present at any given time. The lack of a specific deprivation encourages us to assume a separate drive for the immediate generalized reinforcer. Although we may be willing to give up the notion of a 'taxi drive', we are likely to insist upon a drive for attention, approval, affection, domination, or money. In order to justify assigning separate drives to the behavior so reinforced, we should have to show that it is possible to deprive or satiate an organism with given amounts of attention, approval, and so on, but we should also have to make sure that no satiation or deprivation is taking place in any of the primary areas associated with the generalized reinforcer. For example, we should have to reduce a 'need for affection' by supplying an abundance of affection without supplying any of the primary reinforcers associated with it. Only then would we have evidence of an autonomous drive. But although generalized reinforcers may reinforce when primary reinforcement is not forthcoming – a case exemplified by the behavior of the miser in poring over his gold – we have no reason to assume a corresponding drive. It is one of the more obvious characteristics of the miser that he is not actually satiated by money. The reinforcing effect of money is extraordinarily great, so that most of his behavior which is strong is strong for that reason, but a separate drive implies a separate operation of deprivation or satiation, for which we have little evidence in the behavior of the miser. There are other kinds of misers who specialize in attention, affection, approval, or domination. Although we may show that they are strongly *reinforced* by these generalized reinforcers, even in the absence of primary reinforcement, we do not speak of separate drives because there are no appropriate operations of deprivation or satiation.

The drives appropriate to conditioned reinforcers are not to be confused with acquired drives for nicotine, alcohol, morphine, or other drugs. The effects induced by drugs of this sort reinforce the behavior of consuming them. The drug may bring release from some aversive condition such as anxiety, fear, or a sense of guilt, or it may produce some condition which is positively reinforcing. The reinforcement may become more and more powerful if repeated use leads to physiological changes which increase the aversive condition which the drug reduces. This sort of 'addiction' is an acquired drive for which well-marked processes of deprivation and satiation are evident. A potent technique of control is the development of an addiction. A drug is administered repeatedly until its reinforcing power becomes great. It is then used to reinforce desired behavior – for example, the behavior of a prisoner of war in answering questions. The drug is then withheld, and the probability of the behavior increases greatly.

An event can be a positive reinforcer even though it does not reduce a level of deprivation. There is a related point to be made here: behavior which is strengthened through deprivation need not reduce that deprivation. The Freudian process of *sublimation* raises this issue. Through either stimulus or response induction an operation which strengthens a response also strengthens other responses having similar properties or the same response upon similar occasions. Deprivation is an example of such an operation. Thus a childless couple may 'sublimate' their parental behavior by treating a pet dog as a child. The artist 'sublimates' sexual behavior in working on pictures or models of the human body. If we believe that behavior always takes place 'for good reason' – that is, because of some conceivable biological advantage – many instances of this sort seem puzzling. But a response strengthened through induction may very well have no effect upon the deprivation, even though the response from which it borrows its strength does have such an effect. In many examples of sublimation the behavior itself is automatically satiating.

There is another area in which it is advantageous to deal with the processes of satiation and deprivation rather than with any drive. Efforts have been made to reduce all motivation to one primary drive. Freud, for example, emphasized sex. The contention that a given activity is 'essentially sexual in nature' may be translated in either of two ways depending upon whether we emphasize the dependent or the independent variable. To say that artistic and musical activities 'express sexual impulses' may mean that characteristic behavior in this field *resembles* sexual behavior in topography. The sculptor modeling a human figure is behaving to some extent as he would behave toward a human body; certain temporal aspects of musical behavior resemble the temporal pattern of sexual behavior. This is simply induction from one stimulus to another or from one response to another on the basis of similarity. But it is often difficult to decide whether two situations or two actions are similar enough to warrant such an explanation. Often we have to infer the importance of a point of similarity from its effect upon behavior. On the other hand the issue may be expressed in a question of this form: Does the probability of an act which is asserted to be sexual in nature change with sex deprivation or satiation? If so, it may be regarded as sexual even though it is not topographically similar to obviously sexual behavior.

An alternative contention is that the basic human drive is 'domination'. This generalized reinforcer is certainly very important. The more specific biological reinforcers are frequently received only after precurrent behavior has been effective in 'dominating' the physical or social environment, and to this extent we may bring all behavior together under the rubric of domination. We have seen, however, that a corresponding *drive* is not required when the reinforcer is generalized. Domination may be *reinforcing* and hence very important as a controlling variable. A man may come to dominate 'for the sake of dominating', just as the miser collects money for its own sake. But apparently there is no independent deprivation or satiation concerned with domination itself. To deprive a man of domination would mean to arrange circumstances in which he dominated neither physical nature nor society, but under such circumstances he would presumably suffer other deprivations, to which any general strengthening of his behavior could then be attributed. Conversely, when we change a man's behavior by 'letting him have his own way', we may appear to be satiating his 'need for domination', but we almost certainly also change some primary deprivations or some of the aversive conditions. The surprisingly general effect of many specific satiations or deprivations makes the generality of the drive to dominate questionable. A man who tends to dominate in many walks of life may undergo an extensive change as the result of a successful marriage or, on a shorter time scale, a satisfying meal.

Attempts to reduce all human motivation to a single need for approval, affection, and so on, are subject to the same criticism.

Part Two   GOAL DIRECTION

Common sense considers 'purpose' to be an entirely subjective concept. For the layman, purpose is synonymous with the experience of intent or a preconceived plan to do something. Defined in these subjective terms, it is of little value in the explanation of behaviour. Therefore, psychologists have been concerned with finding some concrete and reliable operations for defining this intuitive concept. They have adopted the term *goal direction* to refer to the observable purposive aspects of behaviour, leaving the terms such as 'purpose' and 'intention' for the common-sense notion of consciousness of some aim. One of the central problems in the study of motivation is the way in which behaviour becomes organized in relation to goals. The view now generally held is that goals are reinforcers which, through response shaping, direct the flow of actions toward themselves.

V   From Purpose to Goal Direction

McDougall drew attention to the purposive aspect of behaviour,
listing certain objective features of behaviour as evident
correlates of subjective purpose. However, he treated
'purposive striving' as a completely subjective phenomenon
and linked it to his metaphysical principle of purposivism.
It remained for Tolman to define goal direction in purely
objective terms. Statements of McDougall and Tolman are
presented below. These are followed by a statement by
Bindra on the quantitative description of goal direction
(appropriateness) and one by Skinner on how prior
reinforcement makes behaviour goal directed.

21 W. McDougall

Purposiveness, a Characteristic of Living Things

Excerpts from W. McDougall, *Outline of Psychology*, Scribners, New York, 1923. Chapter 2.

By reflecting upon a variety of actions, we may realize that our actions may be arranged in a scale; at the upper end of the scale may be put such actions as are most deliberately purposive, the goal and means having been pondered, developed in imagination, and deliberately chosen among various alternative possibilities, before overt action began. Lower in the scale would be those actions the goal and the steps toward which we have thought of, clearly perhaps, but without pondering and choosing. Lower still are such actions as we perform with only a very vague and sketchy foresight of the goal and of the means, or perhaps of the goal only. And, at the lower end of the scale of purposiveness, would be such impulsive actions as the snatching the child from imminent danger. As regards action of this last class, although we cannot give any retrospective account of our experience which would include the foreseeing of the goal of the action, we see that the action is such that, if we had acted a little more slowly and deliberately, we should have foreseen the goal we sought or purposed, and perhaps also the steps of the action we actually took. We rightly feel that we did not act as a mere machine, but that the action was a purposive action in which our nature was truly expressed; and we may confidently infer that the goal was foreseen, however vaguely and incompletely, at the moment of action. There is no obvious lower limit to the scale of purposiveness; and we may fairly ascribe to other men in moments of impulsive action the same vague foreseeing that we infer on our own part at such times. And, though here the inference is more debatable, we may ascribe to an animal whose action exhibits the first five marks of behavior the same kind of vague anticipation of the goal.

Purposive action is, then, action that seems to be governed or directed in some degree by prevision of its effects, by prevision of that which still lies in the future, of events which have not yet happened, but which are likely to happen, and to the happening of which the action itself may contribute. *Purposiveness in this sense seems to be of the essence of mental activity*; and it is because all actions which have the marks of behavior seem to be purposive, in however lowly and vague a degree, that we regard them as expressions of Mind.

We cannot provide any final and conclusive proof of the truth of this ascription of purposive or mental quality to the action of any animal. Some of the mechanists would scornfully repudiate the claim that we may reasonably regard animal behavior as purposive; they would stigmatize such interpretation as anthropomorphic; and this word is one of their strongest terms of reproach for those who do not agree with them. Logically they should equally repudiate the attribution of purpose to their fellow-men, or to those men who give no introspective account of their purposive actions; and some of them do not hesitate to do this, and to deprecate as 'anthropomorphic' such interpretation of human action. If they admit the word 'purposive', they define it in a non-psychological manner, and describe as purposive all actions which seem to be serviceable to the life of the animal or the species. Applying this objective and non-psychological criterion, they point out that simple reflex actions, such as the withdrawal of the foot from a sharp contact, or the scratch-reflex of the dog's hind-leg, are serviceable, and therefore purposive. Yet we see that such reflex actions may be provoked by suitable stimulation in an animal whose brain has been destroyed; or in a man in whom the part of the spinal cord concerned in the action is severed from the brain, and who remains entirely unaware of the whole process. They argue from these facts as follows: such serviceable reflex actions appear to be purposive; yet they are accompanied by no experience and are purely mechanical processes of which the successive steps can be traced in the nerves and muscles as purely chemical and physical events; hence, when we observe the more complicated trains of action in which the processes of the brain play some essential part, we are justified in regarding them as merely more complex processes of the same mechanical type; and, if the actions are those of a man who tells us that he foresaw the end of his action and desired it, and directed his action in such a way as to attain this goal, that makes no essential difference; the brain mechanisms, the complicated arrangements of nervous paths laid down in his brain, would have brought about the serviceable train of action of his limbs just as securely and effectively, if he had not foreseen or desired the end.

Now, if the mechanist could point to any processes or movements of inanimate things which presented all the foregoing marks of behavior, his argument would be a strong one. We might feel compelled to admit that he was right in assimilating all animal and all human behavior to the type of the mechanical reflex, and in explaining behavior from below upwards; leaving the relation of experience to such actions a blank mystery, as the 'parallelists' do in their formula that experience runs parallel with brain-action in a relation of temporal concomitance merely, like two parallel rays of light projected into space, which continue to run parallel, but which never meet or influence one another.

But it is impossible to find any instance of such movements of lifeless objects; and for this reason we are justified in claiming, provisionally at least in the present state of science, that nature presents two classes of things, the non-living and the living, and two classes of movements, the mechanical and the purposive, characteristic of the two classes of things respectively.

The psychologist should and must choose the fundamental categories appropriate to his science, if he is to make progress toward his proper goal, the better understanding and control of human nature and human behavior. *Purposive action is the most fundamental category of psychology*; just as the motion of a material particle according to the mechanical principles of Newton's laws of motion has long been the fundamental category of physical science. Behavior is always purposive action, or a train or sequence of purposive actions.

22 E. C. Tolman

Objective Definition of Purpose

Excerpts from E. C. Tolman, Purpose and cognition: the determiners of animal learning, *Psychological Review*, 1925, Vol. 32, pp. 285–97.

Goal-Seeking (Purpose)

When a rat runs a maze, it is to be observed that his running and searching activities *persist until food is reached*. And it appears that this persistence is the result of the physiological condition of hunger. We do not know whether the rat, in so 'persisting' is 'conscious'; we do not know whether he 'feels a purpose' (to use the terminology of the mentalists); but we do know that, given (1) the physiological condition of hunger and given (2) the objective conditions of the maze, the rat thus *persists until the food is reached*. It is this purely *objective* fact of persistence until a certain specific type of goal-object is reached that we define as a *goal-seeking*. And as thus defined, a goal-seeking is a wholly objective and a wholly behaviouristic phenomenon. There is nothing 'mentalistic' about it.

The one important experiment already in the literature directly oriented toward this question is that of Dr Simmons (1924) on 'The Relative Effectiveness of Certain Incentives in Animal Learning'. In this experiment, she found that the rate of maze learning may be varied by using different types of goal-objects. She found, for example, that bread and milk, as food, caused a more rapid learning than sunflower seed. She found also that complete satisfaction of hunger immediately at the end of the run is more effective than merely partial satisfaction (followed by delayed feeding an hour later). Such findings indicate gross facts concerning the importance of goal-seeking. They indicate that the nature and strength of this goal-seeking and its satisfaction have important effects upon the learning rate. They do not indicate, however, in just what qualitative ways the different goals produce their different effects. She did not, for example, devise her experiments so as to discover whether the different effects are a matter of calling out more and better initial exploratory impulses or rather of a more rapid 'stamping in'. Nor do her results indicate whether the one type of food was better than the other because the one food was less lasting and hence the animal was more *hungry* at the beginning of each new trial, or whether it was rather a matter of the greater satisfactoriness (pleasantness) of one food as such. These are all important points left as problems for further investigation.

Under the head of such further investigations we might suggest the following. First, we might, perhaps, test the 'satisfactoriness' of the goal-object *per se*. Suppose a maze were so constructed that the living cage of the animal were directly connected with the food box. Our experiment would then attempt to use the desire to get back home (i.e. to the living-cage *per se*) as a *standard* against which to measure strengths of the food-desire. We might, perhaps, measure the time spent in the food-box as against the time spent in the living-cage in any fixed period allowed for eating, or in some similar way measure the relative strengths of the food-box-getting-to tendency as over against the home-going tendency. Having such a method of measurement, we could then discover to what extent this food-getting-to tendency *per se* varied in terms of the home-going tendency with different sorts of foods and at different stages of learning. What, for example, would be the results, given the same physiologically defined degree of hunger, for bread and milk and for sunflower seed? What those as regards the initial and the final stages of learning? Etc., etc.?

It is obvious that after gathering such data together we would have infinitely more information for explaining and describing a maze learning-curve than we have at present.

A second line of investigation might be directed toward discovering the nature of the goal features. What feature of a given goal-object is it which makes the latter a goal-object? Experimentally, that is, we would want, by varying the stimuli which a given food presents, to discover just what are its essential and defining goal-features. Is it, for example, its color, its taste, its smell or its what, which determines its acceptance as a goal? And does this necessary feature perhaps vary with the different stages of learning?

Finally, a third sort of investigation suggests itself. For it appears that goal-seeking must be defined not only as a tendency to *persist* in more or less random fashion *until food is reached* but also as a tendency to *select* within limits the *shorter* (and probably also the easier and pleasanter) of two or more alternative ways. This appeared first in De Camp's (1921) classical experiment. For it will be remembered that he found that a rat will, within certain limits, discriminate between and prefer the *spatially* shorter of two alternative routes to food.

At California we have now done a further experiment from which it has been discovered that a rat will also select, other things being equal, the *temporally* shorter of two routes. Mr Sams, in an experiment soon to be published, found that a rat, when given the choice between two ways to food, one temporally longer and the other temporally shorter, will, within limits, select the latter.

Summing up, then, from De Camp's experiment and from this experiment of Mr Sams' we conclude that the goal-seekings (purposes) which govern a rat's maze-learning include not only the tendency toward such and such a goal-object as such but also a further selective tendency to get to this goal-object by the shortest route both (*a*) spatially and (*b*) temporally.

Finally, it appears probable that in addition to these spatial and temporal preferences, further investigations might indicate that a rat will also prefer a 'physiologically easier' route when spatial and temporal distances are rendered constant.

Final Object-Adjustments (Final Cognitions)

What are the defining elements of, and the causal factors determining, the acquisition of the final object-adjustments (cognitions)? We must note, in the first place, that such final object-adjustments seem to be made up of two phases or aspects: (1) what we may call their intent or noëtic aspects, and (2) what we may call their sensory-cue or sensory aspects. We shall consider these separately.

(1) The intent or noëtic aspect of an object-adjustment we will define as the object-structure (i.e. that behavior possibility) which the animal's behavior can be observed quite definitely to *impute* (whether correctly or incorrectly) to such and such a particular part of the maze. Thus, for example, the behavior of the rat who runs straight into the end of the shortened maze-blind may be said quite objectively to impute an object-structure (a behavior possibility) to this part of the maze which the latter does not possess. It imputes, that is, a greater length to the alley than it has. Or, again, when a rat, at a given stage of learning, tends to enter alleys pointing in the general direction of the food-box more often than those pointing in the opposite direction, such a predominance of entrances obviously states, exhibits, an imputation that the food-box lies in the general direction of such alleys. Given, in short, that the animal is dominated by the food-seeking impulse, his various behaviors in the successive parts of the maze can be said, at any stage of learning, quite objectively to express

his thereunto acquired object-adjustments (cognitions) with respect to the 'getting-on-toward-food' possibilities of such maze parts. It must be emphasized that these object-adjustments to the maze structure have meaning only with reference to the task of *getting to the food and getting there as quickly, both spatially and temporally, as possible.* What the animal's behavior exhibits in the way of object-adjustments to (cognitions of) the maze structure are not, of course, comparable to what the physicist would tell us about the maze, but are merely (cognitions of) adjustments to the maze from the one point of view of getting to the food-box.

So much for an indication of the intent or noëtic aspect of the animal's object-adjustments.

(2) It appears however, that learning consists not merely in the acquisition and improvement of these intent or noëtic aspects of the animal's adjustment to the maze, but it involves also the attachment of such intents to the *right stimulus-cues.* The functioning of any given object-adjustment requires the presence of stimuli. The rat imputes a behavior-possibility to a particular part of the maze as a result of particular stimuli presented by that maze part. And the phenomenon of learning consists in large part in the attaching of the object-adjustment intents to these stimuli.

Finally, it is to be pointed out that the above discussion, in spite of its use of the terms *purpose* and *cognition* is *behavioristic.* For in no place in using these concepts have we defined them 'mentalistically'. We have not in some mysterious fashion 'looked within' and so discovered them. Rather have we looked without at the rat in the maze and merely proceeded to describe the behavior which we saw. And the animal's cognitions (object-adjustments) and his purposes (goal-seekings) as we have observed them have been described and *defined* in purely *objective* terms; in terms, that is, of (*a*) the objective maze situation itself, and of (*b*) purely objective and descriptive aspects of the rat's behavior in the presence of that situation.

References
De Camp, J. E. *Psychobiology.* 1921, 2, 245–253.
Simmons, R. *Comp. Psychol. Monog.*, 1924, 2, Serial No. 7.

23 D. Bindra

Meaning and Measurement of Goal Direction

Excerpt from D. Bindra, *Motivation, a Systematic Reinterpretation*,
Ronald Press, New York, 1959, Chapter 3.

Ordinarily, when we describe behavior as goal-directed or
adaptive, we have in mind one or both of two different types of
situations. The first involves the presence of a number of different
modes of behavior which are (known to be) connected with one
and the same goal. Thus, we say that a cat's behavior is adaptive
when we have evidence that it can reach a given goal by a variety
of different courses of action. If, for some reason, one course of
action proves unsuccessful (e.g. if one path to the goal is blocked)
or is likely to prove unsuccessful, the cat follows another course
of action to the same goal. The second variety of situations called
adaptive is one in which the organism's behavior in some way
corresponds to variations in the goal itself. Consider a cat chasing
a rat. If the rat runs to the left, so does the cat; if the rat dashes to
the right, the cat also leaps in that direction; if the rat walks into
a tiny hole, the cat puts its paw into the hole or anticipates and
'waits' for the rat's emergence from it. The cat's behavior in this
case is goal-directed in the sense that the cat's course of action
follows and anticipates, or, in general, corresponds to the variations in the location of the goal (rat).

A moment's reflection will show that both these types of situations have one important feature in common, and this feature is
the essence of goal-directed behavior. In both cases the course of
action of the organism with respect to the given goal changes with
variations in the goal itself or in the location of the goal, and it
changes in a way that, on the whole, increases the probability that
the organism will reach the goal. In the first example above, the
cat, when faced with an obstruction, changes its course of action
to one that would be more effective under the changed circumstances. Similarly, in the second example, the cat responds to the
variations in the stimulus situation (location of the rat) by changing its own behavior to a potentially more effective course of
action. We can employ Sommerhoff's (1950) concept of *appropriateness* to designate this essential feature of what we ordinarily
refer to as adaptiveness of behavior. In general terms, appropriateness of behavior refers to the characteristic of adjusting to

changing circumstances by changing one's course of action in such a way that it is likely to be effective in reaching the goal.

Thus we can say that an organism's behavior is appropriate with respect to a given goal to the extent that the organism shows an effective course of action for the various *possible* changes in the circumstances surrounding the goal. By 'circumstances surrounding the goal' is meant the stimuli that, for the given organism, are connected with the goal in some way or another. Thus, for a rat which has had considerable training in the Skinner box, the walls of the Skinner box, the lever, the food trough, as well as the smell and sight of food, are all stimuli connected with the goal (food). For such an animal, variations in any one of these stimuli would constitute a change in the circumstances surrounding the goal.

Now, we can define *appropriateness* as *the extent to which the organism adopts effective courses of action in response to variations in the stimuli connected with the goal*. This definition can be clarified with reference to an example. Suppose we have a given organism, O, a specified goal, G, and a specified experimental situation. Let us designate the stimuli that in O's experience have been connected to G, as Sg, and variations in these stimuli as $Sg1$, $Sg2$, $Sg3$, and so on. Finally, let R stand for the acts or course of action of O, and $R1$, $R2$, $R3$, and so on, for the variations in the course of action. Now, we can illustrate the meaning of appropriateness with reference to the following diagram:

$Sg1$	$R1$	G
$Sg2$	$R2$	G
$Sg3$	$R3$	G

The statement that O's behavior in this situation is appropriate means that if $Sg1$ occurs, then O responds by the corresponding effective response, $R1$; if $Sg2$ occurs, then the organism gives the effective response, $R2$; and so on. The extent to which each variation of the stimuli connected with the goal ($Sg1$, $Sg2$, ...) elicits an effective course of action ($R1$, $R2$, ...) indicates the degree of appropriateness of the particular sample of behavior. It should be clear that the concept of appropriateness is applicable only to a sample of behavior which represents repeated trials under conditions of controlled variations in Sg. Thus, it is meaningless to say that any one act is appropriate; we can only say that a sample of behavior obtained under prescribed conditions is more or less appropriate than another sample of behavior similarly obtained.

The concept of appropriateness is, of course, quite different from that of *stereotypy* proposed by Miller and Frick (1949). Their concept refers to the extent to which *any* sequence of responses is repeated in a given sample of behavior. Appropriateness, on the other hand, refers to the extent to which the *effective* sequences occur in a given sample of behavior. Thus, behavior that is highly appropriate may, under certain circumstances, also be high in stereotypy, but all highly stereotyped behavior will not necessarily be high in appropriateness. For example, in the above example, if the animal repeated one and the same response (*R1* or *R2* or *R3*) no matter what variations of *Sg* were presented, its behavior would be scored high on stereotypy but low on appropriateness. But if variations in *Sg* were repeated in exactly the same order (e.g., *Sg1, Sg2, Sg3, Sg1, Sg2, Sg3, Sg1, . . .*) again and again and, in each case, the animal responded with the effective response (*R1, R2, R3, R1, R2, R3, R1, . . .*) its behavior would be high in both stereotypy and appropriateness. Stereotypy and appropriateness describe different aspects of behavior; they do not necessarily covary, directly or inversely.

References

Miller, G. A., & Frick, F. C. Statistical behavioristics and sequences of responses. *Psychological Review*, 1949, 56, 311–324.

Sommerhoff, G. *Analytical Biology*. London: Oxford Univ. Press, 1950.

24 B. F. Skinner

Reinforcement and the Emergence of Goal Direction

Excerpt from B. F. Skinner, *Science and Human Behavior*, Macmillan, New York, 1953, Chapter 5.

Goals, Purposes, and Other Final Causes

It is not correct to say that operant reinforcement 'strengthens the response which precedes it'. The response has already occurred and cannot be changed. What is changed is the future probability of responses in the same *class*. It is the operant as a class of behavior, rather than the response as a particular instance, which is conditioned. There is, therefore, no violation of the fundamental principle of science which rules out 'final causes'. But this principle is violated when it is asserted that behavior is under the control of an 'incentive' or 'goal' which the organism has not yet achieved or a 'purpose' which it has not yet fulfilled. Statements which use such words as 'incentive' or 'purpose' are usually reducible to statements about operant conditioning, and only a slight change is required to bring them within the framework of a natural science. Instead of saying that a man behaves because of the consequences which *are* to follow his behavior, we simply say that he behaves because of the consequences which *have* followed similar behavior in the past. This is, of course, the Law of Effect or operant conditioning.

It is sometimes argued that a response is not fully described until its purpose is referred to as a current property. But what is meant by 'describe'? If we observe someone walking down the street, we may report this event in the language of physical science. If we then add that 'his purpose is to mail a letter', have we said anything which was not included in our first report? Evidently so, since a man may walk down the street 'for many purposes' and in the same physical way in each case. But the distinction which needs to be made is not between instances of behavior; it is between the variables of which behavior is a function. Purpose is not a property of the behavior itself; it is a way of referring to controlling variables. If we make our report after we have seen our subject mail his letter and turn back, we attribute 'purpose' to him from the event which brought the behavior of walking down the street to an end. This event 'gives meaning' to his performance, not by amplifying a description of the behavior as such, but by indicating an independent variable of which it may have been a function. We cannot see his 'purpose' before seeing that he mails a letter, unless we have observed similar behavior and similar consequences before. Where we have done this, we use the term simply to predict that he will mail a letter upon this occasion.

Nor can our subject see his own purpose without reference to similar events. If we ask him why he is going down the street or what his purpose is and he says, 'I am going to mail a letter,' we have not learned anything new about his behavior but only about some of its possible causes. The subject himself, of course, may be in an advantageous position in describing these variables because he has had an extended contact with his own behavior for many years. But his statement is not therefore in a different class from similar statements made by others who have observed his behavior upon fewer occasions. He is simply making a plausible prediction in terms of his experiences with himself. Moreover, he may be wrong. He may report that he is 'going to mail a letter,' and he may indeed carry an unmailed letter in his hand and may mail it at the end of the street, but we may still be able to show that his behavior is primarily determined by the fact that upon past occasions he has encountered someone who is important to him upon just such a walk. He may not be 'aware of this purpose' in the sense of being able to say that his behavior is strong for this reason.

The fact that operant behavior seems to be 'directed toward the future' is misleading. Consider, for example, the case of 'looking for something'. In what sense is the 'something' which has not yet been found relevant to the behavior? Suppose we condition a pigeon to peck a spot on the wall of a box and then, when the operant is well established, remove the spot. The bird now goes to the usual place along the wall. It raises its head, cocks its eye in the usual direction, and may even emit a weak peck in the usual place. Before extinction is very far advanced, it returns to the same place again and again in similar behavior. Must we say that the pigeon is 'looking for the spot'? Must we take the 'looked-for' spot into account in explaining the behavior?

It is not difficult to interpret this example in terms of operant reinforcement. Since visual stimulation from the spot has usually preceded the receipt of food, the spot has become a conditioned reinforcer. It strengthens the behavior of looking in given directions from different positions. Although we have undertaken to condition only the pecking response, we have in fact strengthened many different kinds of precurrent behavior which bring the bird into positions from which it sees the spot and pecks it. These responses continue to appear, even though we have removed the spot, until extinction occurs. The spot that is 'being looked for' is the spot which has occurred in the past as the immediate reinforcement of the behavior of looking. In general, looking for something consists of emitting responses which in the past have produced 'something' as a consequence.

The same interpretation applies to human behavior. When we see a man moving about a room opening drawers, looking under magazines, and so on, we may describe his behavior in fully objective terms: 'Now he is in a certain part of the room; he has grasped a book between the thumb and forefinger of his right hand; he is lifting the book and bending his head so that any object under the book can be seen.' We may also 'interpret' his behavior or 'read a meaning into it' by saying that 'he is looking for something' or, more specifically, that 'he is looking for his glasses'. What we have added is not a further description of his behavior but an inference about some of the variables responsible for it. There is no *current* goal, incentive, purpose, or meaning to be taken into account. This is so even if we ask him what he is doing and he says, 'I am looking for my glasses.' This is not a further description of his behavior but of the variables of which his behavior is a function; it is equivalent to 'I have lost my glasses,' 'I shall stop what I am doing when I find my glasses,' or 'When I have done this in the past, I have found my glasses.' These translations may seem unnecessarily roundabout, but only because expressions involving goals and purposes are abbreviations.

Very often we attribute purpose to behavior as another way of describing its biological adaptability. This issue has already been discussed, but one point may be added. In both operant conditioning and the evolutionary selection of behavioral characteristics, consequences alter future probability. Reflexes and other innate patterns of behavior evolve because they increase the chances of survival of the *species*. Operants grow strong because they are followed by important consequences in the life of the *individual*. Both processes raise the question of purpose for the same reason, and in both the appeal to a final cause may be rejected in the same way. A spider does not possess the elaborate behavioral repertoire with which it constructs a web because that web will enable it to capture the food it needs to survive. It possesses this behavior because similar behavior on the part of spiders in the past has enabled *them* to capture the food *they* needed to survive. A series of events have been relevant to the behavior of web-making in its earlier evolutionary history. We are wrong in saying that we observe the 'purpose' of the web when we observe similar events in the life of the individual.

Part Three   NATURE OF REINFORCERS

When certain events occur immediately following a response,
the future probability of the occurrence of that response may
be increased or decreased. Events (e.g., giving food to a hungry
animal) whose presentation increases the future probability of
response occurrence are called *positive reinforcers*: events (e.g.,
giving an electric shock to an animal) whose presentation
decreases the future probability of response occurrence are
called *negative reinforcers*. An important question in psychology
concerns the nature of reinforcers. What makes reinforcers
reinforce (i.e., alter the probabilities of response occurrence)?
Thousands of events exhibit reinforcing properties, under
certain circumstances. What is common to all these events?
What is the source of their reinforcing effects? This is perhaps
the most important problem of psychology, and has been the
subject of a great many theoretical analyses and experimental
investigations.

VI Pleasure and Pain as the Basis of Reinforcement

It is true that actions that lead to pleasure tend to be continued or repeated and those that lead to pain tend to be discontinued and abandoned. But it is one thing to note this and quite another to hypothesize that reinforcers derive their reinforcing effects (i.e., capacity to change response probability) from the pleasure or pain they cause. Borrowing from psychological hedonists, Spencer attributed the capacity of reinforcers to produce learning to the associated pleasure and pain. This idea was elaborated and refined by Thorndike, Troland, and Young. Skinner has pointed out what he considers to be the weakness common to all these positions, namely, lack of a definition of pleasure and pain that is objective and independent of the learning (reinforcement effects) it is supposed to explain.

25 H. Spencer

On Pleasure and Pain

Excerpt from H. Spencer, *The Principles of Psychology*, Appleton & Co.,
New York, 1872, Vol. 1, Chapter 9.

Let us first glance at the fact, sufficiently obvious and sufficiently
significant, that the extreme states, positive and negative, along
with which pains occur, are states inconsistent with that due
balance of the functions constituting health; whereas that medium
state along with which pleasure occurs is consistent with, or
rather is demanded by, this due balance. This we may see *a
priori*. In a mutually-dependent set of organs having a *consensus*
of functions the very existence of a special organ having its
special function implies that the absence of its function must
cause disturbance of the *consensus* – implies, too, that its function
may be raised to an excess which must cause disturbance of the
consensus – implies, therefore, that maintenance of the *consensus*
goes along with a medium degree of its function. The *a priori*
inference involved, that these medium actions productive of
pleasure must be beneficial, and the extreme actions productive of
pain detrimental, is abundantly confirmed *a posteriori* where the
actions are of all-essential kinds. Here are a few cases.

Intense cold and intense heat both cause acute suffering, and
if the body is long exposed to them both cause death; while a
moderate warmth is pleasurable and conduces to physical well-
being. Extreme craving for food accompanies a hurtful inaction
of the digestive organs, and if this craving and this inaction persist
the result is fatal. Conversely, if solid food, or liquid, continues
to be swallowed under compulsion, regardless of the painful
sensations produced, the effect is also detrimental, and may even
kill. But between these pains attending deficient and excessive
action there are the pleasures of eating, which are keenest when
the benefit to be derived is greatest. To a person in health duly
rested, the feeling that accompanies absolute inaction of the
muscles is unbearable; and this inaction is injurious. On the
other hand, extreme exertion of the muscles in general is alike
distressing and productive of prostration, while exertion of a
particular muscle pushed to a painful excess leaves a temporary
paralysis, and occasionally, by rupturing some of the muscular
fibres, entails prolonged uselessness. Arrest of breathing by

forcible closure of the air-passages causes an intolerable state of consciousness; and life soon ceases if there is no relief. The breathing of foul air is injurious as well as repugnant; while the breathing of air that is exceptionally fresh and pure is both pleasurable and physically advantageous. So, too, is it with the feelings caused by contacts with objects. Though, as above pointed out, we cannot be debarred from these, and therefore have no craving for them and little or no pleasure in them, yet we are liable to excesses of them and the accompanying pains; and these pains are the correlatives of detrimental results – crushings, and bruises, and lacerations. It is even so with extremely strong tastes and smells. The intense vegetal bitters are poisonous in any considerable quantities, and the intensest are poisonous in very small quantities. Powerful acids, too, are poisonous – being, indeed, immediately destructive of the membranes they touch. And gases that violently irritate when inhaled, as concentrated ammonia, or as pure chlorine, or as hydrochloric acid, work deleterious effects.

These facts should of themselves suffice to produce the conviction, in spite of apparent exceptions, that pains are the correlatives of actions injurious to the organism, while pleasures are the correlatives of actions conducive to its welfare. We need not, however, rest satisfied with an induction from these instances yielded by the essential vital functions; for it is an inevitable deduction from the hypothesis of Evolution that races of sentient creatures could have come into existence under no other conditions.

If we substitute for the word Pleasure the equivalent phrase – a feeling which we seek to bring into consciousness and retain there, and if we substitute for the word Pain the equivalent phrase – a feeling which we seek to get out of consciousness and to keep out; we see at once that, if the states of consciousness which a creature endeavours to maintain are the correlatives of injurious actions, and if the states of consciousness which it endeavours to expel are the correlatives of beneficial actions, it must quickly disappear through persistence in the injurious and avoidance of the beneficial. In other words, those races of beings only can have survived in which, on the average, agreeable or desired feelings went along with activities conducive to the maintenance of life, while disagreeable and habitually-avoided feelings went along with activities directly or indirectly destructive of life; and there must ever have been, other things equal, the most numerous and long-continued survivals among races in which these adjustments of feelings to actions were the best, tending ever to bring about perfect adjustment.

If we except the human race and some of the highest allied races, in which foresight of distant consequences introduces a complicating element, it is undeniable that every animal habitually persists in each act which gives pleasure, so long as it does so, and desists from each act which gives pain. It is manifest that, for creatures of low intelligence, unable to trace involved sequences of effects, there can be no other guidance. It is manifest that in proportion as this guidance approaches completeness, the life will be long; and that the life will be short in proportion as it falls short of completeness. Whence it follows that as, other things equal, the longer-lived individuals of any species will more frequently produce and rear progeny than the shorter-lived, the descendants of the one must tend to replace those of the other – a process which, equally operative among the multiplying families of these surviving descendants, cannot but work towards maintenance and improvement of the guidance.

How then, it will be asked, does it happen that animals sometimes die from eating poisonous plants, or surfeit themselves fatally with kinds of food which, though wholesome in moderate quantities, are injurious in large quantities? The reply is that, by natural selection, the guidance of pleasures and pains can be adjusted only to the circumstances of the habitat within which the special type has been evolved. Survival of the fittest cannot bring the inclinations and aversions into harmony with unfelt conditions. And since each species under pressure of increasing numbers is ever thrusting itself into adjacent environments, its members must from time to time meet with plants, with prey, with enemies, with physical actions, of which neither they nor their ancestors have had experience, and to which their feelings are unadapted. Not only by migration into other habitats, but also by changes, inorganic and organic, within its own habitat, does each species suffer from failures of adjustment. But mis-adjustment inevitably sets up re-adjustment. Those individuals in whom the likes and dislikes happen to be most out of harmony with the new circumstances are the first to disappear. And if the race continues to exist there cannot but arise, by perpetual killing-off of the least adapted, a variety having feelings that serve as incentives and deterrents in the modified way required.

The Law of Effect

Excerpts from E. L. Thorndike, *Animal Intelligence*, Macmillan, New York, 1911, Chapter 6.

The Law of Effect is that: *Of several responses made to the same situation, those which are accompanied or closely followed by satisfaction to the animal will, other things being equal, be more firmly connected with the situation, so that, when it recurs, they will be more likely to recur; those which are accompanied or closely followed by discomfort to the animal will, other things being equal, have their connections with that situation weakened, so that, when it recurs, they will be less likely to occur. The greater the satisfaction or discomfort, the greater the strengthening or weakening of the bond.*

For more detailed and perfect prophecy, the phrases 'result in satisfaction' and 'result in discomfort' need further definition, and the other things that are to be equal need comment.

By a satisfying state of affairs is meant one which the animal does nothing to avoid, often doing such things as attain and preserve it. By a discomforting or annoying state of affairs is meant one which the animal commonly avoids and abandons.

The satisfiers for any animal in any given condition cannot be determined with precision and surety save by observation. Food when hungry, society when lonesome, sleep when fatigued, relief from pain, are samples of the common occurrence that what favors the life of the species satisfies its individual members. But this does not furnish a completely valid rule.

The satisfying and annoying are not synonymous with favorable and unfavorable to the life of either the individual or the species. Many animals are satisfied by deleterious conditions. Excitement, overeating, and alcoholic intoxication are, for instance, three very common and very potent satisfiers of man. Conditions useful to the life of the species in moderation are often satisfying far beyond their useful point: many conditions of great utility to the life of the species do not satisfy and may even annoy its members.

The annoyers for any animal follow the rough rule that alterations of the animal's 'natural' or 'normal' structure – as by cuts, bruises, blows, and the like – and deprivations of or inter-ference with its 'natural' or 'normal' activities – as by capture, starvation, solitude, or indigestion – are intolerable. But inter-ference with the structure and functions by which the species is perpetuated is not a sufficient criterion for discomfort. Nature's adaptations are too crude.

Upon examination it appears that the pernicious states of affairs which an animal welcomes are not pernicious *at the time, to the neurones.* We learn many bad habits, such as morphinism, because there is incomplete adaptation of all the interests of the body-state to the temporary interest of its ruling class, the neurones. So also the unsatisfying goods are not goods to the neurones at the time. We neglect many benefits because the neurones choose their immediate advantage. The neurones must be tricked into permitting the animal to take exercise when freez-ing or quinine when in a fever, or to free the stomach from certain poisons.

Satisfaction and discomfort, welcoming and avoiding, thus seem to be related to the maintenance and hindrance of the life processes of the neurones rather than of the animal as a whole, and to temporary rather than permanent maintenance and hindrance.

The chief life processes of a neurone concerned in learning are absorption of food, excretion of waste, reception and conduction of the nerve impulse, and modifiability or change of connections. Of these only the latter demands comment.

The connections formed between situation and response are represented by connections between neurones and neurones, whereby the disturbance or neural current arising in the former is conducted to the latter across their synapses. The strength or weakness of a connection means the greater or less likelihood that the same current will be conducted from the former to the latter rather than to some other place. The strength or weakness of the connection is a condition of the synapse. What condition of the synapse it is remains a matter for hypothesis. Close con-nection might mean protoplasmic union, or proximity of the neurones in space, or a greater permeability of a membrane, or a lowered electrical resistance, or a favorable chemical condition of some other sort. Let us call this undefined condition which parallels the strength of a connection between situation and res-ponse the intimacy of the synapse. Then the modifiability or connection-changing of a neurone equals its power to alter the intimacy of its synapses.

As a provisional hypothesis to account for what satisfies and what annoys an animal, I suggest the following:—

A neurone modifies the intimacy of its synapses so as to keep intimate those by whose intimacy its other life processes are favored and to weaken the intimacy of those whereby its other life processes are hindered. The animal's action-system as a whole consequently does nothing to avoid that response whereby the life processes of the neurones other than connection-changing are maintained, but does cease those responses whereby such life processes of the neurones are hindered.

This hypothesis has two important consequences. First: Learning by the law of effect is then more fully adaptive for the neurones in the changing intimacy of whose synapses learning consists, than for the animal as a whole. It is adaptive for the animal as a whole only in so far as his organization makes the neurones concerned in the learning welcome states of affairs that are favorable to his life and that of his species and reject those that are harmful.

Second: A mechanism in the neurones gives results in the behavior of the animal as a whole that seem beyond mechanism. By their unmodifiable abandonment of certain specific conditions and retention of others, the animal as a whole can modify its behavior. Their one rule of conduct causes in him a countless complexity of habits. The learning of an animal is an instinct of its neurones.

I have limited the discussion to animals in whom the connection-system is a differentiated organ, the neurones. In so far as the law of effect operates in an animal whose connection-system is not anatomically distinguishable and is favored and hindered in its life by the same conditions that favor and hinder the life of the animal as a whole, the satisfying and annoying will be those states of affairs which the connection-system, whatever it be, maintains and abandons.

The other things that have to be equal in the case of the law of effect are: First, the frequency, energy and duration of the connection – that is, the action of the law of exercise; second, the closeness with which the satisfaction is associated with the response; and, third, the readiness of the response to be connected with the situation.

The first of these accessory conditions requires no comment. A slightly satisfying or indifferent response made often may win a closer connection than a more satisfying response made only rarely.

The second is most clearly seen in the effect of increasing the interval between the response and the satisfaction or discomfort. Such an increase diminishes the rate of learning. If, for example, four boxes were arranged so that turning a button caused a door to open (and permit a cat to get freedom and food) in one, five, fifty and five hundred seconds, respectively, a cat would form the habit of prompt escape from the first box most rapidly and would almost certainly never form that habit in the case of the fourth. The electric shock administered just as an animal starts on the wrong path or touches the wrong mechanism is potent, but the same punishment administered ten or twenty seconds after an act will have little or no effect upon that act.

Close temporal sequence is not the only means of insuring the connection of the satisfaction with the response producing it. What is called attention to the response counts also. If a cat pushes a button around with its nose, while its main occupation, the act to which its general 'set' impels it, to which, we say, it is chiefly attentive, is that of clawing at an opening, it will be less aided in the formation of the habit than if it had been chiefly concerned in what its nose was doing. The successful response is as a rule only a part of all that the animal is doing at the time. In proportion as it is an eminent, emphatic part of it, learning is aided. Similarly discomfort eliminates most the eminent, emphatic features of the total response which it accompanies or shortly follows.

The third factor, the susceptibility of the response and situation to connection, is harder to illustrate. But, apparently, of those responses which are equally strongly connected with a situation by nature and equally attended to, some are more susceptible than others to a more intimate connection.

27   L. T. Troland

Pleasure-Pain and Facilitation-Inhibition

Excerpts from L. T. Troland, *The Principles of Psychophysiology*, Van Nostrand, New York, 1932, Vol. 3, Chapter 23, Sections 87 and 88.

Sherrington (1911) has signalized a class of receptive systems which he calls *nociceptive*, because they are particularly attuned to noxious or injurious agencies. His interest, however, seems to have been restricted mainly to the observation that the arousal of such sense channels gives rise to particularly energetic reactions on the motor side. The outstanding examples of this class of afferent mechanisms are, of course, the pain nerves, but many other special sensory systems can be added, as we shall see below. Nociceptive afferent paths can be contrasted with those which have no special sensitivity to injurious forces, by designating the latter as *neutroceptive*. However, in order to make the classification complete, we must define a third group to include those afferent channels which are specially attuned to beneficial stimuli. I have suggested the term, *beneceptive*, to designate systems of this sort. The sweet sensibility of the tongue may be cited as an example.

The definition and identification of nociceptive or beneceptive sensory systems can be carried out quite independently of any reference to consciousness. We have only to note whether or not the agencies which characteristically arouse the given receptors are typically injurious or beneficial. The concepts of injury and of benefit must, of course be established from a general biological standpoint; injury means reduction of the chances of species survival and multiplication, while benefit has the opposite significance. However, in applying criteria of this sort, we must recognize that we are dealing only with average tendencies, and not with rules which allow of no exception. In the state of nature, tissue lesions are typically injurious, even if, at the hands of a surgeon, they may be highly beneficial. Similarly, sexual relations are favorable to the maintenance of a species, although in human civilization they frequently lead to venereal infection and death.

Using such criteria, we may classify the various departments of sensation somewhat as follows. The principal neutroceptive systems are those of vision, audition, cutaneous touch, and attitudinal kinaesthesis. Among the nociceptive systems, we may include the various forms of pain sensibility, bitter taste, salt and sour at high intensity, the olfactory responses which correspond to the alliaceous, caprillic, repugnant, and nauseating items of the Zwaardemaker classification, cold, excessive heat, the senses of hunger, thirst, and numerous other visceral afferent processes. The latter include the desires to micturate, to defecate, afferent processes underlying the feeling of suffocation, etc. Each of these sense mechanisms is to be conceived in purely physiological terms, although the nomenclature may be suggested by the psychical accompaniments in many instances. The class of beneceptors has a somewhat smaller number of representatives. The erotic sensibility heads the list, followed by gustatory sweet response, the olfactory reactions corresponding to ethereal, aromatic and balsamic items of Zwaardemaker's classification, salt and sour at low intensities, warmth at low intensity, and certain viscerally aroused afferent currents, such as those underlying coenaesthesia and the satisfaction of organic needs.

We must note, furthermore, that whether or not a given afferent excitation should be regarded as nociceptive, beneceptive, or neutroceptive may not be determined exclusively by the anatomical identity of the sensory channel. It may also depend upon the intensity of the process, and upon the given temporary condition of the organism. Thus, in the gustatory cases of salt and sour, low intensity excitation is beneceptive, while stimulation at a higher intensity must be classed as nociceptive. This distinction is not made primarily upon the basis of any physiological criterion, but wholly from a general biological standpoint. We know that small amounts of salt and acid are beneficial, but that large quantities of either of these substances will upset the metabolic equilibrium. Similarly, in the case of thermal sensibility, a low degree of warmth is beneceptive, whereas a higher degree must be regarded as nociceptive. Cold, on the other hand, is always nociceptive except when it follows excessive exposure to heat, but in this latter case it may be regarded as a beneceptive reponse. With the passage of time, as the body cools off, it must go over into the nociceptive category again.

Considerations of this sort lead us to define more or less abstract functions of *nociception* and *beneception*, which are not rigidly attached to any special afferent channels. However, a study of the general biological situation should enable us to state the conditions under which any given sensory department will be operating in either of these two ways. Intensity, adaptation, organic condition, anatomical identity, and even spatial extent and temporal rhythm may be features in determining the answer.

We are now in a position to note a rather reliable psycho-physiological relationship. This is to the effect that beneception tends to be accompanied by pleasantness in consciousness, while nociception ordinarily brings unpleasantness. Neutroceptive processes, on the other hand, are uniformly inclined to yield an indifferently affective experience. This correlation applies not only to the rough classification of sensory departments on an anatomical basis, but to the quantitative dependency of nociception and beneception upon such factors as intensity and adaptation. Pains of all kinds, bitterness, hunger, nausea, etc., are practically always unpleasant; sexual excitation, sweet taste, etc., quite reliably yield pleasure. But also: low intensity saltiness is pleasant, while high intensities of the same process give unpleasantness. Cold is normally unpleasant, but is accompanied by pleasure when it follows excessive exposure to heat. We do not need to claim that this psychophysical correlation between affectivity and nociception-beneception is perfect, and exceptions can easily be found. Nevertheless, the magnitude of the correlation is such as to make it strikingly significant.

Relation of Affection to Facilitation and Inhibition

In seeking out an appropriate determinant for affectivity, we may find our first clue in the logical nature of the affective variable. We have noted that the latter presents two algebraically opposed modes of variation, with a zero point of indifference between them. Although it is by no means a logical necessity that the cortical determinant of affection should have a similarly algebraic constitution, nevertheless, we shall naturally make this assumption unless reasons appear to the contrary. Now, a very superficial glance at the general physiology of the nervous system immediately reveals a set of functions having the required properties, namely *facilitation* and *inhibition*. These processes are very wide-spread and of extreme importance. They are definitely opposed to each other in an algebraic manner, and are bound up with the dynamics of nervous activity in a very intimate way. Indeed, we can readily note a correlation between these processes and affective experience, on the basis of everyday observations. Everyone will recognize that pain and other forms of discomfort are inhibitory whereas pleasures facilitate concurrent modes of action.

It is very reasonable to suppose that the operations of the

essential thalamic nuclei upon the cortex have general facilitative or inhibitory effects, as the case may be.

When we come to consider the more intimate nature of these processes, we note, first, that facilitation is closely allied to excitation. In fact, it seems, superficially, to involve a mere summation of concomitant excitatory values. Inhibition, on the other hand, apparently stands for a decrease in excitation, as if the combination were of negative with positive amounts. It is thus evident that, although facilitation may possibly involve no elementary features in addition to excitation, inhibition must incorporate an additional feature, to account for the interference. This suggests that facilitation, also, may have a basis which is distinct from that of mere nerve activity. Such a conception is provided in the notion of *Bahnung*, or an opening up of conduction pathways, the reduction of resistance or the raising of *conductance*. Inhibition can be defined in the same fundamental terms, as the opposed process of augmenting resistances or of depressing conductances. It is by no means necessary to insist that all cases of facilitation and inhibition must be explained in this manner, but there is plenty of evidence that such changes in conducting power actually do occur and play a part in the phenomena which we have been considering above. At any rate, they provide the most fruitful basis for developing a psychophysiological theory of affectivity.

References

Sherrington, C. S. *The integrative action of the nervous system.* New Haven: Yale Univer., 1911, pp. 227–231.

Affective Processes and Motivation

Excerpts from P. T. Young, The role of affective processes in learning and motivation, *Psychological Review*, 1959, Vol. 66, pp. 104–25.

The common sense hedonistic explanation of learning implies that subjective feelings of pleasantness and unpleasantness influence behavior. This view involves the mind-body tangle. Thorndike tried to give a better formulation with his law of effect and concepts of satisfiers and annoyers; he later revised the theory, attempting to make it more objective. Troland introduced the concepts of bene- and noci-ception, but his views have never been widely accepted.

The aim of the present paper is to show that affective processes can be studied within a strictly objective frame of reference. I will argue that the affective processes are intervening variables, in Tolman's sense. For the present they may be viewed as logical constructs which bring together in an orderly way a large body of facts. Eventually affective processes will be described in physiological terms; current research indicates that their bodily nature and locus will some day be known. In the meantime the affective processes can be anchored firmly to events within the physical world.

The Construct of Affective Processes

Let us begin by postulating that affective processes have an objective existence within the organism and that their nature and functions can be discovered.

Definition of the affective processes by their attributes

Affective processes can be defined objectively in terms of their attributes: sign, intensity, duration:

1. *Sign.* – What one observes in laboratory situations is that naive animals develop approach-maintaining or avoidance-terminating patterns of behavior. If they develop the approach-maintaining pattern, I would assume that the underlying affective process is positive in sign. If they develop the avoidance-terminating pattern, I would assume that the affective process is negative in sign. If neither positive nor negative behavior develops, I would make no assumption concerning the sign of affective arousal.

It is important to note that the bare existence of adient or abient behavior is not a sufficient ground for inferring affective processes. Approach-maintaining and avoidance-terminating behavior may be habitual, automatic and affectively indifferent; but the *development* of approach-maintaining or avoidance-terminating patterns by *naive animals* is the criterion for the sign of affective processes.

2. *Intensity.* – In addition to sign, affective processes differ in intensity, or degree. Affective processes vary along a bipolar continuum between the extremes of maximal negative and maximal positive intensity.

One way to demonstrate the relative intensity of affective processes is to give animals a brief-exposure preference test with foods. A brief-exposure test is recommended because with prolonged exposures the level of acceptability of test-foods declines as the terminal state of satiation is approached.

In the brief-exposure test the animal is offered a series of choices between two test-foods (A and B). The series of choices reveals whether a preference for one food (A) or the other (B) develops. There is no way to force an animal to show a preference. Either a preference develops, with repeated choices, or it does not develop. Weak preferences, strong preferences, alternating preferences, and no preferences at all, have been found. In some tests the preference is obvious but, in others, statistical methods are needed to determine whether or not a particular body of data indicates a significant preference or a mutation of preference.

If both test-foods are accepted, I would assume that the preferred food arouses a higher intensity of positive affectivity than the nonpreferred. This is what is meant, objectively, by the statement that the preferred food is the more palatable. Again, it must be emphasized that the *development* of a preference *in naive animals* indicates relative hedonic intensity and not the bare existence of a preference, since a preferential discrimination can be purely habitual and automatic.

3. *Duration.* – In addition to sign and intensity, affective processes differ in duration and temporal course. Insofar as affective processes are induced by taste solutions, the duration of stimulation can be used to control the duration of affective arousal. The number of seconds that an animal is in contact with a food can be controlled or the number of individual licks of a fluid can be counted by an electronic device. The frequency and schedule of affective processes can also be controlled.

With painful stimulations it would seem that the intensity, frequency, and schedule are all subject to precise experimental control. In addition to direct stimulation, negative affectivity can be produced by frustration and conflict; but these conditions can be controlled less precisely than the conditions of sensory stimulation.

The hedonic continuum

The sign, intensity, and temporal changes of affective processes can be represented upon the hedonic continuum. Figure 1 shows this continuum extending from the extreme of negative affectivity (distress) to the extreme of positive affectivity (delight). Different intensities of affective arousal are represented by arbitrary units marked off upon the continuum. Midway between negative and positive affectivity is the range of indifferent, neutral processes and others that are weakly affective.

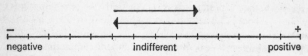

Figure 1 The hedonic continuum

The arrows represent two opposed directions of hedonic change. The upper arrow, pointing away from the negative end and towards the positive end of the continuum, represents a kind of hedonic change that is of great importance in the organization of behavior. According to the hedonic hypothesis, neurobehavioral patterns are organized that minimize negative affectivity (distress) and maximize positive affectivity (delight). That is to say, organization is dependent upon hedonic change in the positive direction. Changes in the negative direction necessarily and frequently occur, and the lower arrow represents such changes. The total figure implies a principle of affective opposition or antagonism: There can be a change towards either pole but not a change in opposite directions at the same moment of time.

Although there are two opposed directions of change, there are, logically and psychologically, four main kinds of affective change that need to be considered: (a) increasing positive affectivity, (b) decreasing positive affectivity, (c) increasing negative affectivity, (d) decreasing negative affectivity. The first kind of hedonic change (increasing positive affectivity) is present when an animal tastes a sugar solution and organizes an approach-maintaining pattern of behavior. The fourth kind of change (decreasing negative affectivity) is present when an animal succeeds in relieving the 'distress' associated with an electric shock or reducing a need produced by dietary depletion. 'Distress reduction' is the hedonic equivalent of 'drive reduction' in the organization of instrumental behavior.

Changes in the negative direction occur under various circumstances. When an organism continues eating an acceptable food, the level of acceptability gradually declines as the final state of satiation is approached. Hedonic changes in the negative direction are also produced by shocks, burns, cuts, shrill sounds, and similar conditions. When negative affectivity is present the organism tries to reduce it. The very attempt to escape from inducing conditions is the earmark of negative affectivity.

The distinction between sensory and hedonic intensity

To a psychology that is limited by stimulus-response concepts the postulate of central affective processes may appear superfluous. I believe, however, that any theory of behavior which ignores the concept of affectivity will be found inadequate as an explanation of the total facts. To prove the point let us consider the following facts which are difficult, if not impossible, to explain in strictly S-R terms:

If pairs of sucrose solutions are presented to rats briefly for choice, the animals select the higher of two concentrations in preference to the lower. Scale values based upon preference tests show that the level of acceptability is directly proportional to the logarithm of the concentration. The relation holds all the way up the intensive scale from the preferential threshold to a saturated solution (Young & Greene, 1953).

From the facts about sucrose solutions one might argue that *sensory* intensity or physical concentration of solution is the critical determinant of behavior. But difficulty with the sensory interpretation appears when one considers the relative palatability of solutions of sodium chloride.

Young and Falk (1956a) ran a series of preference tests between distilled water and sodium chloride solutions of different concentrations, and between pairs of sodium chloride solutions. They found that need-free rats revealed an optimal concentration for sodium chloride within the range of 0·75 to 1·5%. When concentrations were below this range, need-free rats preferred the higher concentration; when above this optimal range, they preferred the lower concentration. Within the optimal range there were marked individual differences in preference and there was much indiscriminate behavior. The experimenters concluded that there is a *range of acceptance* within which acceptability increases with rising concentration of NaCl and a *range of rejection* within which the level of acceptability falls as concentration rises. The optimum of acceptability appears to be determined by the intersection of two gradients – one of acceptance and one of rejection. Incidentally, this finding agrees well with the work of Bare (1949), and others, who relied upon an intake method of studying acceptability of NaCl solutions.

It is clear, therefore, that with solutions of sodium chloride, hedonic intensity does not have a one-to-one relation with sensory intensity. *Sensory* intensity is an increasing monotonic function of concentration of solution; *hedonic* intensity is a discontinuous function of concentration.

In another experiment, Young and Asdourian (1957) selected a 1% sodium chloride solution as representative of the optimal range of NaCl concentrations. This near-optimal concentration was tested for preference against distilled water and four concentrations of sucrose solutions (54, 18, 6, 2%). The 1% NaCl solution was preferred to distilled water by need-free rats; but *all* sucrose solutions were preferred to the standard 1% NaCl solution. In the study it was estimated that a 1% NaCl solution is isohedonic to a sucrose concentration of 0.38%, which is very near to the preferential taste threshold for sucrose (about 0.50%). In other words, practically all sucrose solutions are more palatable to need-free rats than all NaCl solutions. The hedonic intensity of all NaCl solutions is so low, in fact, that it is impossible to discover isohedonic pairs of sucrose and NaCl solutions.

It is difficult at best to equate sensory intensities across modalities but it is impossible to equate hedonic intensities if we employ solutions of sucrose and NaCl. High concentrations of sucrose are hedonically positive and high concentrations of NaCl are hedonically negative. This finding underscores the principle that *sensory* intensity is very different from *hedonic* intensity.

The scaling of hedonic intensities through preference tests yields an order of fact quite different from the facts of sensory intensity. This comes to light clearly in tests (unpublished) by Kent Christensen, who worked with compound solutions containing both sucrose and NaCl. When the sucrose concentration was 1% and the NaCl 0.75% (near optimal), the rats preferred the compound solution to both the 1% sucrose solution and the

0·75 % NaCl solution. In other words, the two solutes – sucrose and NaCl – made independent additive contributions to palatability. The experiment demonstrated summation of two positive hedonic intensities. But, to take an extreme example, when the sucrose concentration was 4 % and the NaCl concentration was also 4 %, the rats showed a marked and consistent preference for the sucrose solution to the compound (very salty) solution. In this instance, positive and negative hedonic values summated algebraically. Christensen demonstrated, therefore, that the palatability of some sucrose solutions can be raised by adding small quantities of NaCl and lowered by adding larger quantities. Although he did not succeed in mapping out isohedonic contours for compound solutions, in an area determined by the concentration of sucrose and the concentration of sodium chloride, he demonstrated their existence and the possibility of charting them.

I believe that these facts demonstrate convincingly the necessity of distinguishing between *sensory* intensity and *hedonic* intensity and hence between the sensory and affective aspects of neural excitation. Stimulation of the taste receptors has both sensory and affective consequences.

Objective Principles of Experimental Hedonism

Some of the objective principles of experimental hedonism are stated briefly below. These statements should be regarded as tentative formulations and as a basis for further experimental studies:

1. *Stimulation has affective as well as sensory consequences.* – Along with gustatory stimulation by sugar solutions, for example, there is a positive affective arousal which, by its very nature, is something to be prolonged and intensified. Along with painful stimulation, there is a negative affective arousal which, by its very nature, is something to be avoided.

2. *An affective arousal orients the animal toward or against the stimulus-object.* – This orientation can be readily observed. For example, when a rat, in the course of exploratory activity, makes contact with a sugar solution he may pause for a moment, then continue to explore. Sooner or later, however, he returns to the solution and takes more. After repeated sips he becomes oriented toward the solution. If an experienced animal is delayed in his approach to the cup, he shows a postural orientation toward the cup and approaches it quickly when released. If, however, the animal is offered a quinine solution, he fails to develop a positive orientation or an existing positive orientation is inhibited.

3. *Affective processes lead to the development of motives.* – An orientation toward the goal-object is a motive that instigates and regulates behavior. The sign of an affective arousal determines whether an approach-maintaining motive or an avoidance-terminating motive will develop. This principle can be illustrated by numerous runway experiments in which animals acquire, through affective arousals, motives that lead to approach or to avoidance.

4. *The strength of a recently acquired motive is correlated with the intensity, duration, frequency, and recency of previous affective arousals.* – On the positive side, at least, the speed with which need-free rats approach a sucrose solution is related to the concentration and to the duration, frequency, and recovery of contact. With practice, however, animals speed up their running as they approach a physiological limit. This speeding up with practice may obscure initial differences due to affective arousals.

5. *The growth of motives is dependent upon learning as well as upon affective arousals.* – Learning of a simple pattern such as running down a straight alley or running back and forth upon the preference tester is dependent directly on exercise (practice, drill, training); but affective arousals play an essential motivating role in the organizing, activating, regulating, and sustaining of neurobehavioral patterns.

It is necessary, therefore, to distinguish between learning through exercise (practice, drill, training) and the hedonic regulation of behavior. Affective processes regulate and organize neurobehavioral patterns in the sense that they determine what will be learned and what not; but such hedonic regulation and organization are not to be confused with learning through practice. Learning is here defined as a change in neurobehavioral pattern that depends upon exercise. Affective processes do not *cause* learning. They are motivational in nature and they influence performance.

6. *The laws of conditioning apply to affective processes.* – Psychologists ordinarily describe conditioning in terms of S-R bonds, but this view is inadequate unless it can be made to include central affective processes.

An environmental situation, through conditioning, comes to arouse affective processes directly. To illustrate: If a rat is placed upon a piece of apparatus, he learns to respond to the stimulus-pattern of his surroundings; but, in addition to the usual S-R patterns, the stimulus-situation produces an affective arousal. If there is a positive affective arousal, the whole situation becomes hedonically positive so that the animal comes to react positively to environmental stimulus-cues. If the situation is hedonically negative, the environmental stimulus-cues come to arouse negative affectivity – call it distress, anxiety, fear, or whatever you will.

There is definitely an internal conditioning of affective processes along with the usual conditioning described in S-R terms. By human analogy it can be said that the animal learns how to *feel* in the situation as well as what cognitive discriminations to make and what acts to perform.

7. *Affective processes regulate behavior by influencing choice.* – Numerous experiments upon the development of food preferences show that the sign and intensity of affective processes influence choice. The development of a food preference between two acceptable foods indicates which food-stimulus arouses the more intense affective process.

The acquisition of a preferential discrimination is not an instance of pure learning because affective processes determine whether one preference or its opposite will develop and, further, the relative hedonic intensities associated with two stimuli determine the rate of growth of a preferential pattern.

8. *Neurobehavioral patterns are organized according to the hedonic principle of maximizing the positive and minimizing the negative affective arousal.* This principle has a very wide range of application. It is seen most clearly in situations that involve choice. The stimulus associated with the more intense affective arousal dominates the preferential discrimination.

Conclusion

Although feelings of pleasantness and unpleasantness are known directly only in human experience, the facts of animal behavior make it necessary to postulate that affective processes have an objective existence. Since affective processes are not directly observed in behavior, they must be postulated as intervening variables. The postulate brings together in an orderly way a large and complex body of interrelated facts. Moreover, there are indications that the hypothetical construct of affective processes can some day be replaced by a physiological account of the intervening events.

Affective processes are motivational in the sense that they arouse, sustain, regulate, direct, and organize neurobehavioral patterns. Reinforcement and extinction are viewed as changes in performance dependent upon affective processes. Reinforcement must be distinguished from a change in habit strength due to exercise (practice, drill, training).

The postulate that affective processes have an objective existence is demanded by the facts of food acceptance but the postulate has a wider range of possible application – to sexual behavior, play, manipulation, and exploration, as well as to human action. Some principles of experimental hedonism have been tentatively formulated and it is suggested that they be tested in the laboratory.

References

Bare, J. K. The specific hunger for sodium chloride in normal and adrenalectomized white rats. *J. comp. physiol. Psychol.*, 1949, 42, 242–253.

Young, P. T., & Asdourian, D. Relative acceptability of sodium chloride and sucrose solutions. *J. comp. physiol. Psychol.*, 1957, 50, 499–503.

Young, P. T., & Falk, J. L. The acceptability of tap water and distilled water to nonthirsty rats. *J. comp. physiol. Psychol.*, 1956, 49, 336–338. (a).

Young, P. T., & Greene, J. T. Quantity of food ingested as a measure of relative acceptability. *J. comp. physiol. Psychol.*, 1953, 46, 288–294.

29 B. F. Skinner

Why is a Reinforcer Reinforcing?

Excerpts from B. F. Skinner, *Science and Human Behavior*, Macmillan, New York, 1953, Chapter 5.

The Law of Effect is not a theory. It is simply a rule for strengthening behavior. When we reinforce a response and observe a change in its frequency, we can easily report what has happened in objective terms. But in explaining *why* it has happened we are likely to resort to theory. Why does reinforcement reinforce? One theory is that an organism repeats a response because it finds the consequences 'pleasant' or 'satisfying'. But in what sense is this an explanation within the framework of a natural science? 'Pleasant' or 'satisfying' apparently do not refer to physical properties of reinforcing events, since the physical sciences use neither these terms nor any equivalents. The terms must refer to some effect upon the organism, but can we define this in such a way that it will be useful in accounting for reinforcement?

It is sometimes argued that a thing is pleasant if an organism approaches or maintains contact with it and unpleasant if the organism avoids it or cuts it short. There are many variations on this attempt to find an objective definition, but they are all subject to the same criticism: the behavior specified may be merely another product of the reinforcing effect. To say that a stimulus is pleasant in the sense that an organism tends to approach or prolong it may be only another way of saying that the stimulus has reinforced the behavior of approaching or prolonging. Instead of defining a reinforcing effect in terms of its effect upon behavior in general, we have simply specified familiar behavior which is almost inevitably reinforced and hence generally available as an indicator of reinforcing power. If we then go on to say that a stimulus is reinforcing *because* it is pleasant, what purports to be an explanation in terms of two effects is in reality a redundant description of one.

An alternative approach is to define 'pleasant' and 'unpleasant' (or 'satisfying' and 'annoying') by asking the subject how he 'feels' about certain events. This assumes that reinforcement has two effects – it strengthens behavior and generates 'feelings' – and that one is a function of the other. But the functional relation may be in the other direction. When a man reports that an event is pleasant, he may be merely reporting that it is the sort of event which reinforces him or toward which he finds himself tending to move because it has reinforced such movement. One could probably not acquire verbal responses with respect to pleasantness as a purely private fact unless something like this were so. In any case, the subject himself is not at an especially good point of vantage for making such observations. 'Subjective judgments' of the pleasantness or satisfaction provided by stimuli are usually unreliable and inconsistent. As the doctrine of the unconscious has emphasized, we may not be able to report at all upon events which can be shown to be reinforcing to us or we may make a report which is in direct conflict with objective observations; we may report as unpleasant a type of event which can be shown to be reinforcing. Examples of this anomaly range from masochism to martyrdom.

It is sometimes argued that reinforcement is effective because it reduces a state of deprivation. Here at least is a collateral effect which need not be confused with reinforcement itself. It is obvious that deprivation is important in operant conditioning. We used a *hungry* pigeon in our experiment, and we could not have demonstrated operant conditioning otherwise. The hungrier the bird, the oftener it responds as the result of reinforcement. But in spite of this connection it is not true that reinforcement always reduces deprivation. Conditioning may occur before any substantial change can take place in the deprivation measured in other ways. All we can say is that the *type* of event which reduces deprivation is also reinforcing.

The connection between reinforcement and satiation must be sought in the process of evolution. We can scarcely overlook the great biological significance of the primary reinforcers. Food, water, and sexual contact, as well as escape from injurious conditions, are obviously connected with the well-being of the organism. An individual who is readily reinforced by such events will acquire highly efficient behavior. It is also biologically advantageous if the behavior due to a given reinforcement is especially likely to occur in an appropriate state of deprivation. Thus it is important, not only that any behavior which leads to the receipt of food should become an important part of a repertoire, but that this behavior should be particularly strong when the organism is hungry. These two advantages are presumably responsible for the fact that an organism can be reinforced in specific ways and that the result will be observed in relevant conditions of deprivation.

Some forms of stimulation are positively reinforcing although they do not appear to elicit behavior having biological significance. A baby is reinforced, not only by food, but by the tinkle of a bell or the sparkle of a bright object. Behavior which is consistently followed by such stimuli shows an increased probability. It is difficult, if not impossible, to trace these reinforcing effects to a history of conditioning. Later we may find the same individual being reinforced by an orchestra or a colorful spectacle. Here it is more difficult to make sure that the reinforcing effect is not conditioned. However, we may plausibly argue that a capacity to be reinforced by any feed-back from the environment would be biologically advantageous, since it would prepare the organism to manipulate the environment successfully before a given state of deprivation developed. When the organism generates a tactual feed-back, as in feeling the texture of a piece of cloth or the surface of a piece of sculpture, the conditioning is commonly regarded as resulting from sexual reinforcement, even when the area stimulated is not primarily sexual in function. It is tempting to suppose that other forms of stimulation produced by behavior are similarly related to biologically important events.

When the environment changes, a capacity to be reinforced by a given event may have a biological *disadvantage*. Sugar is highly reinforcing to most members of the human species, as the ubiquitous candy counter shows. Its effect in this respect far exceeds current biological requirements. This was not true before sugar had been grown and refined on an extensive scale. Until a few hundred years ago, the strong reinforcing effect of sugar must have been a biological advantage. The environment has changed, but the genetic endowment of the organism has not followed suit. Sex provides another example. There is no longer a biological advantage in the great reinforcing effect of sexual contact, but we need not go back many hundreds of years to find conditions of famine and pestilence under which the power of sexual reinforcement offered a decisive advantage.

A biological explanation of reinforcing power is perhaps as far as we can go in saying why an event is reinforcing. Such an explanation is probably of little help in a functional analysis, for it does not provide us with any way of identifying a reinforcing stimulus as such before we have tested its reinforcing power upon a given organism. We must therefore be content with a survey in terms of the effects of stimuli upon behavior.

VII Drive Reduction as the Basis of Reinforcement

Hull was the first to put forward an hypothesis about the nature of reinforcers that avoided any reference to subjective states of pleasure and pain, and that did not define the reinforcer in terms of its effects on response probability. His idea was that events that reinforce do so by virtue of the fact that they reduce drive. Contrary to the earlier views that required two different mechanisms of reinforcement (pleasure and pain) to account for increases and decreases in response probability, Hull attributed the reinforcing powers of all events to the single mechanism of drive reduction. Miller and Dollard clarified and elaborated Hull's main idea. One of the early experiments which raised some doubts about the adequacy of the drive reduction hypothesis was that of Sheffield and Roby. Studies on the reinforcing effects of exploratory behaviour, such as those of Montgomery, also created difficulties for the drive reduction hypothesis.

Law of Primary Reinforcement

Excerpt from C. L. Hull, *Principles of Behavior*, Appleton-Century-Crofts, New York, 1943, Chapter 6.

The infinitely varied and unpredictable situations of need in which the higher organisms find themselves make any form of ready-made receptor-effector connections inadequate for optimal probability of survival. This natural defect of inherited reaction tendencies, however varied, is remedied by learning. Learning turns out upon analysis to be either a case of the differential strengthening of one from a number of more or less distinct re-actions evoked by a situation of need, or the formation of re-ceptor-effector connections *de novo*; the first occurs typically in simple selective learning and the second, in conditioned-reflex learning. A mixed case is found in which new receptor-effector connections are set up at the same time that selective learning is taking place.

An inductive comparison of these superficially rather divergent forms of learning shows one common principle running through them all. This we shall call the *law of primary reinforcement*. It is as follows: *Whenever an effector activity occurs in temporal contiguity with the afferent impulse, or the perseverative trace of such an impulse, resulting from the impact of a stimulus energy upon a receptor, and this conjunction is closely associated in time with the diminution in the receptor discharge characteristic of a need, there will result an increment to the tendency for that stimulus on subsequent occasions to evoke that reaction.* From this principle it is possible to derive both the differential receptor-effector strengthening of simple selective learning and the acquisition of quite new receptor-effector connections, characteristic of condi-tioned-reflex learning as well as of certain forms of selective learning.

31 N. E. Miller and J. Dollard

Drive Reduction and Reinforcement

Excerpts from N. E. Miller and J. Dollard, *Social Learning and Imitation*, Yale University Press, New Haven, 1941, Chapter 2.

A drive is a strong stimulus which impels action. Any stimulus can become a drive if it is made strong enough. The stronger the stimulus, the more drive function it possesses. The faint murmur of distant music has but little primary drive function; the infernal blare of the neighbor's radio has considerably more.

While any stimulus may become strong enough to act as a drive, certain special classes of stimuli seem to be the primary basis for the greater proportion of motivation. These might be called the primary or innate drives. One of these is pain. Pain can reach stabbing heights of greater strength than probably any other single drive. The parching sensation of thirst, the pangs of extreme hunger, and the sore weight of fatigue are other examples of powerful innate drives. The bitter sting of cold and the insistent goading of sex are further examples.

Drive impels the person to make responses to cues in the stimulus situation. Whether these responses will be repeated depends on whether or not they are rewarded. If the response is non-rewarded, the tendency to repeat it to the same cues is weakened. Pavlov called this process *extinction*. In cases of so-phisticated human learning, the process of extinction is facilitated by the learned habit of abandoning unsuccessful responses quickly. Thus in the experiment, the little girl went back to look under the same book only a few times and only on the first trial. The failure to see candy became a cue to abandon looking under that book.

As the dominant response is weakened by the non-reward, next response in the hierarchy becomes dominant. As successive responses are eliminated by non-reward, the individual exhibits variable or what has perhaps been misnamed *random behavior*. It is this variability that may lead to the production of a response which will be rewarded.

If one of the so-called random responses is followed by an event producing a reduction in the drive, the tendency to make this response on subsequent exposure to the same cues is increased. In other words, the connection is strengthened between the stimulus pattern (drive and other cues) and the response. Events producing such strengthening are called rewards. A more technical name for reward is *reinforcement*. Relief from pain is a reward. Drinking water when thirsty, eating food when hungry, and relaxing when tired are other examples of primary, or innate, rewards.

If rewards are thought of as events producing a reduction in the drive, that is, in strength of stimulus, the relationship between satiation and reward becomes clear. Since it is impossible further to reduce the strength of a drive stimulus which is already zero, reward is impossible in the absence of drive. Thus, gulping food is no reward to a satiated animal and may even become painful so that regurgitation is rewarding.

If rewards produce reductions in drive, then too rapid repetition inevitably leads to satiation of the drive, with the result that the rewards lose their rewarding value until the drive reappears. In the absence of reward, the acts which have led to a previously rewarding event tend to be weakened through extinction. Such weakening is one of the factors which eventually cause responses appropriate to a given drive to cease in the absence of that drive. Did rewards not tend to weaken drives, there would be no mechanism for causing the individual to stop one line of satisfying behavior and turn to another.

32 F. D. Sheffield and T. B. Roby

Reward Value of a Non-Nutritive Sweet Taste

Reproduced in full from *Journal of Comparative and Physiological Psychology*, 1950, Vol. 43, pp. 471–81.

The purpose of the present experiments was to help answer the question of what constitutes a 'reinforcing state of affairs' in instrumental conditioning. One of the most systematic positions on this topic (4) holds that ultimate reduction of a survival need is an essential factor, and a closely related position (5) argues for the necessity of ultimate reduction in a primary drive. However, several studies (3, 6, 1) – and at least one theory of reinforcement (10) – suggest the possibility that a sweet taste is reinforcing regardless of whether it is produced by a nutritive or non-nutritive substance. These previous studies demonstrate that sweet-flavored water is preferred to plain water by rats. They do not demonstrate, however, whether a sweet taste, *per se*, will operate as a reward in instrumental conditioning, uncomplicated either by a measurement of purely reflexive ingestion or by acquired reward from nutritive sweet-tasting substances. Also previous studies apparently have not related the sweet preference to the hunger state of the animal. The present experiments demonstrate that a non-nutritive sweet-tasting substance functions as a very effective reward in instrumental conditioning. They also demonstrate that the reward value depends on the degree of hunger present.

The 'reward' used for instrumental conditioning in rats was a solution of saccharine in water. This substance produces a sweet taste in humans which is apparently 'satisfying' to its many users (chiefly diabetics and those on reducing diets). The non-nutritive nature of saccharine is indicated by the fact that it apparently goes through the mammalian body unchanged chemically, and animals ingesting it do not diminish their food intake (3). Throughout all the present experiments the solution used was 1·30 grams of pure saccharine powder per liter of water. This value was chosen on the basis of a previous investigation of sweet preference (1) as likely to be effective with most rats.

Experiment I

Purpose

The purpose of Experiment I was to determine whether a position preference in drinking behavior could be established on the basis of saccharine flavored water and whether the preference varied as a function of degree of hunger.

Method

Six albino rats (age about six months at outset of experiment) were kept hungry by restricting their daily diet to eight grams (dry weight) of ground Purina Dog Chow mixed with 10 cc. of water. Six comparable control animals had food available at all times in the form of standard dry Purina Dog Chow pellets. The living cages were equipped at their rear walls with two 100 cc. graduated cylinders about four inches apart which served as water bottles. The cylinders were held in place by standard steel-clip broom holders, which permitted rapid insertion or removal without dripping of the contents. The water was taken by the rat in the usual way – by lapping from the end of a glass tube. The tips were partially sealed to a diameter small enough to prevent any spontaneous dripping. The laboratory was dimly lighted by a shielded 25-

Table 1

Acquisition of Drinking from the Saccharine Side on Training Days

| | Mean per cent from saccharine side out of total intake of fluid from bottles | | | |
	Preceding day (water in both bottles)	During first 2½ training hours	During first training day	During tenth training day
Hungry	55·2	88·6	98·8	99·5
Satiated	59·5	77·3	95·5	95·8

watt lamp at all times except when readings were made and when the daily food was given, at which times a bright overhead light was turned on. The procedure was as follows:

1. Two habituation days in the cages with both groups satiated for food and water, followed by a day in which the six experimental animals were not fed.

2. Five days with water in both bottles, hunger-drive regime as indicated in the Method section.

3. Nineteen days of alternate training and testing. On *training* days a saccharine solution (1·30 grams per liter) was on a given side

for a given animal, water being on the other side; on the alternate *testing* days water was on both sides. The saccharine side was on the left for half of the animals of each group and on the right for the other half.

Results

Relative consumption of water and saccharine solution. – All animals demonstrated rapid acquisition of a preference for drinking the saccharine solution as compared with the water solution on training days. Regardless of the degree of hunger, the proportion – of total liquid consumed – taken from the saccharine bottle jumped to almost 100 per cent during the first training day. The relevant results are shown in table 1.

Table 1 shows that there was a slight preference in both groups for the 'saccharine' side prior to the introduction of saccharine, as indicated by the per cent of water intake during the preceding day when there was water in both bottles. During the first $2\frac{1}{2}$ hours with saccharine in one of the bottles, however, there was a decided preference in both groups for drinking from the saccharine bottle, and over the entire first 24 hours with saccharine both groups drank almost exclusively from the saccharine bottle. There was little difference between the first and last day of training.

Whereas there was no important difference between hungry and satiated animals in the *per cent* of total intake from the saccharine bottle, there was a large difference in *absolute* intake. Hungry animals drank far more saccharine solution than satiated animals. This is shown in table 2, which also compares saccharine drinking with water consumption prior to the first training day.

It can be seen in table 2 that both hungry and satiated rats markedly increased their fluid intake when the saccharine solution was available. Even satiated animals almost doubled their intake, while the hungry animals increased theirs by a factor of almost nine, drinking over two and one-half times as much of the solution as the satiated animals. It will also be noted that hungry animals drank significantly less water than satiated animals during the five control days before the introduction of saccharine. This may well merely reflect the fact that they received 10 cc. of water in their daily ration of Purina mash. If a constant of 10 cc. is added to the mean it becomes 34·2 and does not differ significantly from that of the satiated group. Thus no clear relation of hunger to water intake is in evidence.

Table 2

Effect of Hunger on Consumption of Saccharine Solution

| | Mean ccs. fluid taken | | | | |
	From both water bottles before training	From saccharine bottle during training	Diff.	*t*	df.
Hungry	24·2	205·4	181·2	9·7	5
Satiated	37·8	78·1	40·3	4·8	5
Diff.	−13·6	127·3			
t	3·7	6·0			
df.	10	10			

Table 3

Mean Per Cent of Water Taken from the 'Saccharine' side on Test Days During Training

| | Mean per cent from 'saccharine' side | | | | |
	Day Before Training	1st Test Day	2nd Test Day	3rd Test Day	9th Test Day
Hungry	55·2	81·1	82·8	76·7	72·8
Satiated	59·5	76·7	80·2	68·0	57·3

Position preference on test days. – All animals showed a preference for the 'saccharine' side during the nine interspersed test days on which there was plain water in both bottles. However, the transfer of position preference was not complete, that is, while all animals drank the *majority* of their water from the reinforced side they did not attain the 100 per cent level. On the contrary, the transfer to test days reached a maximum on the second test day and declined thereafter. The important trends are shown in table 3.

It can be seen in table 3 that transfer of the reinforced position to test days with water only increased to the second test day. At this point both hungry and satiated animals showed reliable transfer (*p* less than ·02 in each group). But the transfer began to decline by the third test day and continued downward through the remainder of training. The decline from the second to the last test day was not significant for either group but at least the failure to progress toward 100 per cent preference indicates either that the reinforcing power of the saccharine solution was extinguishing or that some other factor was interfering with complete transfer of the position preference to the test days with water in both bottles. One such interfering factor might be frustration due to failing to find a sweet taste in the appropriate bottle on test days. Another could be acquisition of a discrimination involving drinking exclusively from the saccharine side on training days and drinking more or less indiscriminately on the test days. The cue for the differential behavior would be presence or absence of a sweet taste. The critical question for the present study was whether or not the sweet taste was losing its reinforcing power as would be the case if it were an acquired reward. Evidence on this question will be considered next.

Did the reinforcing effect extinguish? – Perhaps the most relevant finding on this question has already been shown in table 1, in which it is obvious that an almost 100 per cent preference for the saccharine side was maintained throughout the training days for all animals. If the decline in preference on test days is due to decline of reinforcing effect, a comparable decline would be expected on training days.

Another relevant source of evidence is the course of saccharine drinking throughout the 10 training days. The finding here was

Table 4

Possible Extinction of Saccharine Drinking

		Day of saccharine training		
		1st	2nd	10th
Hungry	Mean ccs.	244·7	195·5	194·8
	Diff.		49·2	0·7
	t		4·3	0·1
	df.		5	5
Satiated	Mean ccs.	94·7	77·3	74·3
	Diff.		17·4	3·0
	t		1·6	0·4
	df.		5	5

an initial drop in saccharine drinking in both groups, but with little change from the second to the tenth training day. These results are shown in table 4. The table shows a significant drop between the first and second training days in the hungry group. None of the other differences shown is significant although the difference in each case is in the direction of extinction of saccharine drinking.

While the results demonstrate some initial extinction of saccharine drinking, they do not provide a convincing explanation of the failure to achieve 100 per cent transfer of position preference on test days. This preference declined *after* the saccharine drinking stabilized. Moreover, a decline in saccharine drinking is not necessarily an index of a decline in its reinforcing power – it could be acquisition of a tendency not to get too full a stomach. It should be noted that ingestion of 245 ccs. of fluid (the mean for the first day for hungry rats) involves considerable stomach distension in a 350-gram animal. The amount consumed is comparable to a 150-pound man's consuming 13 gallons of fluid in a 24-hour period.[1]

Experiment II

Purpose

It had originally been expected that if a sweet taste was reinforcing a progressive acquisition of a position preference on test days would have been shown in Experiment I. This expectation was not borne out; instead the animals showed rapid acquisition of a moderate preference, followed by a tendency toward a decline.

The results might be interpreted as evidence that the reinforcing effect of a sweet taste was relatively weak and tended to extinguish in the course of the experiment. On the other hand the results can be interpreted as evidence that the animal was frustrated by absence of a sweet taste on test days or that a discrimination was being established such that the animals would try both bottles and drink only from the sweet side if one was sweet, but drink more indiscriminately if neither was sweet. Experiment II was designed to test further the reinforcing value of a sweet taste with both of these latter factors – frustration and discrimination – eliminated.

1. The experimenters had no real check on how much of the saccharine solution was actually ingested because the cages had wire mesh floors with sawdust trays underneath. However, in Experiment III, in which drinking was done over solid floors, very little of the saccharine solution taken was found to be spilled on the floor. In any case the measure used was a good index of instrumental tongue movements.

Method

The laboratory was normally kept dimly lighted by a shielded 25-watt lamp. At 9:00 A.M., 11:00 A.M., 1:00 P.M., 3:00 P.M., and 5:00 P.M., the experimenter entered the room, turned on a bright overhead light and inserted the saccharine bottle, always on the same side for a given animal. A bottle of plain water was always present on the opposite side. The subjects were the same ones which had been used in Experiment I, the hunger regime was the same, and the saccharine solution was of the same concentration (1·30 grams per liter) and on the same side as in Experiment I. On each trial the saccharine bottle was left in position for exactly 10 minutes and the measure of instrumental behavior was the amount of the solution consumed. It was expected that if a sweet taste was reinforcing then the turning on of the light, the presence of the experimenter, the sound of the bottle being inserted, and the visual presence of the bottle would be a cue-pattern to which approach and drinking would become conditioned. The ten-minute trials were continued for 18 days – a total of 90 trials.

Results

Acquisition of instrumental drinking in response to the environmental cue-pattern appeared to continue throughout the 18-day period for hungry animals, although approaching an asymptote toward the end of training. Satiated animals on the other hand showed no signs of acquisition. The results are depicted in figure 1, which shows the average ccs. per 10-minute trial per rat. The results are smoothed in the figure by using successive sets of three days' trials (15 trials per rat for each point on the curve).

It is apparent in figure 1 that the satiated rats show no increase in propensity to drink saccharine whereas hungry animals show progressive acquisition. The acquisition in hungry animals is well beyond the one per cent level of confidence (t, for first point versus last point, $= 4·9$, df. $= 5$). Thus when the frustration and discrimination possible in Experiment I are eliminated a conventional acquisition curve is obtained. This argues against extinction of an acquired reward as an explanation of the failure to get progressive acquisition in Experiment I.

It should be borne in mind that the same animals were used in both experiments. Thus a sweet taste was shown to retain its reinforcing value for hungry animals over a lengthy period in which it could have extinguished if it were an acquired reward. Also the rate of ingestion for hungry animals was much higher by the end of Experiment II than it was even on the first day of Experiment I. Over the first day of Experiment I the hungry animals drank at a rate of 0·17 ccs. per minute, whereas the last

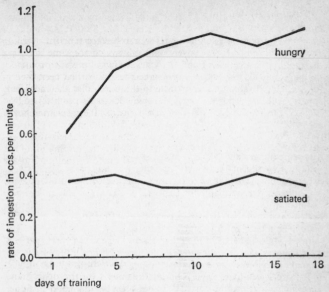

Figure 1 Acquisition of drinking of the saccharine solution (1·30 grams per liter) in response to a specific cue-pattern accompanying availability of the solution

point on the curve for hungry animals in figure 1 represents a rate of 1·09 ccs. per minute.* This difference is complicated by the fact that in Experiment I the animals were asleep part of the time but it probably reflects in addition the fact that the unlimited drinking periods of Experiment I allowed any painful effects of too full a stomach to motivate avoidance of drinking behavior. The difference is in a direction opposed to the hypothesis that a sweet taste is an acquired reward which extinguishes with performance of the instrumental response. The reinforcing effect was still going strong after 10 days of unlimited drinking in Experiment I and 18 days with five 10-minute drinking periods per day in Experiment II.

* A methodological point worth mentioning is that the hungry animals consistently drank the least at the 1:00 P.M. test, which came just before their daily feeding – at a time when they were presumably most hungry. This runs counter to the overall relation between hunger and saccharine drinking and is interpreted by the writers as due to the conflicting habit of loitering at the front of the cage where food was soon to be introduced.

Experiment III

Purpose

The main purpose of Experiment III was to test the reinforcing value of a sweet taste in a more conventional animal-learning situation than that used in Experiments I and II. A second purpose was to continue the same animals in a further learning task to give further opportunity for the reward value of a sweet taste to extinguish if it is an acquired reward. A third purpose was to get a rough idea of the order of magnitude of the reinforcing values of saccharine and food with hungry animals.

Method

The same hungry animals used in Experiments I and II served as subjects in Experiment III. Of the six hungry rats used in the first two experiments, one died of whirling disease between experiments, so only five animals were available for Experiment III. The learning task was acquisition of a position habit in a standard T-maze. The stem and each arm of the maze were 21 inches long and four and one-half inches wide. The interior of the stem was painted grey, that of one arm was painted white and that of the other black. The ends of each goal box were made of wire screening to provide cues very similar to those in the animal's previous experience with drinking from the saccharine bottle in its wire-screen living cage. A Springfield timer recorded running time via a microswitch which started the timer when the door of the starting box was opened and another microswitch which stopped the clock when the animal's weight landed on a hinged floor at the far end of the arm. Retracing was prevented by dropping a door as soon as the animal entered a particular arm. The correct side for a given animal always had a bottle of saccharine solution (1·30 grams per liter); the incorrect side had a bottle of plain water. Throughout Experiment III the animals had a supply of water from a water tray in their living-cages – thus they were satiated for thirst, and the only time they drank from a glass tube during the experiment was in the maze. All trials were run in the evening, starting about 8:00 P.M.; the daily feeding of 8 grams (dry weight) of Purina flour mixed with water was given at noon. The procedure was as follows:

1. Four forced runs, two to the saccharine side and two to the water side. The forced runs were spaced over two days, one of each kind per day, balanced for order. On each trial the rat was confined in the end box for eight minutes.

2. Forty-two free-choice trials, three per day for 14 days, the trials on a given day being spaced about one half-hour apart. On each trial the rat was confined in the end box for four minutes.

Results

All animals showed prompt acquisition in terms of both time and errors. The results are summarized in the three curves shown in figure 2. Curve (a) shows acquisition in terms of frequency of correct choice; the frequency scores plotted use per cent of correct choices on each day's set of three trials for the five animals. Thus the N at each point in the curve is 15 animal-trials. Curve (b) shows acquisition in terms of time to reach the end of the arm on correct choices. Every animal made at least one correct choice per day, and the value plotted in the curve is the median, over the five animals, of each animal's median daily performance. Curve (c) shows the mean rate of consumption of saccharine solution. The daily rate per minute was determined for each animal and these values were averaged over the five animals to get the points plotted.

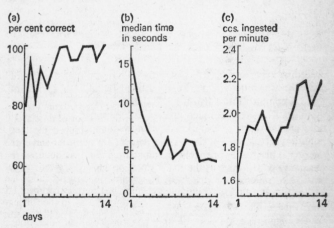

Figure 2 Acquisition in a T-maze with saccharine solution (1·30 grams per liter) as reward: (a) frequency of correct choices, (b) time to reach correct side, (c) rate of ingestion of solution in the goal box

An important relationship was found between rate of ingestion of saccharine solution and maze performance. Animals whose rate of drinking tended to be low during the four minutes of confinement in the goal box also tended to be poor learners both in terms of time scores and frequency scores. In other words if they did not drink the saccharine avidly they also did not perform well in getting to the solution. The relationship is depicted in figure 3.

Another interesting finding was that the average rate of consumption was much greater in Experiment III than in either of the

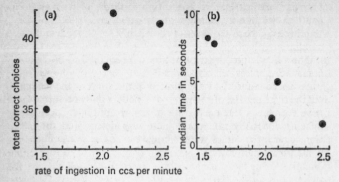

Figure 3 Relation between mean amount of saccharine drinking in the four-minute confinement and (a) frequency of correct choice on all trials and (b) median running time during the last half of training

preceding experiments. It has already been noted that the rate of ingestion was much greater in Experiment II than in Experiment I and a comparison of figure 1 and figure 2-C readily shows that the ingestion rate was much greater in Experiment III. The last point on the curve in Experiment II shows a rate of 1·09 ccs. per minute whereas the last day in Experiment III was 2·16 ccs. per minute. This result probably can be attributed to the greater specificity of the cues in the maze situation and to the fact that only four minutes of drinking were allowed at a time, thus minimizing the chance of filling up and avoiding the bottle. However, this result, like the rest of the findings in Experiment III, argues against extinction of the reward value of the non-nourishing sweet taste.

Moreover, the motivating power of the sweet taste was quite impressive. The two fastest animals appeared to run at top speed and were consistently close to two seconds at the end of training. The final median time of 3·8 seconds is slower than that obtained in the same apparatus by other rats rewarded with food, who achieved a median of about two seconds. However, the time is still of a low enough order of magnitude to indicate considerable reinforcement value of a sweet taste for hungry animals.

Discussion

The experiments prove that a non-nourishing but sweet-tasting substance served as a reinforcement for instrumental learning.

Hunger was presumably in no way reduced by the saccharine solution, yet hungry animals clearly demonstrated acquisition in the three different learning situations in which the reward was a saccharine solution.

The possibility that the sweet taste was an acquired reward seems very unlikely – on two counts. For one thing, previously experienced sweet tastes (e.g., rat's milk, conversion of starch to sugar in the mouth, etc.) are very unlikely to have been as sweet as the concentrated saccharine solution used. Thus the sweet taste used would be at an unfavourable point on the generalization gradient as an acquired reward stimulus if we make the usual assumption that the generalization gradient falls in either direction from the stimulus intensity reinforced. Moreover, the sweet taste did not lose its reward value throughout the three experiments, with the ingestion of thousands of ccs. of saccharine solution and no doubt millions of instrumental tongue movements. Since the visual, kinesthetic, tactile, and gustatory pattern accompanying this ingestion in all three experiments (drinking from a glass tube protruding from a visible graduated cylinder through quarter-inch wire mesh) received no primary reinforcement, it would be expected that any *acquired* reward value of a sweet taste would have extinguished for this pattern.

The findings are thus at variance with the molar principle of reinforcement used by Hull (4), which identifies primary reinforcement with 'need reduction'. Hull admittedly chose need reduction on the grounds that from a Darwinian point of view reduction of a survival need is very likely to be accompanied by a 'reinforcing state of affairs', and at the molar level this principle may be predictive in a high proportion of instances of instrumental learning. However, it does not designate the *mechanism* by which natural selection has managed to make need-reducing events reinforcing, and it is unable to predict the present results in which reinforcement is obtained in the absence of need reduction. The findings highlight the desirability of a theory concerning the mechanism (or mechanisms) by which natural selection has achieved adaptive instrumental learning.

At a more molecular level, Miller and Dollard (5) have proposed *reduction of drive* as the occasion for a reinforcing state of affairs and they tentatively identify drive with intensity of stimulation. The present findings are at variance with their position in that hunger drive, in the usual sense of the concept, is not at all reduced by the saccharine solution. Thus, as mentioned earlier, saccharine is allegedly excreted without chemical change and its ingestion has no effect on food intake (3). However, it may be postulated that part of the total stimulation in the case of hunger consists of proprioceptive return from the striped-muscle tension occasioned by the hunger state. It may further be postulated that a sweet taste relaxes the striped muscles – at the very least the animal stands still while ingesting the solution – and this innate relaxation would provide stimulus reduction and consequent acquisition of instrumental responses. Thus a closer analysis of the physiological effects of a sweet taste may show that the present results are consistent with Miller and Dollard's position.

While the experiments were aimed mainly at providing evidence relevant to the need-reduction and drive-reduction theories, a brief comment should be made on the relation of the results to other positions on the reinforcement process. The results in no way conflict with or provide support for the relatively empirical and circular systems of Skinner (7), Thorndike (8), and Tolman (9). The results merely demonstrate that with hungry animals a saccharine solution is a 'reinforcing stimulus' in Skinner's terms, is a 'reward' or 'satisfier' in Thorndike's terms, and probably is 'demanded' in Tolman's terms. The results are also consistent with Guthrie's (2) more theoretical and less circular position involving the mechanism of stimulus change and protection of the last response from relearning. In Guthrie's terms the results demonstrate that ingesting the sweet substance innately produces a stimulus change which can be observed to be very much the same as that produced by presenting food to the hungry animal (i.e., cessation of exploration, maintained ingestion, and so forth) and it is therefore not surprising that the change is big enough to protect the instrumental response. Another theory which cannot escape mention in the present context is the unpopular 'beneceptor' theory of Troland (10), which holds that the reinforcing value of a reward lies in the quality of the stimulation produced by the reward. The findings are a natural fit to his theory – which argues that stimulation of receptors for sweet is all that is needed to strengthen an instrumental act.

In conclusion the question should be answered as to whether any novel hypotheses concerning the reinforcement process are indicated by the results. The chief suggestion the authors have to make is that stimulation and performance of a consummatory response appear to be more important to instrumental learning – in a primary, not acquired, way – than the drive satisfaction which the consummatory response normally achieves. The present experiments were essentially sham-feeding experiments in which the animal was innately stimulated to ingest a substance which did not change his state of hunger, and the result was acquisition, without extinction, of the instrumental responses. Thus it would appear that *eliciting* the consummatory response of ingestion was the critical factor. This suggestion is in line with Wolfe and Kaplon's (11) finding that with total food intake held constant, the reward value of eating is a function of amount of consummatory activity required to ingest the food.

Summary

1. A non-nourishing but sweet-tasting substance was shown in three successive learning situations to be an effective reward for instrumental learning, its reward value depending on the state of hunger present.

2. The possibility that the sweet taste was an acquired reward rather than a primary reward was shown to be extremely unlikely.

3. The findings demonstrate the expected limitations of Hull's molar 'need reduction' theory of reinforcement and the necessity of exploring indirect reduction of striped-muscle tension as a drive-reduction factor in Miller and Dollard's theory of reinforcement. The results are consistent with Guthrie's last-response theory of reinforcement, and demonstrate that a sweet taste is 'reinforcing' in Skinner's system, 'satisfying' in Thorndike's system, and 'demanded' in Tolman's system.

4. It is suggested that elicitation of the consummatory response appears to be a more critical *primary* reinforcing factor in instrumental learning than the drive reduction subsequently achieved.

References

1. Beebe-Center, J. G., Black, P., Hoffman, A. C., and Wade, Marjorie: Relative per diem consumption as a measure of preference in the rat. *J. comp. physiol. Psychol.* 1948, 41, 239–251.
2. Guthrie, E. R.: *The psychology of learning.* New York: Harper, 1935.
3. Hausmann, M. F.: The behavior of rats in choosing food. II Differentiation between sugar and saccharine. *J. comp. Psychol.* 1933, 15, 419–428.
4. Hull, C. L.: *Principles of behavior.* New York: Appleton-Century, 1943.
5. Miller, N. E. and Dollard, J.: *Social learning and imitation.* New Haven: Yale Press, 1941.
6. Richter, C. P. and Campbell, Kathryne: Taste thresholds and taste preferences of rats for five common sugars. *J. Nutrition.* 1940, 20, 31–46.
7. Skinner, B. F.: *The behavior of organisms.* New York: Appleton-Century, 1938.

8. Thorndike, E. L.: *Animal intelligence.* New York: Macmillan, 1911.
9. Tolman, E. C.: *Purposive behavior in animals and men.* New York: Appleton-Century, 1932.
10. Troland, L. T.: *The fundamentals of human motivation.* New York: Van Nostrand, 1928.
11. Wolfe, J. B. and Kaplon, M. D.: Effect of amount of reward and consummative activity on learning in chickens. *J. comp. Psychol.* 1941, 31, 353–361.

33 K. C. Montgomery

The Role of Exploratory Drive in Learning

Reproduced in full from *Journal of Comparative and Physiological Psychology*, 1954, Vol. 47, pp. 60–4.

In previous papers the author has presented evidence that novel external stimulation evokes the exploratory drive which leads to exploratory behavior, that continued exposure to such stimulation results in a decrease in the strength of the exploratory drive, and that the exploratory drive is a primary drive largely independent of other primary motives (5, 6, 7).

The present investigation is concerned with the role of the exploratory drive, as a primary drive, in learning. According to drive-reduction theory, behavior followed by a reduction in amount of exploratory drive should be strengthened. However, qualitative observation by the author has repeatedly suggested an alternative hypothesis: behavior which results in an *increase* in amount of exploratory drive is strengthened. In other words, it is possible that behavior which produces novel stimulation is reinforced, not because exposure to that stimulation reduces the strength of the exploratory drive, but because the novel stimulation produces an increase in, or at least maintains, the strength of the exploratory drive. Results reported by Mote and Finger (4), by Schiller (9), and, in particular, by Harlow *et al.* (1, 2) tend to support the latter hypothesis.

The present experiment is designed (*a*) to test the hypothesis that novel stimulation can function as a reinforcing agent, and (*b*) to provide evidence relevant to the question of whether exploratory-drive reduction or exploratory-drive increase (or maintenance) is the mechanism underlying this kind of reinforcement.

The experimental conditions had to meet two major requirements. First, drives other than the exploratory drive and reinforcements other than those provided by novel stimulation had to be eliminated or controlled. Second, a situation had to be devised in which the exploratory drive could be evoked and then either reduced or increased (maintained) in strength after a response had occurred. These requirements were met by running rats satiated for food and water, with a control for the activity drive, in a Y maze so constructed that one arm was a blind alley and the other opened into a large Dashiell-type maze offering a much greater amount of intra- and extramaze stimulation. On any given trial an animal was free to enter either arm of the Y; as soon as it did so, a sliding door was closed behind it, and approximately 2 min. later it was removed from the maze.

Thus, the situation (a) provides an opportunity for learning to occur, and (b) permits of a rough test between the exploratory-drive reduction and the exploratory-drive increase hypotheses. According to the former, the animals should learn to enter the blind alley of the Y because continued exposure to that arm produces an appreciable decrease in the strength of the exploratory drive it evokes originally (5). According to the latter hypothesis, the animals should learn to enter the arm leading to the Dashiell maze because it provides a large amount of novel stimulation which increases, or at the very least maintains, the strength of the exploratory drive evoked by the Y-maze arm. An additional test for learning consisted of reversing the Dashiell maze from one arm of the Y to the other midway through the experiment. Preferences developed for either arm of the Y maze should shift accordingly if they are under the control of either of the above two kinds of reinforcement.

Method

Subjects

The Ss were 12 female albino rats of the Wistar strain, averaging about 150 days of age at the beginning of the experiment.

Apparatus

A diagram of the apparatus is presented in Figure 1. It consisted of two mazes, a Y maze with L-shaped goal arms and a modified Dashiell maze (D maze) which could be attached to either arm of the Y. The L-shaped arms prevented the animals from seeing the position of the D maze from the choice point of the Y. The mazes were set on a table placed in the center of the experimental room in which the rats were housed. Dim indirect lighting was used during the experimental periods to provide uniform illumination in the apparatus.

Procedure

Housing and adaptation. – On day 1 the animals were placed in the experimental room. Half were housed on the right side of the room and half on the left. Half the rats on each side of the room were housed in small individual cages and the other half in small individual cages attached to activity drums. Throughout the experiment food and water were always available in the living-cages. Daily records were taken of number of activity-wheel revolutions. The animals were given 24 hr. to adapt to the experimental room. All had been thoroughly tamed prior to day 1.

Test for turn of position preferences. – On day 2 each animal was given four widely spaced, free-choice trials in the Y maze, whose arms were made into blind alleys. As soon as the rat entered an arm, the sliding door was closed behind it. It was removed from the maze 30 sec. after entering an arm. The arm entered and the latency of entry were recorded for each trial.

Learning series. – On days 3, 4, and 5 each animal was given eight trials in blocks of four. The D maze was attached to the right side of the Y maze for half the animals and to the left side for the other half. A trial consisted of (*a*) placing a rat in the stem of the Y, (*b*) permitting it to enter either arm, (*c*) closing the sliding door behind it, and (*d*) removing it from the apparatus 2 min. after it was placed in the stem of the Y. The intertrial interval within each block of four trials varied from about 15 to 25 sec.; the interblock interval averaged about 1 hr. On each trial a record was made of the arm of the Y maze entered, the latency of entry, and the number of 12-in. units traversed in the D maze when the animal entered that arm of the Y.

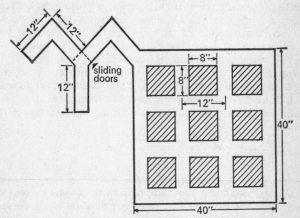

Figure 1 Floor plan of the apparatus. The measurements shown are inside dimensions. All alleys were 4 in. wide and 5 in. high, and were covered with hardware cloth. The walls and floor of the Y maze and the outside walls of the D maze were constructed from unpainted ½-in. plywood; the floor and the inside walls of the D maze were made from unpainted Homosote (a wall board)

Reversal series. – On days 6, 7, and 8 the procedure followed during the learning series was duplicated in all details. The only change in the situation was that the D maze was moved to the other arm of the Y maze.

Experimental Design

The experimental design was such that the following variables were balanced: the type of living cage, the side of the room on which the living cage was placed, and the side of the Y maze on which the D maze was placed during the learning (and reversal) series. All possible combinations of these three variables were used, resulting in eight subgroups of animals. Four subgroups contained two animals each, and the other four contained one rat each. The 12 animals were so assigned that half of them contributed to each of the two 'values' of each of the three variables.

Results

Percentage choice of the D-maze side of the Y maze

For each animal the total number of entries of the Y arm leading to the D maze was tabulated for each block of eight trials during the learning and reversal series. These values were summed for the 12 animals and converted to percentages. The results are summarized in the upper half of Figure 2. The first point represents the percentage choice of the right arm of the Y on the four initial-preference trials. The horizontal lines at 63 and 37 per cent represent the 0·01 fiducial limits based upon chance.

Inspection of the graph reveals that the animals (a) learned to enter the arm of the Y leading to the D maze and (b) reversed their behavior when the position of the D maze was reversed. Individual records are consistent with the performance of the group.

Latency data

The mean latency for the group was computed for the four initial-preference trials and for each succeeding block of eight trials. Also, the common logarithm of each rat's latency on each trial was obtained, and averages corresponding to the latency means were computed. The results are summarized in the lower half of Figure 2. Both curves resemble typical learning curves. The decreases in mean log latency from the first to the fourth and from the first to the seventh point on the graph are highly significant. The respective values of t are 5·11 and 7·00; for 11 df both values are significant at beyond the 0·001 level.

Reversing the position of the D maze produced an apparent temporary increase in the latency measures. However, the in-

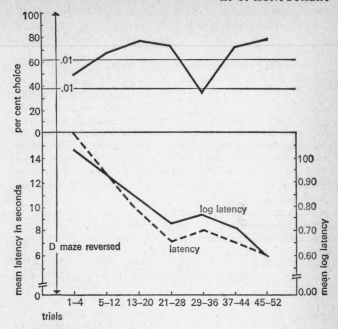

Figure 2 Group learning curves

crease in mean log latency from trials 21 to 28 to trials 29 to 36 does not differ from zero (t of 1.01; 11 df).

Further analyses

On the four initial-preference trials six animals turned either left or right three times; each of the other six rats turned left twice and right twice. There were no differences in performance between these two groups during either the learning or the reversal series.

During the learning series the D maze was attached to the right arm of the Y for half the animals and the left arm for the other half. There were no differences in performance between these two groups. Similarly, these groups did not differ during the reversal series.

It is possible that extramaze stimuli deriving from the side of the room on which the animals lived evoked an acquired drive, or provided secondary reinforcement, for entering the arm of the

Y pointing toward that side of the room. Hence, learning would be either facilitated or hindered, depending upon the relative position of the D maze. The results yield no evidence of such effects.

No differences in performance occurred between the six animals given access to activity drums and the six not given such access. During the learning series the former group entered the Y arm leading to the D maze a total of 108 times and the latter group a total of 101 times. Corresponding totals for the reversal series are 74 and 63. Furthermore, these groups did not differ significantly in amount of activity in the D maze. The average number of 12-in. D-maze units traversed per D-maze entry was 28·1 for the activity-drum group and 24·8 for the other group. On the average the animals in the former group ran about one-third mile per day in the activity drums.

A progressive increase in amount of D-maze activity occurred during the experiment. The mean number of 12-in. D-maze units traversed per D-maze entry was computed for each block of eight trials during the learning and reversal series. These values are 19·5, 24·2, 26·6, 30·6, 29·4, and 30·3. The difference between the first and last mean is significant at the 0·001 level (t of 5·84; 11 df).

Discussion

Both the percentage choice and the latency data indicate that learning occurred. During the learning series the animals developed a preference for the arm of the Y leading to the D maze, and during the reversal series they reversed this preference; average latency decreased systematically as a function of number of trials. Various analyses reveal that performance was not influenced by initial turn or position preferences, by drives or reinforcements acquired in the experimental room, or by the placement of the D maze relative to the Y maze. Moreover, there is no evidence that the general activity drive affected performance in any way.

Thus the results appear to confirm the hypothesis that novel stimulation can function as a reinforcing agent. However, there are three other possible explanations of the present findings that must be considered. Because all the rats were females, it is possible that an activity drive based upon the estrus cycle was present and that the D maze provided a means of partially reducing this drive, thus influencing the Y-maze choices. There is, however, no evidence in the present results of any kind of systematic variation either in amount of D-maze activity or in the latency measures such as would be expected if this motive were important.

Another possible explanation is that a conditioned fear of the blind alley developed because the animals were picked up every time they entered it; hence, they tended to avoid the blind alley and to enter the other arm. There are at least two reasons why this hypothesis is untenable. First, because the arms of the Y were very similar, fear conditioned to one arm should generalize to the other. Thus the animals should tend to avoid both arms, and their average latency should increase with number of trials. Figure 2 shows that mean latency decreased during the experiment. Second, when the rats entered the Y arm leading to the D maze they were almost always picked up in the D maze. If handling results in fear conditioning, then the animals should exhibit an increasing avoidance of the D maze, i.e., a progressive decrease in amount of D-maze activity as number of trials increases. The results show that a progressive increase occurred.

Finally, it is possible that the D maze provided some kind of secondary reinforcement based upon learning that occurred *prior* to the experiment. Available evidence (e.g., 8) indicates that for the rat the secondary reinforcing properties of stimuli extinguish rapidly if primary reinforcement is withheld. Hence one would predict an initial increase followed by a decrease in percentage choice of the Y arm leading to the D maze and an initial decrease followed by an increase in the latency measures. The data presented in Figure 2 contradict both predictions. The preceding considerations apply to secondary reinforcement derived from positive primary reinforcers, e.g., food and water. Miller (3) has demonstrated that secondary reinforcement based upon reduction of an acquired fear drive is effective over a long series of trials. Thus, the present results might be explained by assuming that the Y maze evoked an acquired fear drive, based upon prior learning, that was reduced only when the animals entered the D maze. Qualitative observation yielded no evidence supporting this hypothesis. Only one or two rats defecated or urinated in the stem of the Y, and all the animals ran back and forth between the Y and D mazes freely when they entered the Y arm leading to the D maze.

It is concluded that the present results support the hypothesis that novel stimulation can function as a reinforcing agent. The results are also interpreted as supporting the hypothesis that the mechanism underlying this kind of reinforcement is an increase in the strength of the exploratory drive, and as providing negative evidence for the hypothesis that the mechanism is a decrease in the strength of the exploratory drive.

Summary

Two hypotheses are tested in the present experiment: (a) novel stimulation can function as a reinforcing agent, and (b) the mechanism underlying this kind of reinforcement is an *increase*, rather than a decrease, in the strength of the exploratory drive. Twelve rats were given 48 free-choice trials in a Y maze in which one arm led to a blind alley and the other to a large Dashiell-type maze. On the first 24 trials the D maze was attached to one arm of the Y; on the second 24 trials it was moved to the other arm of the Y. The results show (a) that during the first 24 trials the animals learned to enter the arm of the Y leading to the D maze and that they reversed their choices during the second 24 trials, and (b) that over the 48 trials the animals exhibited a progressive decrease in latency of Y-maze-arm entries. It is concluded that learning occurred, that it is based upon the exploratory drive, and that the results support both the above hypotheses.

References

1. Harlow, H. F. Learning and satiation of response in intrinsically motivated complex puzzle performance by monkeys. *J. comp. physiol. Psychol.*, 1950, 43, 289–294.
2. Harlow, H. F., Harlow, Margaret K., & Meyer, D. R. Learning motivated by a manipulation drive. *J. exp. Psychol.*, 1950, 40, 228–234.
3. Miller, N. E. Learnable drives and rewards. In S. S. Stevens (Ed.), *Handbook of experimental psychology.* New York: Wiley, 1951. Pp. 435–472.
4. Mote, F. A., & Finger, F. W. Exploratory drive and secondary reinforcement in the acquisition and extinction of a simple running response. *J. exp. Psychol.*, 1942, 31, 57–68.
5. Montgomery, K. C. Exploratory behavior and its relation to spontaneous alternation in a series of maze exposures. *J. comp. physiol. Psychol.*, 1952, 45, 50–57.
6. Montgomery, K. C. The effect of the hunger and thirst drives upon exploratory behavior. *J. comp. physiol. Psychol.*, 1953, 46, 315–319.
7. Montgomery, K. C. The effect of activity deprivation upon exploratory behavior. *J. comp. physiol. Psychol.*, 1953, 46, 438–441.
8. Saltzman, I. J. Maze learning in the absence of primary reinforcement: a study of secondary reinforcement. *J. comp. physiol. Psychol.*, 1949, 42, 161–173.
9. Schiller, P. H. Innate constituents of complex responses in primates. *Psychol. Rev.*, 1952, 59, 177–191.

VIII   Reinforcers as Elicitors of Responses

The experiments of Sheffield and his collaborators led them
to postulate that it is the reliable elicitation of responses by
reinforcers which is the critical factor in reinforcement. This
postulate has become known as the *consummatory response
hypothesis*. Though these responses contribute to reinforcement
effects, Miller and Kessen have experimentally refuted the
view that they are essential for reinforcement. Premack has
recently developed a model of reinforcement which states
simply that, for any pair of responses, the independently more
probable or more prepotent response will reinforce the less
probable one. Miller has pointed out some difficulties with this
interpretation of the reinforcing process. However, any
complete theory of reinforcement would have to explain the
observed role of consummatory responses on response
probability.

Reward Effects of Food via Stomach Fistula
Compared with Those of Food via Mouth*

Reproduced in full from *Journal of Comparative and Physiological Psychology*. 1952, Vol. 45, pp. 555–64.

Motivation and reward are closely related. For example, if an animal is not motivated by the drive of hunger, food is not an effective reward. Furthermore, the food that rewards the hungry animal so that it learns also tends to reduce the strength of its hunger drive so that it eventually becomes satiated. These functional relationships have led to the drive-reduction hypothesis of reinforcement which states that a prompt reduction in the strength of a drive has the effect of rewarding immediately preceding responses (2, 6, 7). According to this hypothesis the rewarding effects of food are due to the fact that it reduces the strength of the hunger drive, and the relative ineffectiveness of food as a reward after the animal has become satiated is due to the fact that little if any drive is present to be reduced.

The present experiment is one of a series designed to analyze the mechanism of satiation and its relationship to the rewarding effects of food. The first two experiments in this series compared the hunger-reducing effects of food via stomach fistula with those of food via mouth. The measure of hunger in the first of these, Kohn (4), was the rate of performance of an instrumental response (panel-pushing) periodically reinforced by food; in the second, Berkun, Kessen, and Miller (1), it was a consummatory response (amount of milk drunk). Both measures showed exactly the same pattern of results: (a) 14 cc. of isotonic saline injected by fistula directly into the stomach of hungry albino rats produced relatively little effect, (b) a similar volume of enriched milk injected directly into the stomach produced a prompt reduction in the rate of performance of the instrumental response and the amount of the consummatory response, and (c) the same volume of enriched milk taken normally by mouth produced an even greater reduction in the responses. From these results it seems

* This study was supported by funds from the Institute of Human Relations. A preliminary report of it was given as part of a paper read at the 1951 meetings of the APA (8).

reasonable to conclude that milk injected directly into the stomach produces a prompt reduction in the strength of hunger and that milk taken normally by mouth produces an even greater reduction.

If milk injected directly into the stomach produces a prompt reduction in the strength of hunger, the drive-reduction hypothesis of reinforcement demands that it should act as a reward to produce the learning of new responses. That food injected directly into the stomach may indeed serve as a reward is suggested by the results which Hull *et al.* (3) secured in an exploratory experiment on a dog with an esophageal fistula. Unfortunately, the original data of this experiment were lost, but the authors' notes indicate that the animal learned to choose the side of a simple maze where it received food through the esophageal fistula in preference to the side where a catheter was inserted but no food injected.

The main purpose of the present experiment was to determine whether food injected via fistula directly into the stomach of hungry albino rats would serve as a reward to reinforce the learning of a simple habit. The essential procedure involved giving hungry rats with small plastic fistulas sewn into their stomachs injections of enriched milk when they made the correct choice on a T maze and an injection of isotonic saline when they made an incorrect choice. Learning the correct choice would demonstrate the reward value of an injection of food; it would also serve as a control to rule out the possibility that the reductions in instrumental and in consummatory responses observed in the first two experiments were caused by nausea motivating conflicting responses rather than by a genuine reduction in the strength of the hunger drive. Finally, such learning would not be expected from the hypothesis, recently advanced by Sheffield (9, 10, 11), that the critical factor in reinforcement is the elicitation of a prepotent consummatory response.

A second purpose of the experiment was to compare the rewarding effects of food injected directly into the stomach with those of food taken normally by mouth. This was accomplished by training a second group of animals that received a dish of milk when they went to the correct side of the T maze and a dish of isotonic saline when they went to the incorrect side. From the fact that food by mouth produces a greater reduction in the strength of hunger than food via fistula, the drive-reduction hypothesis predicts that it should serve as a stronger reward and hence produce faster learning. A similar prediction would also be made from the fact that one would expect the cues involved in oral ingestion to have learned reward value.

Since it might be argued that the effect of reward begins with the first sip, when milk is taken by mouth, but only after a considerable volume of milk has been injected directly into the stomach, a third group was run exactly like the second one except that the presentation of the dishes of milk or saline was delayed 7 min. and 35 sec., the time required to complete an injection.

Procedure

The subjects in this experiment were 17 male, albino rats of Sprague-Dawley strain approximately 150 days old at the start of the experiment. All of them had small plastic fistulas sewn into their stomachs, threaded between the skin and the body wall and projecting approximately $\frac{1}{2}$ in. from the back of the neck. These fistulas were inserted according to the procedure described by Kohn (4).

The apparatus is illustrated in Figure 1. It consisted of a T maze. The starting compartment was painted black; it had a slotted lid through which a small rubber tube descended to the animal's fistula, and a false back which could be pushed forward when it was necessary to force recalcitrant subjects to make a choice. The two arms of the maze, which also served as the goal boxes, were made quite distinctive (*a*) so that it would be easy for the cues in the correct one to acquire learned reward value to help compensate for any delay in the effects of the injection, and (*b*) to minimize the generalization of this learned reward value to the cues in the incorrect goal box (12). The goal box to the left (in the diagram) was painted gray and had a floor consisting of $\frac{1}{2}$-in.-gauge wire mesh which was bisected longitudinally by an aluminium covered wooden strip $\frac{7}{8}$ in. high and $\frac{3}{4}$ in. wide. The goal box to the right was painted with vertical black and white stripes 1 in. wide and had a window-screen floor.

In order to allow a $\frac{1}{2}$-in. opening at the top through which the small rubber tube could descend to the fistula, but to discourage the rats from trying to jump up and poke their heads through this opening, the sides of the two goal boxes slanted inward at a 12° angle toward the top. The front of each goal box was a hinged door through which the animals could be removed. In order to allow the experimenter to observe the animals in the goal boxes, the top $7\frac{1}{4}$ in. of this hinged front side was made of transparent plastic.

The starting box has a false back which can be pushed forward by a rod projecting through the back. The starting box and each of the goal boxes have doors sliding up from below, which are operated by foot pedals. Opening the door to the starting box closes a microswitch and starts a clock which is stopped when the animal steps across the small gap in the floor of either goal box and operates an electronic relay.

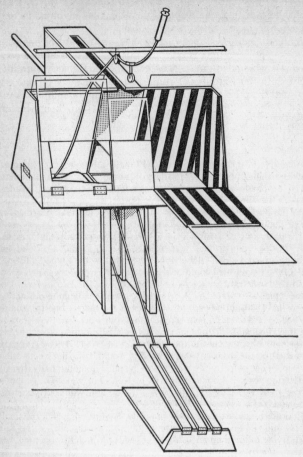

Figure 1 The T Maze

The top $7\frac{1}{2}$ in. of the front of the apparatus is transparent plastic to allow the experimenter to observe the animal. In the diagram the hinged front of the right goal box is opened; a portion of the left one is cut out so that an animal can be seen being injected with milk via fistula. Hinged doors at the end of each goal box allow dishes of milk or saline to be inserted.

Lowering the door at the front of the starting compartment automatically started an electric clock. When it put one of its front feet across a little break in the metal mesh in the floor 4 in. from the entrance of either goal box, the animal completed a circuit allowing a subthreshold current to actuate an electronic relay which stopped the clock. Then the experimenter closed the door behind it so that the animal was confined in the goal box. The experimenter operated the doors by foot pedals.

A small rubber tube ran from the rat's fistula up through the top of the maze over a pulley on the far side of which a light counterweight picked up the slack. Beyond the counterweight the tube was attached to an ordinary hypodermic syringe containing the liquid to be injected.

At the end of each goal box was a small hinged door through which dishes of milk or saline could be inserted. In order to speed up the procedure and to rule out any possibility that drops of spilled milk or the odor of milk could serve as a reward for the injected animals, two pieces of apparatus were used, one for the animals receiving injections via fistula and another for those receiving milk by dish. These T mazes were identical except for the fact that in the first one the striped compartment was on the right and in the second it was on the left. It had originally been planned to reverse the roles of these two pieces of apparatus in the second replication of the experiment as a control on the improbable possibility that differences between them influenced learning. Inasmuch as the results of the first replication were statistically reliable, however, no second one was run.

The diet used in this experiment consisted of milk enriched with cream, starch, casein, vitamins, and minerals according to the formula described in previous articles (1, 4). This supplied 2·1 calories per cc. It was supplemented by a mash of 50 per cent ground Purina Laboratory Chow and 50 per cent water in amounts sufficient to bring the animal's total daily intake to 50 calories.

Habituation

Postoperative care of the animals was similar to that described by Kohn (4). To avoid possible distress (suggested by exploratory work), the experimental animals were first habituated to progressively increasing injections of milk. Each animal was injected with milk twice a day at 11 A.M. and 3 P.M. The first injection was 2 cc. and on each subsequent injection the amount was increased 2 cc. until 12 cc. had been injected. Enough wet mash was given at approximately 4:30 P.M. to bring the total intake to 50 cal. Injections were given on a small perch at the rate the animals normally drank, 1 cc. every 35 sec. The animals to be fed by mouth were habituated in exactly the same way except that they received progressively increasing amounts of milk in dishes in their home cages.

Training

Before habituation the animals were randomly divided into three groups:

1. *Stomach injection* animals received an injection of 14 cc. of enriched milk via fistula when they went to the correct side and 14 cc. of isotonic saline when to the incorrect. For two animals the correct (milk) side was to the right; for three it was to the left. (Seven operated animals were originally prepared for these groups. One, however, was discarded before the first trial because its fistula leaked, and the second had to have a new fistula put in after five training trials, and then died following an operation for a tumor after 26 days of training during which it showed definite signs of learning.) Before being placed in the starting box, the animals had a small rubber tube slipped over their fistula and firmly tied with a thread. In order to avoid injecting air into the animal, this tube was collapsed by gentle suction from a hypodermic syringe after which the free end was sealed off by a little spring clip. As soon as the animal stopped the clock, the door was closed behind it, the syringe containing the proper substance was connected to the tube, the clip was removed, and the first 1 cc. (plus an extra 3·15 cc. required to fill the rubber tube and the plastic fistula) was injected. Thereafter 1 cc. was injected every 35 sec. so that the average rate of injection approximated the rate at which animals had been found to drink normally by mouth. The injection lasted for 7 min. 35 sec.; the animals were allowed to remain in the compartment 3 min. longer and then were removed to their home cages. Approximately 15 min. before the first run each day, while the animals were being weighed, they received an injection of 1 cc. water to clear the fistula and, if the last injection of the day had been milk, another 1 cc. of water was injected before they received their supplementary diet of wet mash.

2. *Mouth, No delay* animals received dishes containing 14 cc. of milk or saline in the correct or incorrect goal boxes, respectively. These dishes were inserted through the hinged door at the end of the sections at the same time that the injections of animals in the preceding group were begun. For three rats the correct side was to the right, and for the other three to the left. The animals in this group remained in the goal boxes the same length of time as those in the first group.

3. *Mouth, Delay* animals received their dishes of 14 cc. of milk for a correct choice or saline for an incorrect one after a delay of 7 min. 35 sec., the time that it normally took to complete an injection. After this delay these animals were left in the goal box with the dish of milk or saline for another period of approximately 7 min. 35 sec. For three of these animals the correct side was to the right, for three to the left.

At approximately 10 A.M. each animal in each of the three groups was given a trial during which it was free to choose either side. As soon as it stepped over the break in the floor of a goal box and stopped the clock, the door was closed behind it and the substance, milk for a correct choice or saline for an incorrect one, was administered. Approximately 4 hr. later, each animal was given a second trial during which the door to the previously chosen side was closed so that it was forced to turn in the opposite direction and receive the other kind of substance. If an animal failed to run within 3 min. on any trial, the false back of the starting box was gradually pushed forward, forcing the animal to the choice point; if it failed to choose within 7 additional minutes, the false back was pushed all the way forward so that the animal was forced out of the choice point into a goal box. Approximately an hour after the forced trial the animals were given enough wet mash in their home cages to bring their daily intake to a total of 50 calories.

Training of the stomach-injection animals was continued for 40 days. Because the other two groups had already learned, their training was discontinued after 25 days.

In some animals there developed an infection along the side of the fistula. Cultures showed that the infections contained a typical intestinal bacteria, *Escherichia coli*, which presumably seeped through the incision where the fistula was sewn into the stomach. Such infections were treated by making a pinpoint incision at the place of infection, draining it and sprinkling powdered sulfathiazole on this area. As a preventive measure the animals were given powdered aureomycin three or four times a week in their diet of wet mash.

Results

Figure 2 shows the percentage of correct choices (to the milk side) made by the animals in the three groups on the morning trials which were free choice. It can be seen that all three groups learned. In order to test the reliability of improvement for the animals which received injections directly into the stomach, the number of correct choices made by each animal on the first 15 free-choice trials was compared with that on the last 15. Chi-square tests, corrected for discontinuity, showed that the improvement was statistically reliable for each one of the five animals in that group. For the individual animals the probability of securing the observed differences in the predicted direction by chance are: 0.05, 0.05, 0.01, 0.001, and 0.001. Furthermore, the three animals tested in the preliminary experiment using a slightly different apparatus (8) also learned to go consistently ($p = 0.02$, 0.01, and 0.001) to the side (two right and one left) on which milk was injected via fistula.

Comparing the different groups shows that milk taken immediately by mouth produced the fastest learning, milk taken by mouth after a delay produced the next fastest learning, and milk injected directly into the stomach produced the slowest learning. In order to test the reliability of these differences each animal was given a score which was the number of correct choices during the first 25 free-choice trials. Then t tests were made. These are

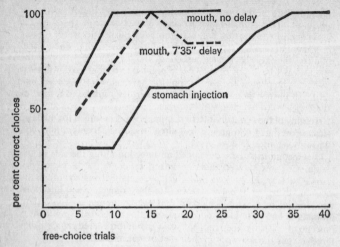

Figure 2 Percentage of choices to the correct (Milk) side on free-choice trials. After making five successive correct choices on the eleventh to fifteen trials, one animal in the Mouth, Delay Group reverted to a consistent position habit on the incorrect side. This one animal contributed all the errors made by this group after the first ten trials

Table 1

Reliabilities of the Differences between the Groups on Days 1 to 25

Group	Errors in free-choice	Log time to milk side
Stomach Injection vs. Mouth, No Delay	·001*	·001
Stomach Injection vs. Mouth, Delay	·038	·001
Mouth, Delay vs. Mouth, No Delay	·070	·003

* Probability of getting by chance as large a difference in the predicted direction.

summarized in Table 1. It can be seen that the superiority of the animals fed milk by mouth (either immediately or after a delay) over those who received it via fistula is statistically reliable.

Figure 3 shows the mean running speed to milk of the animals in the three groups. When the free choice in the morning was correct, this was the running speed on that trial; when it was incorrect, this was the running speed on the afternoon forced trial to the milk side. It can be seen that the differences among the speed scores of the three groups are exactly the same as those among the error scores. In order to test the reliability of these differences, the time scores of each animal on each trial were converted to logs. This conversion was made to normalize the distribution. Then each animal was given a score consisting of the sum of the log times on the first 25 trials, and t tests were made for the differences among the means of the three groups. These are summarized in Table 1, which shows that all the differences are highly reliable.

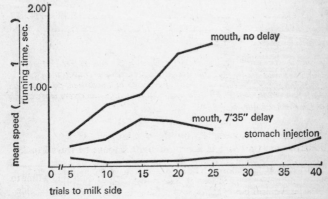

Figure 3 Speed of running to the compartment in which milk was given

Further evidence that the injection of milk directly into the stomach produced learning whereas that of saline did not, is presented in Figure 4. This figure presents the speed of running to the compartment in which milk was injected compared with that to the compartment in which saline was injected. At the beginning of training there was no difference between these two speeds. During the first 15 trials the speed of running to both compartments decreased. It seems probable that this decrease was produced by the extinction of initial exploratory tendencies, but it may have been due to a slight discomfort produced by the injections during the early part of training and gradually adapting out

243

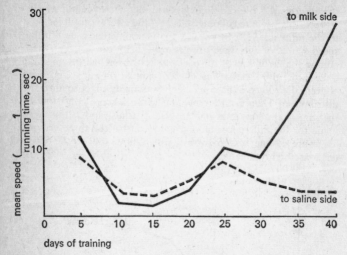

Figure 4 Speed of run to milk versus speed of run to isotonic saline for animals receiving injections via fistula. The curve represented by the solid line in this figure is the same as the bottom curve in Figure 3 except that the scale has been considerably magnified

or becoming counteracted by the reward effects.* From the fifteenth trial on there is a progressive increase in the speed of

* That such discomfort can be produced is suggested by the results of a fourth group of five animals which were run as a part of the original design of this experiment but relegated to this footnote because the behavior and results suggested an artefact from discomfort produced by the injection. These animals were run under exactly the same conditions as the first group except that during habituation and training their injection was given almost ten times faster so that 14 cc. required between 45 sec. and 1 min. During the last 15 free-choice trials, chi-square tests showed that three of these animals were consistently going to the saline side ($p = \cdot01, \cdot001, \cdot001$) and two to the milk side ($p = \cdot01$ and $\cdot001$). Because the avoidance of the milk side showed up so early in training, none of the differences between the first and last 15 free-choice trials is reliable for the animals preferring saline, but for the animals choosing milk these differences are reliable at $\cdot04$ and $\cdot001$ levels, respectively. The fact that the animals preferring the saline side had to be forced (their average speed to saline on the last five trials was somewhat slower than that of the animals injected at the normal rate, but their average speed to milk was much slower) suggests that they were avoiding milk rather than approaching saline. Because milk curdles and leaves the stomach much more slowly than saline, it seems reasonable to assume that the fast injection of large amounts of milk would be more likely to produce distress than similar injections of isotonic saline.

running to the compartment where milk was injected while the speed to the compartment where saline was injected remains at approximately the same low level. The difference in the speeds of running to the milk and saline compartments (as calculated by t tests for the sum of the log times on the last 5 trials to each) would be expected in the predicted direction by chance less than 1 time in 100. It is another indication of the reward effect of injecting milk directly into the stomach.

Discussion

The results show (a) that milk injected directly into the stomach can serve as a reward to produce learning, and (b) that milk taken normally by mouth serves as a stronger reward to produce faster learning. Both results are exactly what was predicted from the drive-reduction hypothesis and the evidence (1, 4) that milk by fistula produces a prompt reduction in the strength of hunger while milk by mouth produces an even greater reduction.

The reward effect of milk injected directly into the stomach would not readily be predicted from Sheffield's (9, 10, 11) hypothesis that reinforcement is critically related to the ability of the goal object to elicit a dependable, prepotent response when presented.

The faster learning of the animals which received milk by mouth would be expected from the fact that this procedure produces a greater reduction in the strength of the drive. It would also be predicted from the fact that one would expect the cues involved in oral ingestion to have learned reward value, but if one holds to a strict drive-reduction hypothesis of learned rewards, this reduces to the same factor of drive-reduction (5, 6, 7). It is also quite possible that the reduction in the strength of drive is not quite as prompt when food is injected into the stomach as when it is taken by mouth.

Finally, the fact that the injected animals learned to choose the milk side serves as a control to rule out the possibility that the effects of the injection of milk into the stomach in the preceding experiments (1, 4) were only the production of nausea rather than a reduction in the strength of the hunger drive.

Summary

1. Seventeen male, albino rats had small plastic fistulas sewn into their stomachs. Then they were given training trials during which they received enriched milk when they went to the correct side of a simple T maze and isotonic saline when they went to the in-

correct side. They were divided into three groups trained respectively under the following conditions:

a. The substances, 14 cc. of milk for a correct or saline for incorrect choice, were injected directly into the stomach at the rate at which the animals normally drank.

b. Dishes containing 14 cc. of milk for a correct or saline for an incorrect choice were inserted into the end of the goal box immediately after the animal had made its choice.

c. Dishes containing 14 cc. of milk or saline were inserted into the end of the goal box after a delay of 7 min. 35 sec., the time required to complete an injection for the animals in *a.*

2. All animals were given two trials a day motivated by hunger. On the first trial the animal was free to go in either direction; this trial was used to measure correct choices. On the second trial, given 4 hr. later, the animal was forced to go in the opposite direction and receive the other substance.

3. The animals which received injections directly into their stomachs learned to choose the milk side within 40 days of training. Both the decrease in errors and the faster speed to the milk side were statistically highly reliable.

4. The animals which received milk by mouth, either immediately or after a delay, learned faster than those which received milk via fistula. The differences in both the speed and error scores were statistically reliable.

5. These results show that milk injected directly into the stomach serves as a reward to produce learning, but that milk taken normally by mouth serves as a stronger reward to produce faster learning. The results confirm the prediction from the drive-reduction hypothesis of reinforcement and fail to confirm the prediction from the prepotent consummatory response hypothesis of reinforcement. They serve as a control to show that the decrements in instrumental and consummatory responses observed in preceding experiments were produced by reductions in hunger rather than by nausea.

References
1. Berkun, M. M., Kessen, M. L., & Miller, N. E. Hunger-reducing effects of food by stomach fistula versus food by mouth measured by a consummatory response. *J. comp. physiol. Psychol.*, 1952, 45, 550–554.
2. Hull, C. L. *Principles of behavior.* New York: D. Appleton-Century, 1943.
3. Hull, C. L., Livingston, J. R., Rouse, R. O., & Barker, A. N. True, sham, and esophageal feeding as reinforcements. *J. comp. physiol. Psychol.*, 1951, 44, 236–245.

4. Kohn, M. Satiation of hunger from stomach versus mouth feeding. *J. comp. physiol. Psychol.*, 1951, 44, 412–422.

5. Miller, N. E. Learnable drives and rewards. In S. Stevens (Ed.), *Handbook of experimental psychology.* New York: Wiley, 1951.

6. Miller, N. E. Comments on multiple-process conceptions of learning. *Psychol. Rev.*, 1951, 58, 357–363.

7. Miller, N. E., & Dollard, J. *Social learning and imitation.* New Haven, Conn.: Yale Univer. Press, 1941.

8. Miller, N. E., Kessen, M. L., & Kohn, M. The drive-reducing and reinforcing effects of food injected via fistula into the stomach. *Amer. Psychologist*, 1951, 6, 280–281. (Abstract.)

9. Sheffield, F. D., & Roby, T. B. Reward value of a non-nutritive sweet taste. *J. comp. physiol. Psychol.*, 1950, 43, 471–481.

10. Sheffield, F. D., Wulff, J. J., & Backer, R. Reward value of copulation without sex drive reduction. *J. comp. physiol. Psychol.*, 1951, 44, 3–8.

11. Sheffield, F. D. The contiguity principle in learning theory. *Psychol. Rev.*, 1951, 58, 362–367.

12. Spence, K. W. The role of secondary reinforcement in delayed reward learning. *Psychol. Rev.*, 1947, 54, 1–8.

35 D. Premack

Reversibility of the Reinforcement Relation

Reproduced in full from *Science*, 1962, Vol. 136, pp. 255–57.

Abstract. – Parameters were identified for the rat which both made drinking more probable than running and running more probable than drinking. In the same subjects, depending upon which parameters were used, running reinforced drinking and drinking reinforced running. This relationship suggests that a 'reward' is simply any response that is independently more probable than another response.

Food or water are used customarily to reinforce the bar press or running, but it is not asked, Can this relation be reversed? Will the bar press or running reinforce eating or drinking? The traditional account of reinforcement does not generate this question, for it assumes categorical reinforcers, food and water being prime examples (1). Furthermore, the traditional account was not changed basically even by the finding that light and sound also reinforce (2). To incorporate these 'new' reinforcers the reward category was simply enlarged, admitting unforeseen kinds of stimulation, and inferring additional drives and needs. The logic of the traditional account remains one that distinguishes between categories of positive and neutral events; only the events to which this logic is applied have changed.

We have proposed a model of positive reinforcement (3) whose major assumption is simply that, for any pair of responses, the independently more probable one will reinforce the less probable one. In this model the traditional vocabulary of drive, reward, and goal becomes either meaningless or misleading, for the model leads to the predictions that (i) the eating or drinking response is itself reinforcible (4) and, more important, (ii) the reinforcement relation is reversible.

Are there intervals of time in which eating or drinking are less probable than certain other responses, as well as other intervals in which the probabilities are reversed? Although the present model cannot make such predictions, but predicts only after the response probabilities are given, parameters were recently found in the rat that satisfy both conditions.

With free access to both food and an activity wheel, but access to water for only 1 hour per day, mean total drinking time for a group of six female rats was about 4 minutes, and mean total running time in the same period was only about 0·9 minute. With free access to both food and water, but access to the wheel for only 1 hour per day, mean total drinking time per hour was only about 28 seconds, and mean total running time in the same period was about 329 seconds. Thus it should be possible, according to the present model, not only to reinforce drinking with running but also to reverse the reinforcement relation in the same subject merely by changing from one set of parameters to the other.

Apparatus used to test these predictions was a modified Wahmann activity wheel equipped with a brake and a retractable drinkometer. Joint access to the wheel and water was provided by releasing the brake on the wheel and moving the drinkometer up to a hole on a stationary plate enclosing the open face of the wheel. Drinking contingent upon running was arranged by retracting the drinkometer, freeing the wheel, and making availability of the drinkometer contingent upon running. Conversely, running contingent upon drinking was arranged by locking the wheel, moving in the drinkometer, and making release of the wheel contingent upon drinking.

Because the outcome for the conventional experiment was not in doubt, the case of running contingent upon drinking was tested first. Four female albino rats, about 200 days old, Sprague-Dawley strain, were given daily 1-hour conditioning sessions, followed by daily 1-hour extinction and reconditioning sessions. A fixed ratio schedule was used in which each five licks freed the wheel for 10 seconds. Throughout this training, food and water were continuously available in the home cage; after the last reconditioning session, water was removed from the home cage, and on the next day training was begun with the reverse contingency – drinking contingent upon running.

With running contingent upon drinking, total drinking time was increased in all subjects by a factor of from three to five. For operant-level drinking, with only the tube present, mean total drinking time was about 28 sec/hr; with both tube and wheel present, it was 23 sec/hr; and with running contingent upon drinking, 98 sec/hr. Moreover, the first extinction session further increased mean total drinking time to about 175 sec/hr.

Samples of all phases of training are shown in the Esterline Angus records of Fig. 1. The top records show the reinforcement of drinking by running in rats S-4 and S-6, characterized by alternating bursts of licking and running. A representative example of extinction – drinking no longer producing the oppor-

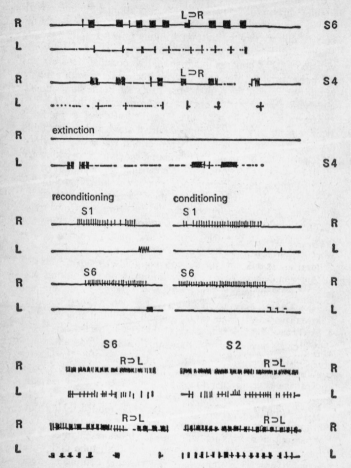

Figure 1 Esterline Angus samples of all phases of training. Top three records show the reinforcement of drinking by running $(L \supset R)$ and subsequent extinction of drinking. Middle records compare the lick pattern for conditioning and reconditioning. Bottom records show the reinforcement of running by drinking $(R \supset L)$. R designates running, where each 90 degrees of turn deflected the needle, and L represents drinking, where each lick deflected the needle. Records read from right to left

tunity to run – is provided by the record for rat S-4; both the atypical periodicity and brevity of the lick bursts have largely disappeared. Of interest in the middle records, which show fine-grain examples of conditioning and reconditioning, is the recovery of the noninstrumental lick pattern that followed extinction. Throughout the original conditioning, the five licks or more that were required for running tended to be dispersed, whereas during reconditioning, licking occurred in bursts typical of routine drinking. The picture is completed by the two bottom records; these provide examples of the evident increase in running subsequently produced by the conventional case, where 450 degrees of wheel turn were required for first 10 seconds, and later, 5 seconds of tube-time. Hence parameters were demonstrated which made running more probable than drinking, and vice versa, and subsequently, that it was possible not only to reinforce drinking with running, but also to reverse the reinforcement relation in the same subjects merely by changing from one set of parameters to the other (5).

References and Notes

1. C. L. Hull, *Principles of Behavior* (Appleton-Century, New York, 1943), pp. 68–83; B. F. Skinner, *The Behavior of Organisms* (Appleton-Century, New York, 1938), pp. 61–115.
2. G. W. Barnes, G. B. Kish, *J. Exptl. Psychol.* 62, 164 (1961); R. A. Butler, *J. Comp. and Physiol. Psychol.* 46, 95 (1953); G. B. Kish, *ibid.* 48, 261 (1955); M. H. Marx, R. L. Henderson, C. L. Roberts, *ibid.* 48, 73 (1955).
3. D. Premack, *Psychol. Rev.* 66, 219 (1959); *J. Exptl. Psychol.* 61, 163 (1961).
4. D. R. Williams and P. Teitlebaum [*Science* 124, 1294 (1956)] have reported the negative reinforcement of drinking – drinking turning off electric shock – but I can find no report of the positive reinforcement of eating and drinking responses.
5. This report is based on a paper read at the meeting of the Psychonomic Society, New York, 1961. This work was aided by grant M-3345 from the National Institute of Mental Health and by grant G-19574 from the National Science Foundation.

Limitations of the Consummatory Response
Hypothesis of Reinforcement

Excerpt from N. E. Miller, Some reflections on the law of effect produce
a new alternative to drive reduction. In M. R. Jones (Ed.), *Nebraska
Symposium on Motivation*, University of Nebraska Press, Lincoln, 1963,
pp. 65–112.

Sheffield, Roby, and Campbell (1954) have proposed a drive-induction hypothesis. According to this hypothesis, the consummatory response tends to be conditioned to responses immediately preceding it, but since it cannot occur in the absence of the goal object, frustrational excitement is elicited which serves as an increase in drive that energizes whatever response is occurring at that time. The cues involved in responses leading most directly to the consummatory responses are conditioned most strongly to it. Hence, when the subject is oscillating at a choice point, the responses leading most directly to the goal produce the most exciting cues, are more invigorated by this excitement, and are most likely to be continued. Such responses are also conditioned by contiguity and hence are more likely than others to be elicited immediately on subsequent trials. It can be seen that this hypothesis accounts for the increase in vigor which is difficult for Guthrie.

One of the main difficulties with this hypothesis is that it places too much emphasis on the peripheral consummatory response. For example, an animal's consumption of a new food is not necessarily avid immediately after the feedback from the initial bite, but increases gradually with experience. How is this increase in the consummatory response learned? The problem is still more pointed in an experiment like the one performed by Harris, *et al.* (1933) in which animals deficient in Vitamin B apparently did not have any immediate preference for a solution containing a minute amount of the purified extract, but could learn to prefer such a solution, provided it was given a distinctive flavor. That this consummatory response was not controlled by immediate feedback from the taste of the vitamin was shown by the fact that, when the vitamin was put in a different solution, they only gradually learned to abandon the original one and go to the new one. It is difficult to account for such learning on the assumption that the vigor of performance of the peripheral consummatory response is the crucial factor in determining reinforcement. Observations by Weiskrantz and Cowey (1963) present a similar difficulty. Such results suggest that reinforcement is the crucial factor in determining the vigor of the consummatory response.

Furthermore, Marion Kessen and I (1952) have shown that rats will learn to go to the side of a T maze where milk is delivered directly into their stomachs, thereby completely by-passing the consummatory response. It is barely possible that the slight amount of reflex licking sometimes observed while milk is being given via fistula could be considered enough of a consummatory response to mediate such learning. But this way out is not very adequate because such licking occurs in the absence of the goal object, and hence presumably could become anticipatory without being blocked by absence of a goal object. Therefore, Sheffield's frustrational mechanism for inducing excitement does not seem to be present.

It would be still more difficult to account for learning reinforced by injecting sugar or water directly into the bloodstream of a hungry or thirsty animal. But I do not like the techniques that Coppock and Chambers (1954) have used to get presumably positive results on this problem, because they involve measuring the total time spent on one of two sides of an apparatus in which the injection is given. To give an extreme example, if subjects continue to explore randomly, but are completely knocked out every time they go to the injection side, it is obvious that they will spend more time there, without necessarily having learned to go there. That is why techniques for measuring frequency of choice are better. A recent experiment by Clark, *et al.* (1961) indicates that a thirsty monkey will learn to press a bar to get isotonic saline injected into his bloodstream, but will not press when he is satiated on water. We need more experiments of this kind.

Finally, in an addendum to a mimeographed paper for which he should not be held too accountable because it is unpublished, Sheffield (1954) deals with the problem of learning to escape and avoid painful shocks by assuming that the conditioned induction of the drive of fear functions as excitement. Therefore, it would lead to approach to an electric shock if it were not for the incompatible responses elicited by the shock. With admirable clarity he says: 'Any punishment situation which could be rigged to prevent the moving forward of an incompatible terminal response would be expected to produce the paradoxical strengthening of the response that leads to punishment.'

Incidentally, any hypothesis that attributes generalized reinforcing value to *the elicitation of a prepotent response* may have trouble by predicting that the subject will learn the response leading to an electric shock which elicits a prepotent wild leap. The same difficulty applies to Premack (1959) who concludes that whenever a strong response, emitted at a higher rate, is made contingent upon the prior occurrence of a weaker response, emitted at a lower rate, the latter is reinforced by the former. A rat's rate of running in an activity wheel can be greatly increased by avoidance training in which every time that he stops he receives a shock that can be turned off only by running. But I do not believe that such an increase in the rate of wheel turning would increase the rate at which rats would press a bar to unlock the wheel and turn on the shock which would produce the fast rate. Nevertheless, the experiment should be tried.

References

Clark, R., Schuster, C. R., & Brady, J. V. Instrumental conditioning of jugular self-infusion in the Rhesus monkey. *Science*, 1961, 133, 1829–1830.

Coppock, H. W., & Chambers, R. M. Reinforcement of position preference by automatic intravenous injections of glucose. *J. comp. physiol. Psychol.*, 1954, 47, 355–357.

Guthrie, E. R. *The psychology of learning* (Revised). New York: Harper, 1952.

Harris, L. J., Clay, J., Hargreaves, F. J., & Ward, A. Appetite and choice of diet. The ability of the vitamin B deficient rat to discriminate between diets containing and lacking the vitamin. *Proc. Roy. Soc.*, B113, 1933, 161–190.

Miller, N. E., & Kessen, M. L. Reward effects of food via stomach fistula compared with those of food via mouth. *J. comp. physiol. Psychol.*, 1952, 45, 550–564.

Premack, D. Toward empirical behavior laws: I. Positive reinforcement. *Psychol. Rev.*, 1959, 66, 219–233.

Sheffield, F. D. A drive-induction theory of reinforcement. Mimeographed manuscript of paper read at Psychology Colloquium, Brown University, November, 1954.

Sheffield, F. D., Roby, T. B., & Campbell, B. A. Drive-reduction versus consummatory behavior as determinants of reinforcement. *J. comp. physiol. Psychol.*, 1954, 47, 349–354.

Weiskrantz, L., & Cowey, A. The aetiology of food reward in monkeys. *Anim. Behav.*, 1963, 11, (in press).

IX Sensory Effects as the Basis of Reinforcement

Exposure of animals to the onset of mild lights and sounds, as well as to the taste of non-nutritive sweet substances, have been shown to have positive reinforcing properties. On the other hand, intense stimuli lead to responses that would terminate such stimuli. These observations have led to the suggestion that qualitative and quantitative aspects of *sensory* stimulation *per se* may be the prime determinants of reinforcement. Among the investigators who have studied such 'sensory reinforcement' are Hurwitz, Guttman, and Pfaffmann.

37 H. M. B. Hurwitz

Conditioned Responses in Rats Reinforced by Light

Reproduced in full from *British Journal of Animal Behaviour*, 1956, Vol. 4, pp. 31–3.

It has been generally held that rats, being primarily nocturnal animals, are light shy. A number of investigators have used strong light as an adversive stimulus to set up and sustain avoidant conditioned responses. However, recent research completed in our laboratory shows that weak light may serve as an incentive and lead to the formation of strong adient conditioned responses. Both Girdner (1953) and Henderson (1953) have made similar observations in recently reported, independently conducted, investigations.

In our experiments twelve male hooded rats, $2\frac{1}{2}$ months old, drawn from the inbred colony maintained by the Department, were placed on a rigorous feeding schedule. Unlimited food was made available once daily between 6 and 8 p.m. During feeding time, the laboratory was darkened, so as to minimise the association of food and light. This regime was started six weeks before the beginning of the experiments and was maintained throughout the experimental period. The animals were allocated at random to three groups, each of four animals. Each group underwent a different series of tests in a very simple apparatus, consisting of a rectangular box (of base $8\frac{1}{2}'' \times 12\frac{1}{2}''$ and $12\frac{1}{2}''$ high), placed into a sound-proofed dark chamber. A lever ($\frac{1}{2}'' \times \frac{1}{2}''$) responding to 3 g. pressure was mounted $3''$ above floor level in one corner. A 6-volt light bulb was mounted on a wall at the opposite end of the box, $10''$ above floor level.

Three experimental conditions were set up.

Box totally dark except that when the lever was pressed a light (5·2 candle power) was switched on for as long as the lever was held down; alternatively, the lever switched a light off.

Box illuminated by a 5·2 c.p. lamp except that for the period the lever was held down, the light was extinguished.

Box in total darkness at all times.

Each animal subjected successively and for a varying number of trials to the experimental conditions indicated in Table 1.

After six weeks of the feeding schedule each animal was placed into the box for a half-hour daily session before feeding time. At

Table 1

Survey of the Design of the Study

Group	Successive order of experimental conditions	No. of ½-hour trials	Experimental Conditions
A (4 animals)	A I	10	Lever pressing in dark box has no after-effect
	A II	12	Lever turns a light on
	A III	10	Lever turns light off
B (4 animals)	B I	5	Lever turns a light off
	B II	10	Lever turns a light on
C (4 animals)	C I	16	Lever turns a light on
	C II	6	Lever pressing in dark box has no after-effect
	C III	10	Lever turns a light on

the conclusion of each trial, the animal was placed in a darkened feeding cage, to exclude any association between light and food. This procedure should favour the association of darkness and food. Records were obtained of the total *number* of lever pressing responses on each trial, the *duration* of each lever pressing response and the *rate* of lever pressing response in successive trials. The present report deals mainly with the first of these measures, which are summarised in Figures 1-3.

Two features of the results should be noted.

Experiment A-I shows that when the lever pressing is unattended by any perceptible after-effect in a dark box, the frequency of response stabilises in the present instance at about 30 responses per half-hour. When, subsequently, the response is instrumental in switching on the light response frequency immediately increases and after an initial high value stabilises at about 85 responses per half-hour. The scores under condition A-II and A-III or A-II and B-I show that the higher response frequency observed under

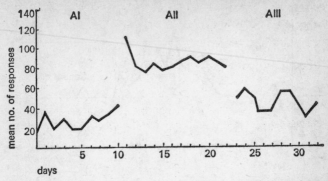

Figure 1 Mean number of Responses per daily half-hour trial.
AI: lever → no after-effect; AII: lever → light on; AIII: lever → light off

conditions A-II, B-II, C-I and C-III is correlated with the *onset* of light: when the animal's actions turn off the light, as in experiments A-III and B-I, the response frequency does not differ significantly from conditions A-I. An interpretation of similar results proposed separately by Girdner (1953) and Marx, *et al.* (1955) that the animals' performance and learning is due to curiosity or novelty, cannot readily be reconciled with these observations. Such an interpretation predicts no difference in the frequencies of response between conditions of switching on or switching off the light.

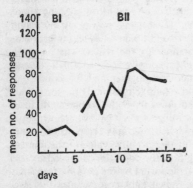

Figure 2 Mean number of Responses per daily half-hour trial.
BI: lever → light off; BII: lever → light on

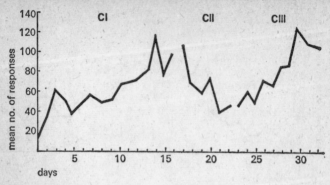

Figure 3 Mean number of Responses per daily half-hour trial.
CI: lever → light on; CII: lever → no after-effect; CIII: lever → light on

The results of experiments A-II and C-I contrast sharply, despite identical conditions of observation. Throughout the 16 trials of experiment C-I, the frequency of response per trial increased and again increased in experiment C-III, whereas the response occurred most frequently on the very first trial of experiment A-II. A tentative explanation of this difference will be attempted elsewhere. For the present, our main interest lies in the steady increase of the frequency score throughout successive trials in experiment C-I, the decline in response frequency during experiment C-II and the recovery of high response frequency in the final experiment C-III. These results are comparable to conditioning, experimental extinction and reconditioning phenomena described by Skinner (1938) and previously by Pavlov (1927) in his classic studies of conditional reflex learning, and are being interpreted in this manner by the writer. The increasing frequency of response during successive trials in C-I is regarded as indicative of the systematic strengthening of a conditioned response based on the incentive (and reinforcing) function of light. When the incentive is dissociated from the response, as in experiment C-II, a gradual waning of the response (shown by a decrease in frequency) is predicted, the rate of response deterioration being a joint function of the incentive value of the reinforcing stimulus and the strength of the conditioned response.

These interpretations are supported by the data of *duration* on the lever-holding response. When light accompanies the lever-response, the average duration of the response is significantly longer than under conditions A-I. We have recorded durations extending up to 5 minutes, although the mean value in experiment C-I is 2·3 seconds as compared to 0·3 seconds in A-I.

When the light is kept on for extended periods, the animal vigorously surveys the box, making rapid, scanning-like head movements. The rate of pressing was not regular. Responses tended to be bunched, each 'burst' being separated by periods of 'silence'. During a response burst the animal would stand on its hind legs in front of the lever, resting one or both of its paws on the lever, the head held at right angles pointing to the light source. An infra-red film is being made to discover the animal's behaviour during 'silent' periods. The analysis of the animal's total activity during the response-bursts and silent periods should help to clarify the obviously puzzling problem inherent in the experimental results so far cited.

The above results are relevant to the controversy about the importance of homeostatic mechanisms in animal learning which continues to feature prominently in the literature on the psychology of learning. Some writers (Hull, 1943) hold that the conditioning of responses is only possible in the presence of stimuli representative of need stabilisation. So far, at least, it has been extraordinarily difficult to adduce evidence inimical to this theory. However, since it is not obvious how light – in the case of rats – is instrumental to the stabilisation of organic needs, it seems that the experiments reported here, as well as those reported by Girdner (1953), Henderson (1953) and Marx *et al.* (1955) call for an alternative approach to the central problems of conditioning.

Acknowledgement

This study has been supported by a grant from the Central Research Fund, University of London.

References
Girdner, J. B., Ph.D. Thesis, Duke Univ. Library (1953).
Henderson, R. K., Ph.D. Thesis, Missouri Univ. Library (1953).
Hull, C. L. (1943). *Principles of behavior*.
Marx, M., Henderson, R., & Roberts, C. (1955). *J. comp. physiol. Psychol.*, 58, 73–76.
Pavlov, I. P. (1927). *Conditional reflexes*.
Skinner, B. (1938). *The behavior of organisms*.

Equal Reinforcement Values for Sucrose and Glucose
Solutions Compared with Equal Sweetness Values[1]

Reproduced in full from *Journal of Comparative and Physiological
Psychology*, 1954, Vol. 47, pp. 358–61.

A previous study of sucrose as a reinforcing agent (4) has shown
that the rate of bar pressing of rats under periodic reinforcement
is a logarithmic function of the percentage sucrose concentration
used as reinforcing agent, over the range of 4 per cent to 32 per
cent. On the hypothesis that the reinforcing effects of sapient
substances are related to the magnitude of their effects upon
taste receptors, it should be possible to predict, for example, the
relative reinforcing effects of solutions of two sweet substances
if their relative sweetness is known. For humans, isosweetness
curves for many nutrient and nonnutrient chemical compounds
have been obtained (2), and MacLeod (7) has recently redeter-
mined the sucrose-glucose isosweetness function over the lower
portion of the solubility ranges of these substances.

In this study, the reinforcing effects of sucrose and glucose
solutions for rats are studied in the aperiodically reinforced bar-
pressing situation. For both substances, rate-concentration
functions over the range from 2 per cent to 32 per cent are sought
in the same group of Ss. Quantitative predictions concerning the
relationships of such rate-concentration functions are based upon
two premises: that equally sweet substances used as reinforcing
agents will yield equal rates of responding, and that the taste
receptors for sweet are very similar in rats and humans. The latter
is a tenable assumption on the evidence that rat preference
thresholds and human sweet-taste thresholds for sucrose and
glucose are comparable (9). These premises jointly lead to the
highly specific prediction that if an isosweetness curve is constructed from the rate-concentration curves by selecting pairs of
concentration values of the two substances which result in

1. This investigation was supported by research grant M-631 from the
National Institute of Mental Health of the National Institutes of Health,
Public Health Service, and by a grant from the Duke University Research
Council. Acknowledgment is made of the assistance of Maurice Siskel, Jr.
in carrying out the pilot studies prior to this experiment and of Mrs Paula L.
Kipnis and Norman J. Wilson in obtaining the data reported here.

equal rates of responding, the form and constants of such a curve will closely reproduce the curve obtained by psychophysical means.

Method

Apparatus

A set of four identically constructed Skinner boxes was used. These boxes and associated recording and control units are very similar to those described by Guttman and Estes (5). The animal is housed in a metal chamber with a transparent roof and a grill floor. This chamber is enclosed in a plywood and Celotex box to provide sound insulation. The animal's compartment is 10 in. long by 8 in. wide by $7\frac{3}{4}$ in. high. The bar is a rod of $\frac{3}{16}$-in. brass which projects 2 in. into the box through a hole near one side of the front wall and extends along the side wall. The magazine is a solenoid-operated dipper which delivers approximately 0·1 ml. of solution. The dipper opening is at floor level $\frac{1}{2}$ in. in front of the front wall and $2\frac{1}{2}$ in. from the side wall opposite the bar. Bar-pressing responses are recorded by means of a set of graphic cumulative recorders and also by means of magnetic counters. The aperiodic schedule of reinforcements (1-min. mean interreinforcement interval) was provided by a Skinner-Gerbrands punched-film programmer.

Subjects

Eight male white rats bred in the Duke University Medical School colony were used as Ss. They were 305 to 315 days old at the start of the experiment, and had been used in exploratory studies related to the present experiment. All Ss were trained to bar press for water under 22-hr. thirst and were given 1100 continuous water reinforcements at ages 107 to 121 days. This was followed by 1 hr. of periodic reinforcement on a 1-min. schedule. All Ss were then food deprived and water sated and tested under periodic reinforcement with various sucrose and glucose solutions for twelve days. Four Ss were then used in a series of further exploratory studies in which they were run a total of approximately 87 hr. under periodic and aperiodic reinforcement with sucrose, glucose, or water as reinforcing agents. The other group of four Ss was not used again until the present study, approximately five months after their initial tests. The four very experienced Ss will be referred to as the VE group, and the other four as the ME (moderately experienced) group. All Ss were treated identically in the present experiment.

Procedure

Each S was given one 50-min. session of aperiodically reinforced bar pressing with each of seven sucrose solutions and seven glucose solutions as reinforcing agents. In addition, each S received two 50-min. sessions with distilled water. For both sucrose and glucose the concentrations used were: 2·0, 3·2, 5·0, 8·0, 12·7, 20·1, and 32·0 per cent by weight. 'Percentage by weight' here means:

$$\frac{\text{weight of solute}}{\text{weight of solute} + \text{solvent}} \times 100.$$

This follows the terminology suggested in (8). The sucrose used was Franklin brand commercial granulated cane sugar. The glucose was C.P. d-glucose (Pfanstiehl). Distilled water was used as solvent. On a $\log_{10}$ scale these values are separated by ·2 log unit steps. The 16 experimental sessions occurred on successive calendar days, except for session 16 for the VE group, which was run on the seventeenth calendar day.

To determine the order of presentation of solutions, two 8 by 8 orthogonal random latin squares were selected, one for the seven sucrose concentrations, plus water, and one for the seven glucose concentrations, plus water. Animals were assigned to one margin of each square, experimental days to the other margin, and concentrations were substituted for the cell entries. The first day's treatment for four animals was taken from the sucrose square, and for the other four animals from the glucose square. On succeeding days, the Ss alternated between the squares. Two of the VE and two of the ME animals were started on sucrose, and the remaining four on glucose.

During the experiment and for several days preceding, Ss were restricted to 1-hr. eating of dry Purina pellets immediately after the running time. They had free access to water in their home cages.

Results and Discussion

The empirical rate-concentration curves based on the data for all Ss are shown in Figure 1. It can be seen that rate of responding for sucrose is everywhere above the rate for the corresponding concentration of glucose. This is the general relation which must obtain if the prediction based upon relative sweetness is to hold, since sucrose is sweeter for the human observer.

The rate-concentration curves for the VE and ME groups separately are quite similar to those in Figure 1. The curves for the ME group contain irregularities not present in the data for the VE group, indicating that in this type of experiment the effect of practice is largely to improve the smoothness of the functions.

The degree of correspondence between the present data and those obtained in human equal-sweetness experiments may be seen in Table 1, where the four pairs of sucrose and glucose concentrations judged equally sweet by MacLeod's three Ss are listed (7). Since MacLeod specified his concentrations in terms of grams of solute in 100 cc. of solution, his percentages have been converted to the present scale by the use of specific gravity tables. For sucrose, the density table in the *Handbook of Chemistry and Physics* (10) was used. For glucose, densities were obtained by means of the formula: $d = 0.99840 + 0.003788p + 0.00001412p^2$,

sucrose and glucose functions were monotonic up to 40 per cent. In effect, questions of reliability of both sets of data preclude for the present any final statement regarding the confirmation of the experimental hypothesis for higher concentration values.

A point of interest concerns the reinforcement thresholds for sucrose and glucose. The reinforcement threshold has been defined (4) as that value of reinforcing stimulation which will produce conditioned response strength just in excess of the unconditioned strength of that response. In the present instance, reinforcement thresholds might be estimated by extrapolating the rate-concentration functions toward the origin and finding their respective intercepts with the base line established by the background stimulation provided by water and the operation of the magazine. Since the present curves are not linear, such extrapolations have not been attempted, but it can nonetheless be seen that the reinforcement threshold for sucrose is probably lower than that for glucose. This is consistent with the relation between the absolute sensory thresholds for these substances in humans. Moreover, it is not incautious to suggest that the values of the absolute limens (about 0·5 per cent for sucrose, and about 1 per cent for glucose) would provide approximately correct intercepts for the present rate-concentration curves on the water + magazine sound base line (Fig. 1).

Summary and Conclusions

An attempt was made to see whether the relative reinforcing values of sucrose and glucose solutions for rats in the aperiodically reinforced bar-pressing situation are consistent with the relative sweetness of various concentrations of sucrose and glucose for human observers. Four very experienced and four moderately experienced rats were given one 50-min. test on each of seven sucrose and seven glucose concentrations, plus two tests with water reinforcement. Rate of bar pressing was found to be an increasing function of concentration of both substances, with the rate for sucrose always above that for glucose at a given concentration. Between about 2 per cent and 15 per cent sucrose, and between about 4 per cent and 20 per cent glucose, the pairs of concentrations which yield equal rates of responding are in close agreement with the pairs judged equally sweet by human Ss. Above these ranges, the correspondence is relatively inexact. The findings are considered compatible with the theoretical expectation that the effects of reinforcing stimuli upon receptors are closely related to their reinforcing properties.

References
1. Bates, F. J., and associates. *Polarimetry, saccharimetry and the sugars.* Washington: U.S. Government Printing Office, 1942.
2. Cameron, A. T. The sweet sense and the relative sweetness of sugars and other sweet substances. *Sci. Rep. Sugar Res. Found,. N.Y.,* 1947, No. 9.
3. Dahlberg, A. C., & Penczek, E. S. The relative sweetness of sugars as affected by concentration. *N.Y. St. Agric. Exp. Sta. tech. Bull.,* 1941, No. 258.
4. Guttman, N. Operant conditioning, extinction, and periodic reinforcement in relation to concentration of sucrose used as reinforcing agent. *J. exp. Psychol.,* 1953, 46, 213–224.
5. Guttman, N., & Estes, W. K. A modified apparatus for the study of operant behavior in the rat. *J. gen. Psychol.,* 1949, 41, 297–301.
6. Lichtenstein, P. E. The relative sweetness of sugars: sucrose and dextrose. *J. exp. Psychol.,* 1948, 38, 578–586.
7. MacLeod, S. The construction and attempted validation of sensory sweetness scales. *J. exp. Psychol.,* 1952, 44, 316–323.
8. Pfaffmann, C., Young, P. T., Dethier, V. G., Richter, C. P., & Stellar, E. The preparation of solutions for research in chemoreception and food acceptance. *J. comp. physiol. Psychol.,* 1954, 47, 93–96.
9. Richter, C. P., & Campbell, K. H. Taste thresholds and taste preferences of rats for five common sugars. *J. Nutrition,* 1940, 20, 31–46.
10. *Handbook of chemistry and physics.* (25th Ed.) Cleveland: Chemical Rubber Publishing Co., 1941.

39   C. Pfaffmann

The Pleasures of Sensation*

Reproduced in full from *Psychological Review*, 1960, Vol. 67, pp. 253–68.

That the senses are the channels of communication between the external environment and the nervous system is so much a truism that, except for those who espouse ESP, the senses are held to be the sole mediators of transactions between the organism and its environment. But students of the senses tend to emphasize primarily the nature of their information handling function, their discriminative capacities and limits as well as the physiological processes upon which they are based. Behavior theorists have given heed to such function in another context when they speak of the cue function of stimuli. According to these conceptions discriminative stimuli serve to steer behavior, to guide it or set the stage for the response. But in this paper I do not plan to elaborate upon such processes. Rather I wish to call attention to certain other aspects of sensory function.

In recent years, neurophysiologists have emphasized that sensory systems may mediate important functions other than discrimination. Attention has been focused on such generalized effects as arousal or alerting of the nervous system as a whole. Bremer (1935) first showed that a state of cerebral somnolence could be produced in experimental animals in which the cerebrum had been surgically isolated from the brainstem and its incoming afferent pathways. He attributed this to the interruption of sensory influx itself. Later analysis (Magoun, 1958) showed that the somnolence resulted largely from interference with the centripetal influence exerted by the reticular system, the ascending reticular activating or arousal system. Much subsequent research has shown that this system controls not only the state of arousal of the 'higher centers' of the nervous system, but that it can also modulate and influence activity within the classical sensory pathways themselves (Galambos, 1956; Hagbarth & Kerr, 1954; Hernandez-Peon, 1955). The reticular system may also be significant

* Slightly revised version of Presidential Address presented at the Annual Meeting of the Eastern Psychological Association, Atlantic City, April 13, 1959.

for a variety of other psychological processes (Lindsley, 1951; Schlosberg, 1954).

Most sense organs were found to have at least two central neural pathways. One, the well-known primary projection pathway via the thalamic sensory relays to the cerebral cortex, and the second, a nonspecific pathway by way of the reticular activating system with diffuse projections to the cortex and other neural structures. The reticular system is multimodal and intramodal, for it receives inputs from many modalities. The classical projection systems are specific to one modality and may be said to mediate primarily the cognitive or discriminatory sensory functions, the nonspecific system to mediate physiological and behavioral arousal (Magoun, 1958).

Psychologists especially have emphasized that stimuli may have still other functions, especially that of reinforcement (Hebb, 1958b; Keller & Schoenfeld, 1950; Skinner, 1953; Spence, 1956). This concept has most often been discussed in purely behavioral terms until the more recent studies of direct reinforcement by intracranial stimulation (Brady, 1958; Miller, 1957; Olds, 1958; Olds & Milner, 1954). In the ensuing discussion I shall limit myself to the so-called *primary reinforcement* for there is almost no limit to the range of previously neutral stimuli that, by one method or another, can be made to acquire reinforcing properties. That *primary aversive reinforcement* has been a function of stimuli has long been known, particularly for those stimuli of high intensity which elicit defense reactions or 'reflexes'. Certain of these seem qualitatively more prepotent as, for example, the pain of electric shock; 'rat runners' have frequently used shock as a primary negative reinforcer in their mazes or lever boxes. Some theorists hold that the pain reduction by shock termination provides the prototype of all reinforcement in the form of drive or tension reduction (Miller, 1959). The study of stimuli as *positive primary reinforcers* has, until recently, been restricted to those stimuli which are naturally related to such biologically functional activities as eating, drinking, or sexual activity. These stimuli could often be assigned a role in processes that mediated the satisfaction of a need or 'homeostatic drive'. Thus they were said to be related in some way to the primary biological drives. But there has been increasing evidence of late that sensory stimulation, divorced from its need or drive reducing concomitants, may function as a reinforcer in its own right. 'Exteroceptive motivation' sometimes called by such names as curiosity or stimulus change (Harlow, 1953; Hebb, 1958a; Kling, Horowitz, & Delhagen, 1956; Montgomery, 1952) has been demonstrated in a number of situations. And one theorist (Hebb, 1958a, pp. 451–467, 1958b) has attempted to link such reinforcement to the reticular activating system on the grounds that changes in level of activation are reinforcing, *per se*, depending upon the prevailing level at the time of stimulation. Thus, in sensory isolation experiments, 'the subject experienced great swings of motivation, which alternated between periods of apathy and intense desire to get back to a normal environment.' Hebb concludes, 'clearly man's motivation is a function of his exteroceptive stimulation.' Thus, although the reinforcing function of stimuli has long been recognized and is the stock in trade of many experimentalists, there is still considerable debate as to the basis for this effect. Does it depend upon some secondary effect as need reduction, drive reduction, or change in arousal patterns in the reticular activating system? Or can we attribute these effects to sensory stimulation directly?

In this paper I shall discuss the proposition that sensory stimulation *per se* together with its ensuing central neural events be considered as a prime determinant of reinforcement. In this context I shall discuss our experiments on the sense of taste with emphasis on the sensory physiology of taste-mediated motivation as revealed in the correlation between gustatory nerve discharges and food preferences in animals. This will lead into a consideration of the relation between hedonic processes and afferent nerve discharges, preference behavior, and taste reinforcement. Finally the relation between affective sensory processes and discriminative functions will be discussed in the light of some speculations on the physiological bases for these two aspects of sensory function and their significance in behavior.

Taste as a Model System

Although I began my studies of the sense of taste with a traditional sensory emphasis, it became increasingly apparent that the gustatory sense has certain unique features for the further understanding of behavior in general. Not only does the sense of taste possess selective receptor sensitivity that permits the discrimination of different taste stimuli, but these stimuli will elicit a number of specific consummatory responses: drinking and eating or, on the other hand, rejection. It is a relatively simple matter to demonstrate the control of behavior that taste stimuli can manifest by giving the animal a choice of water and taste solutions as Richter (1942) showed in his classic studies of self-selection. In

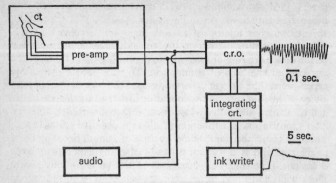

Figure 1 A block diagram of the recording apparatus showing two types of record. The upper trace shows a typical asynchronous, multifiber discharge from a large number of nerve fibers; the lower trace shows how such activity appears when processed through the integrator. (After a diagram in the American Journal of Clinical Nutrition)

addition, these stimuli can act as powerful reinforcers of instrumental responses leading to ingestion. Thus one and the same sense modality possesses easily demonstrable discriminative and reinforcing functions. In this respect it is an ideal model sensory-behavioral system in which to examine the relation between sensory stimulation and the reinforcing mechanisms in behavior as well as to permit the manipulation of the state of the organism by certain deprivation operations. I should, therefore, like to review briefly some of the methods we have employed and some of our experiments on taste,[1] to show how we look at the sensory continuum and its afferent neural input to the CNS which both motivates and directs behavior. In so doing I shall make use of the behavioral data of other workers, as well as the results of our own physiological and behavioral experiments. Our behavioral studies to date have utilized primarily the preferential ingestion method.

The Gustatory Afferent Discharge and Preference

Afferent nerves, like all nerves of the body, carry a series of electrical pulses which are the signs of impulse traffic up the sensory nerve. These can be recorded by appropriate electronic

1. These experiments have been supported in part by projects and grants from the Office of Naval Research, National Science Foundation, and the General Foods Corporation.

devices as shown in Figure 1 (cf. Pfaffmann, 1959). I shall present only data for the over-all activity in the taste nerve as afforded by the integrating circuit illustrated in the lower trace in Figure 1. The gustatory response curves for the cat are shown in Figure 2 in terms of the magnitude of the electrical signal generated in the nerve when each of the basic taste stimuli is applied to the tongue receptor surface. By such curves we can map out the taste sensitivity of different animals (Pfaffmann, 1955). These curves do not tell us about 'qualitative' differences in the nerve response. For that, analysis of the activity of single nerve fibers in the nerve is required (Pfaffmann, 1959).

From the point of view of behavior, the basic response to taste solutions is either one of acceptance or rejection so that the classical manifold of four tastes, salt, sour, bitter, and sweet, may be reduced to two behavioral classes: acceptance and rejection. We have used a typical two-bottle Richter-type preference situation to study such behavior in different species (Bare, 1949; Carpenter, 1956; Pfaffmann, 1957). Certain substances may be accepted at low, but rejected at the higher concentrations. This is so for NaCl in the rat where the well-known preference-aversion response can

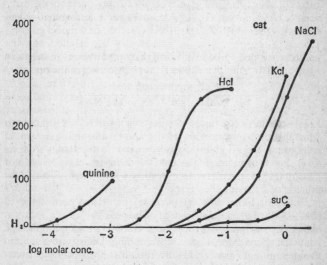

Figure 2 Curves of taste responses in the cat to four different taste stimuli as indicated by the integrated response method. (After a graph in the Journal of Neurophysiology)

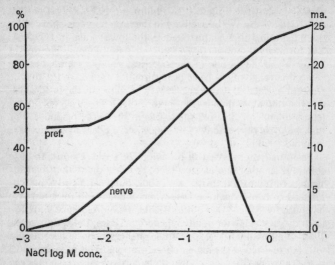

Figure 3 Preference response to different salt concentrations and magnitude of the chorda tympani nerve discharge in the rat. Ordinate to the left corresponds to preference response, ordinate to the right shows magnitude of integrator deflection. (After Pfaffmann 1958)

be demonstrated to be a function of concentration as shown in Figure 3. The solid line shows relative preference behavior

$$\frac{\text{cc. intake taste sol.}}{\text{cc. intake taste} + \text{cc. intake } H_2O}$$

Most acceptable solutions including sugar will follow this pattern when ingestion measures are used. Figure 3 also shows the neural response in the rat chorda tympani nerve to the same salt solutions. The broken line shows the integrated neural responses as a percentage of the maximum response observed. Clearly the preference behavior (i.e., response greater than 50%) is not apparent until some substantial neural input has been achieved (20%–30% of maximal discharge). The peak preference occurs at about 60% of maximal input, and the aversion rapidly sets in while the afferent discharge is still climbing. There is no change in the afferent input signal that corresponds to the behavioral inversion point – at least we have not been able to detect any such change. Up to the inversion point, the behavior parallels the afferent discharge curve as if the positive approach to the stimulus were due directly to the afferent input. The inversion and the subsequent aversion suggest the intrusion of a secondary 'stop' system. The fact that the inversion point is close to the isotonic point for sodium chloride solutions (0·9% NaCl [0·15M] is isosmotic with the body fluids) suggests that some postingestion or metabolic factor related to water balance has become operative.

Indeed Stellar, Hyman, and Samet (1954) have shown that the salinity of the gastric contents does affect the salt preference. Strong salt solutions intubated directly into the stomach depress the drinking of the more concentrated salt solutions. On the other hand, this is not the only stop factor for, in the same study, animals with an esophageal fistula showed the preference for hypotonic solutions and aversions for hypertonic ones even though the solutions never reached the stomach. Taste factors alone appear capable of eliciting the typical salt preference-aversion function. Thus the stop may indicate a change in 'sign' of the afferent input merely as a consequence of its increasing intensity. Perhaps there is a central-neural switching when the intensity of the afferent salt discharge reaches a critical value. Most intense sensory stimuli have aversive effects.

The relation of behavior to sensory afferent discharge for some of the other basic taste stimuli is shown in Figure 4. The upper figure shows the preference response curves for sugar, acid, and quinine as well as salt. We show here only the intakes above 50% for salt and sugar, remembering that at higher concentrations, the curves fall below the 50% value. The responses for acid and quinine are both aversions; no preference is shown. Note in the lower curves that the absolute magnitudes of neural response are quite different for the electrolytes as compared with the non-electrolytes. The behavioral response to quinine is quite definite and appears before there is a clear signal 'greater than the noise' for the nerve response. Here the behavioral indicator is the more sensitive. In an analogous way, the response to sucrose behaviorally is clear and definite, yet the neural response is disappointingly small. Intrinsic differences in the magnitude of the neural response, due in part to fiber size, etc., mean that sheer size of electrical signal itself cannot be correlated with behavioral effect. On the other hand, the range of effective stimulus concentration values in the two sets of determinations for each stimulus shows good agreement. The exact form or position of the preference aversion curves along the abscissa may be shifted depending upon such factors as order of presentation of stimuli, degree of hunger or physiological need, and amount of experience

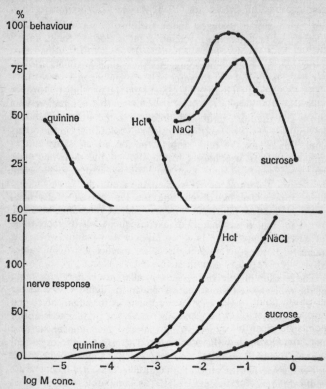

Figure 4 Composite graph of behavioral and electrophysiological responses in the rat. Upper graphs show the percentage preference (or aversion) as a function of stimulus concentration. The integrator responses in the chorda tympani nerve to the same stimuli are shown in arbitrary units in the lower graph

with the taste stimuli. It is the general nature of the relations between sensory input and preference that is shown in Figure 4.

The behavioral response to sugar solutions has been studied rather extensively, and it now seems possible to give an account of the start and stop factors in relation to sensory input. The preference curve just shown is based on ingestion of sugar over a 24-hour or longer period. Ingestion is a rising function of concentration to a peak preference when the typical inflection occurs and intake declines. This relation is found also in the single stimulus method. McCleary (1953) was one of the first to show that the intake of sugar solution is limited by an osmotic post-ingestion factor. Others have shown similar effects of gastric factors by studying the effects of intubation upon intake (Le-Magnen, 1955; Miller, 1957; Smith & Duffy, 1957; Stellar, Hyman, & Samet, 1954). The relative frequency of choice in the brief exposure preference method, however, does not show the inflection (Young & Greene, 1953). Here there appears to be a linear relation between the level of acceptability and logarithm of concentration. Guttman's (1953) study of the rate of bar pressing as a function of concentration of sucrose solution used as the reinforcement showed that, on a continuous schedule, rate increased for the weaker concentrations but showed an inversion at the higher value. On a periodic schedule, however, the rate of bar press was found to be linear with the log of the concentration. The latter schedule provides relatively little drinking per response. But bar press rate also can be depressed by intragastric injections (Smith & Duffy, 1955).

The relations between bar pressing on the two schedules and the preference ingestion data of Richter and Campbell (1940) are shown in Figure 5 together with the electrophysiological response curve for the rat (Hagstrom & Pfaffmann, 1959). Note that the inversion point in the two-bottle preference test is close to the inversion point of the continuous reinforcement schedule. Both points lie close to the top of the electrophysiological sensory function. On the periodic schedule, rate rises as the sensory function increases. The fact that there is no inversion where the amount ingested is small appears to implicate the postingestion factor as a primary stop mechanism (Collier & Siskel, 1959; Shuford, 1959). Such a formulation would agree with Young's (1959) statement 'that sugar solutions are basically hedonically positive for the rat as compared with salt which is first positive but then negative.'

Studies which compared the effect of two different sugars, glucose and sucrose, on consummatory behavior, choice response, and rate of bar press likewise point to the importance of post-ingestive factors. Isohedonic concentrations, equally accepted in short comparative tests, were not consumed in equal amount when presented singly for longer periods. The glucose solutions were consumed in less volume than their isohedonically matched sucrose solutions, and the cumulative mean intake of both sugars was linearly related to osmotic pressure for the longer periods (Shuford, 1959). In the Skinner box the concentration of these

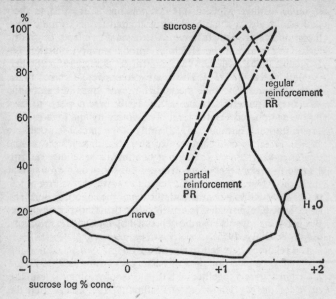

Figure 5 Composite graph showing the neural response to sucrose and the behavioral measures obtained by three different procedures in the rat. Pref. is the typical two bottle 24-hour ingestion preference method. Both the sucrose and water intakes are shown as smoothed curves, based on data by Richter and Campbell. RR is the rate of bar pressing during a test period for a small drop of sucrose on a regular reinforcement schedule, and PR is the same on a periodic reinforcement schedule, both based on Guttman (1953). Ordinates have been adjusted to make the maximum values in the original curves equal to 100

two sugars which give equal rate of response on an aperiodic schedule (i.e., have equal reinforcing value) corresponds to the isohedonic concentrations (Shuford, 1959; Young, 1957). Guttman (1954) previously showed that the equal reinforcing solutions correspond to the equally sweet concentrations found in psychophysical experiments (Cameron, 1947; MacLeod, 1952).

Hagstrom and I (1959) have also compared the relative efficacy of sucrose and glucose as gustatory stimuli for the rat, using the electrophysiological recording method. This could be done even though the magnitude of response to sugar is relatively small. Figure 6 shows the relative responses to the two sugars, and Figure 7 shows the comparison of the equi-effective concentrations of the two sugars as determined in the bar pressing experiment, in the preference choice test, and by the electrophysiological measure. All measures agree that sucrose is more effective than glucose of equimolar concentration, although the quantitative relation is not precise, for the electrophysiological data is curvilinear, the behavioral data, linear. However, it should be remembered that the physiological data reflect only the chorda tympani response and not the taste receptors at the back of the mouth. Perhaps the curvilinear relation between the behavioral and physiological measures arises from this.

Where ingestion is minimal, behavior and sensory effectiveness seem to go together. Actually the postingestion factor seems to be especially significant in preferences based on ingestion. The glucose preference threshold is lower than that for sucrose and the intake of glucose greater than that predicted by the sensory measures. Soulairac (1947) has shown that the relative preference for sugars in a typical two-bottle preference test is correlated with their relative rates of absorption from the gastrointestinal tract.

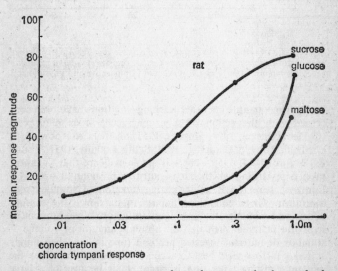

Figure 6 Integrator response magnitudes to three sugars for the rat chorda tympani nerve. Ordinate is relative magnitude, 100 equals the response to 0·01 M NaCl. (After graph in Journal of Comparative and Physiological Psychology)

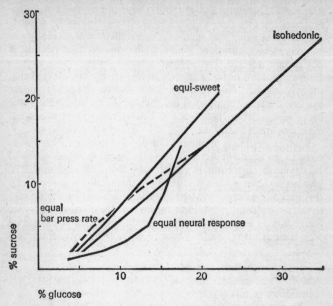

Figure 7 Equal response concentrations of glucose and sucrose for electro-physiological measures, equal bar press rates, equi-sweet solutions and iso-hedonic solutions. (After graph in Journal of Comparative and Physiological Psychology)

Experiments utilizing other learning situations have been concerned with the action of sugar or saccharin as reinforcers (Collier & Siskel, 1959; Hughes, 1957; Sheffield & Roby, 1950; Sheffield, Roby, & Campbell, 1954; Smith & Duffy, 1957; Young & Shuford, 1954, 1955). There is ample evidence that the sweet taste is rewarding whether it is nutritive or nonnutritive. Performance here too is an increasing function of stimulus concentration where conditions appear to maximize the sensory effects and minimize the postingestion factor. When amount or temporal factor is such that the absolute amount or volume of stimulus or nutrient ingested per unit time is low, then purely stimulus factors seem best to account for the results. When the amount consumed per unit is large, either because of a large amount of reinforcing agent or short time between presentations, then the secondary postingestive factors intrude. As Collier and Siskel (1959) point out, it should be possible with the proper combination of concentration, volume, interval between reinforcement, and number of reinforcements to obtain a monotonic stimulus function, a nonmonotonic function with inversion points at different volumes or concentrations, or even no relation at all between amount of reinforcement and performance.

These considerations presumably apply to Campbell's (1958) measurements of the JNR, the just noticeable reinforcing difference for sucrose solutions. He determined the minimal concentration increment necessary to produce a 75% preference for the stronger of a pair of sucrose solutions in a two-bottle preference situation. Stronger solutions required a larger concentration increment than did the weak ones, and the plot of JNR against stimulus concentration showed a U-shaped function reminiscent of the more familiar Weber intensity discrimination functions. The resemblance may be due only in part to the properties of the sensory input because, as we have just shown, preference is the composite of sensory as well as postingestion factors. The osmotic effects of the stronger sugar solutions might be particularly strong. This situation contrasts with the JNR functions for the noxious stimuli where the stimulus itself may be more directly the source of the reinforcement uncomplicated by secondary factors (Campbell, 1958).

Thus we see that sensory stimulation of the mouth receptors, especially of taste, has a direct relevance for the control of ingestive behavior and the instrumental responses which lead to ingestion. Although a number of investigators have provided evidence that the mouth receptors may be bypassed and that learning can still take place, all such evidence shows that such learning is not as effective as when stimulation of the mouth receptors is included (Coppock & Chambers, 1954; Miller, 1957). Nearly all workers, whatever their theoretical predilections, have shown the importance of stimulation and 'sensory contact', some would say 'sensory satisfaction' (Smith & Duffy, 1957) in the reinforcement process. Indeed as Bindra (1959) concludes in his recent monograph on motivation: 'Whatever the interpretation, it seems clear that, up to a certain point, an increase in sensory stimulation is a positive reinforcer' (p. 134).

The fact that certain taste stimuli control ingestion directly appears to be biologically determined. Frings (1946) has pointed out that nearly all organisms accept sugar solutions. There are exceptions perhaps related to certain aspects of metabolic or other biochemical divergences among the species. Cats cannot taste or discriminate sugar solutions (Carpenter, 1956; Pfaffmann,

1955), and birds (Pick & Kare, 1959) do not appear to show strong sucrose preferences; but these examples are remarkable largely for their divergence from what otherwise appears to be a general rule. Further there is no convincing evidence that the 'sweet tooth', where it does exist, depends upon the concomitant nourishment. The drinking of nonnutritive saccharin solutions under prolonged exposure to them shows no sign of extinction such as might be expected if the preference for saccharin or 'sweet' were acquired by past association with nourishment (Sheffield & Roby, 1950). Here we have 'sweet for sweet's sake.'

On the other side of the coin, we have been able to show that a 'bitter' aversive stimulus can be made more acceptable *only temporarily* when it is paired with the alleviation of thirst in early infancy (Warren & Pfaffmann, 1958). Newborn guinea pigs were raised on a normally avoided solution of sucrose octaacetate (SOA) as the only source of water for a three-week period. At an older age these organisms showed the usual rejection of SOA. Gustatory stimuli, therefore, appear to be biologically determined as the instigator of consummatory or avoidance responses and as primary positive or negative reinforcing stimuli.

So far I have discussed the mechanisms of a variety of behaviors which appear to be under the control of sensory stimulation qua 'sensory stimulation'. I have not discussed the question of the affective or hedonic aspects of sensory stimulation, the pleasure of sensation, so to speak. To do so, I should now like to turn to other kinds of data derived from studies of man.

Hedonic Aspects of Sensory Stimulation

Of all the applied psychophysical fields, none has made greater use of the affective or hedonic rating scale methods, along with purely sensory testing procedures, than has the field of flavor technology. In a series of carefully controlled tests the Army Quartermaster Food Acceptance Laboratory (Pilgrim, 1957), using a ninepoint hedonic rating scale, has been able to predict, with good reliability, the actual choices of food and the acceptance of menus on the part of soldiers in the field. These ratings frankly ask such questions as the following:

like extremely – like very much – indifferent – dislike very much – etc.

In this case the hedonic ratings are not determined solely by stimulus properties of food, for other studies by the Quartermaster group have documented the important role played by familiarity and past experience. None the less, the frankly hedonic rating initiated by the sensory stimulation is a good predictor of actual acceptance and ingestion.

I have been impressed by the apparent similarity of our rat preference curves with those of hedonic value obtained many years ago by Engel (1928). In those experiments, subjects were asked to rate different intensities of taste stimuli as either pleasant, unpleasant, or indifferent. The data can be treated in a number of ways, but in Figure 8 we see the ratings of four different taste modalities expressed as percentage of pleasant ratings minus the percentage of unpleasant ratings for a group of seven observers

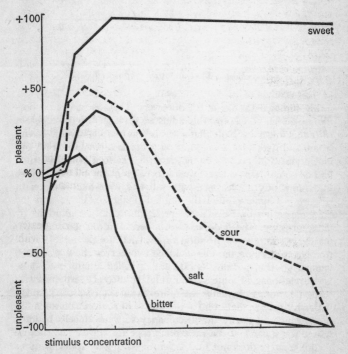

Figure 8 The preponderance of 'pleasant' or 'unpleasant' judgments in relation to the concentration of taste solution. Ordinate gives percentage 'pleasant' minus percentage 'unpleasant'. The abscissa is proportional to concentration, the full length of the base line standing for 40% cane sugar, 1·12% tartaric acid, 10% NaCl, and 0·004% quinine sulphate (by weight). (After Pfaffmann 1958)

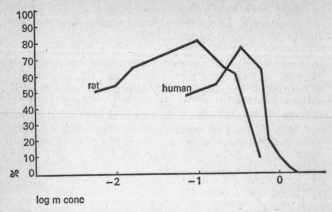

Figure 9 Comparison of animal preference and hedonic ratings of man in response to sodium chloride solutions. (After Pfaffmann 1958)

using summed ratings of all observers. The abscissa is proportional to the concentrations adjusted for each of the different stimulus solutions. Note that sugar begins at a slightly unpleasant value and rises with concentration to reach a plateau. Sour, bitter, and salt all start from indifference, rise to a peak, and then fall off to unpleasantness. Sweet is predominantly pleasant, bitter predominantly unpleasant, with salt and sour intermediate. In Figure 9 I have plotted the animal preference curve and the hedonic rating by Engel's Ss for sodium chloride solutions by concentration. The hedonic ratings here were computed simply as the percentage of the total ratings that are pleasant. Except for position along the abscissa, the two curves show a striking similarity. Beebe-Center (1951) earlier called attention to these same relations and compared the animal preference responses with hedonic ratings. Actually the more recent analysis of the postingestive factors that control the intake of sucrose solutions has done much to clarify the discrepancy between Engel's hedonic curve for sugar and the rat's preference for sugar. The sucrose hedonic curve does not turn down at the higher concentrations (see Figure 8). As noted earlier, rate of bar pressing on a periodic schedule and frequency of choice in the brief exposure test are likewise monotonically related to concentration. Thus hedonic rating and reinforcement bear the same relation to stimulus concentration.

284

In the preference-aversion curves for other substances, the stop mechanism may be sensory (gustatory) in origin or might arise from other than postingestive effects. If the taste of strong salt solutions is aversive *per se*, then we might expect that, regardless of reinforcement schedule, response will fall off above the optimal salt concentration in a manner resembling the 'falloff' in Engel's curves. The same might hold for saccharin which has a 'bitter' sensory component at the higher concentrations. Further study of these effects is needed.

I have been emphasizing stimulus properties as prime determinants of the hedonic effect, but let me hastily point out that specific training and experience may make some unpleasant odors and tastes acceptable or even preferred. I am reminded here of the whiskey drinker's development so aptly described by Brown (1955).

Straight whiskey, when first ingested, typically effects rather violent defense reactions. Because of this, the novice drinker usually begins with sweet liqueurs, 'pink ladies,' and wines, and slowly works his way through a series of beverages characterized by the gradual disappearance of cola and ginger ale additives. Finally, only plain water or even nothing need be mixed with the raw product. To the hardened drinker, straight whiskey does not taste bad—*not bad at all!* (It is thus that a product euphemistically labelled 'neutral spirits' becomes indeed psychologically neutral.)

Although this description appeared in defense of a drive reduction formulation of behavior and learning, the mere fact that drive reduction was supported and buttressed by the use of sweet and 'pleasant' stimuli seems to have been overlooked. There is no convincing evidence that the primary relation between hedonic tone and sensory stimulation is entirely acquired. Indeed, quite the converse seems to be true.

The relation of sensory stimulation to hedonic process has been noted by earlier workers. Sherrington (1906) noted that the stimulation of contact receptors, as contrasted with distance receptors, is characterized by strong affective tone and that the contact receptors stand in very close relation to consummatory responses. Stimulation of the touch receptors of the lips and touch and taste in the mouth initiates reflex movements that precede the act of swallowing. Troland (1928) spoke of three classes of stimulus reception: nociception, beneception, and neutroception. The principal nociceptor system was pain, but other examples were hunger, thirst, the taste of bitter, strong salts and acids, and certain foul or repugnant odors, etc. In the beneceptor class were the sense organs mediating erotic behavior, the taste of sugar, and certain other odors. Vision, hearing, touch, and proprioception were relegated to neutroception. Although Troland's criterion was that of biological utility, Young (1936) pointed to the high correlation between pleasantness and beneception, unpleasantness and nociception. He also notes that there is a frequent correlation between pleasantness and approach, and unpleasantness and avoidance; and further that the affective responses to simple colors and tones are much weaker than those evoked by odors, tastes, cutaneous or organic stimuli.

In his work on palatability, Young espouses a clearly hedonistic theory of reinforcement in which he treats the affective process as a postulate, an intervening variable (Young, 1959). The reactions of animals to taste solutions then can only be described when reference is made to their positive or negative hedonic effects. Thus, sugar solutions are hedonically positive, and the level of acceptability is directly proportional to the logarithm of the concentration. Salt on the other hand does not show this one-to-one correspondence with sensory intensity. Low concentrations of salt are said to be hedonically positive for the rat, but at high concentrations are hedonically negative. Such terminology often appears simply to rename approach or avoidance behavior with hedonistic synonyms for we all know what we mean when we say in laboratory jargon that the rat likes sugar. We know he will take it in preference to water, he may press a

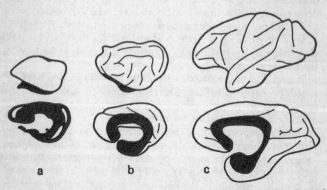

Figure 10 Lateral and medial surfaces of brains of rabbit (a), cat (b), and monkey (c) drawn roughly to scale. The drawings illustrate that the limbic lobe, represented in black, forms a common denominator in the brains of all mammals. (After a drawing in Journal of Neurosurgery)

bar for it, he may take it even when it is adulterated with something he 'doesn't like' such as quinine. But such usage does not necessarily indicate the primacy of the hedonic process; we must have further experimental study of acceptance and rejection and of their relation to hedonic or affective processes.

Thus it is abundantly clear that, instigation of consummatory response (or of rejection), reinforcement of instrumental responses, and elicitation of hedonic effect are all closely related and that reproducible stimulus functions can be demonstrated for each. A definitive choice as to which of these is primary cannot yet be made. I would like to propose that sensory stimulation *per se* together with its ensuring central neural events be considered as a prime determinant in the chain of events culminating in acceptance behavior, reinforcement, and hedonic effect. The further study of such stimulus functions and their analysis particularly at the physiological level is a problem that should merit the highest priority.

I should like to turn to the possible physiological mechanisms in the reinforcing and hedonic functions of stimuli.

The Physiology of Reinforcement and Sensory Affect

The studies of cranial self-stimulation (Brady, 1958; Olds, 1958; Olds & Milner, 1954) show that the reward and punishment systems within the brain itself, but particularly the reward systems, have been found to depend in large measure upon the limbic system. In classical neuroanatomy this was known as the rhinencephalon or smell brain, but its relation to olfaction seems less and less particular. The limbic lobe including the hippocampus completely surrounds the hilus of the hemisphere. Its various subcortical cell stations include the amygdala, septal nuclei, the hypothalamus, anterior thalamic nuclei, etc. The limbic lobe of the rabbit, cat, and monkey is shown in black in Figure 10. The limbic lobe appears to form a common denominator in the brains of all mammals.

Its constancy of gross and microscopic structure throughout the phylogeny of the mammal contrasts strikingly with the mushrooming neopallium which surrounds it. . . . Papez theorized that the experimental evidence also points to the limbic lobe as a cortical common denominator for a variety of emotional and viscerosomatic reactions in the mammal (MacLean, 1954).

There is increasing evidence of a sensory viscerosomatic influx into the limbic system. In pathological involvements, particularly

287

of the temporal lobe, discharges in this part of the brain may be associated with a wide variety of auras involving all the body senses as well as a great number of feeling and emotional states. Among the more purely sensory auras are crude olfactory sensations; alimentary symptoms including taste, thirst, hunger, nausea; and somatic sensations ranging from pains to paresthesia. Prolonged rhythmic responses can be elicited in the pyriform area by olfactory, gustatory, and painful stimulation (MacLean, 1954). MacLean notes that all three of these senses accent the quality and intensity of a stimulus rather than its spatial relationships.

I do not wish to give the impression that this system is essentially one for viscerosomatic sensation, for it is also implicated in a variety of complex effects such as the Klüver-Bucy syndrome (1958), memory losses (Penfield, 1958), the lowering of rage thresholds in some cases or increased docility after ablation in others (Bard & Mountcastle, 1947; Green, 1958; Schreiner & Kling, 1953; Spiegel, Miller & Oppenheimer, 1940), and a variety of cranial self-stimulation effects (Brady, 1958; Olds, 1958; Olds & Milner, 1954). The details of these relations are beyond the scope of the present discourse. What I wish to emphasize is that there are significant sensory inputs into this system which may relate to the hedonic and reinforcing features of stimulation as compared with either the cognitive or arousal functions.

Stellar and his colleagues (Sprague, Chambers, Stellar, Liu & Robson, 1958; Stellar, Chambers, Liu, Levitt, & Sprague, 1958) at the University of Pennsylvania have made some interesting studies of chronic animals with extensive lesions in the lateral lemniscal, primary sensory pathways. I was struck with their description of the lemniscal animals, i.e., the sensorially restricted animals displayed little affect in any situation, except, perhaps the most extreme. They flex and tend to pull away from a pinch, but do not attack or show any autonomic response. They showed little or no aversive reaction to an ether cone, although they lacrimated and sneezed. Prior to the operation, they solicited petting and responded to it well; afterwards they gave no reaction to petting.

These observations suggest that the affective response to sensory stimuli might be mediated by the lemniscal and not the diffuse arousal system, which, it might be noted, already seems to have been theoretically overworked by psychologists. I would like to remind you of the 'thalamic syndrome,' described by

Head and Holmes (1911). Lesions in the region of the thalamus are characterized by 'overreaction', by excessive affectivity, for both pleasurable as well as painful sensations. This is pathology characterized by the affective modification of sensation. Although the 'syndrome thalamique' is well known to clinical neurologists, its exact mechanism is still not clear. For our purposes, it is sufficient to note that in this condition, the basic hedonic responses to sensory stimulation, some of the 'Pleasures of Sensation' as well as the displeasures, can be unmasked. In short, I am suggesting that the affective consequences of sensory stimulation are mediated by processes that depend upon the primary projection systems and their ramifications in thalamic and old brain neural connections. Obviously much work is required to place these speculations upon a more solid foundation.

Summary

And now let me briefly summarize. I alluded briefly to the different roles of stimuli and sensory processes in the behavioral economy of the organism. I pointed out that traditionally sensory processes were studied largely in relation to discrimination or so-called cognitive functions. But stimuli have been shown to have other neural and behavioral functions as arousal and reinforcement. I then went on to discuss in further detail certain of our own experiments on taste as a model system to show the relation of gustatory stimulation to the control of consummatory responses and the reinforcement of instrumental behavior. It was shown that there is increasing support for the idea that gustatory stimulation *per se* is capable of eliciting and reinforcing behavior in its own right. We might say 'sweet for sweet's sake'. I then led into the problem of hedonic or affective responses to such stimuli; and, although a good correlation between affective response and reinforcement could be demonstrated, a statement as to their exact relation must await further study, particularly at the physiological level. Finally, I speculated as to the psychophysiological mechanisms that might underlie reinforcement and the affective responses to sensory stimuli. My basic theme has been that sensory stimulation 'qua stimulation' plays a significant role in the motivation as well as guidance of behavior – euphemistically we might say, in controlling behavior for the 'Pleasures of Sensation'.

References

Bard, P., & Mountcastle, V. B. Some forebrain mechanisms involved in expression of rage with special reference to suppression of angry behavior. *ARNMD*, 1947, 27, 362–404.

Bare, J. K. The specific hunger for sodium chloride in normal and adrenalectomized white rats. *J. comp. physiol. Psychol.*, 1949, 42, 242–253.

Beebe-Center, J. G. 'Feeling and emotion'. In H. Helson (Ed.), *Theoretical foundations of psychology*. New York: Van Nostrand, 1951. Pp. 254–317.

Bindra, D. *Motivation, a systematic reinterpretation*. New York: Ronald, 1959.

Brady, J. V. Temporal and emotional factors related to electrical self-stimulation of the limbic system. In *Recticular formation of the brain*. Boston: Little, Brown, 1958. Pp. 689–704.

Bremer, F. Cerveau 'isole' et physiologie du sommeil. *CR Soc. Biol., Paris*, 1935, 118, 1235–1241.

Brown, J. S. Pleasure-seeking behavior and the drive-reduction hypothesis. *Psychol. Rev.*, 1955, 62, 169–179.

Cameron, A. T. The taste sense and the relative sweetness of sugars and other substances. New York: Sugar Research Foundation, 1947. (*Sci. Rep. Ser.*, No. 9.)

Campbell, B. A. Auditory and aversion thresholds of rats for bands of noise. *Science*, 1957, 125, 596–597.

Campbell, B. A. Absolute and relative sucrose preference thresholds for hungry and satiated rats. *J. comp. physiol. Psychol.*, 1958, 51, 795–800.

Carpenter, J. A. Species differences in taste preferences. *J. comp. physiol. Psychol.*, 1956, 49, 139–144.

Collier, G., & Siskel, M., Jr. Performance as a joint function of amount of reinforcement and interreinforcement interval. *J. exp. Psychol.*, 1959, 57, 115–120.

Coppock, H. W., & Chambers, R. M. Reinforcement of position preference by automatic intravenous injection of glucose. *J. comp. physiol. Psychol.*, 1954, 47, 355–357.

Engel, R., Experimentelle Untersuchungen über die Abhängigkeit der Lust und Unlust von der Reizstärke beim Geschmackssinn. *Arch. ges. Psychol.*, 1928, 64, 1–36.

Frings, H. Biological backgrounds of the 'sweet tooth.' *Turtox News*, 1946, 24, No. 8.

Galambos, R. Suppression of auditory nerve activity by stimulation of efferent fibers to cochlea. *J. Neurophysiol.*, 1956, 19, 424–437.

Green, J. D. The rhinencephalon and behavior. In *Neurological basis of behavior*. Ciba Foundation Symposium. Boston: Little, Brown, 1958. Pp. 222–235.

Guttman, N. Operant conditioning, extinction and periodic reinforcement in relation to concentration of sucrose used as reinforcing agent. *J. exp. Psychol.*, 1953, 46, 213–224.

Guttman, N. Equal reinforcement values for sucrose and glucose solutions compared with equal sweetness values. *J. comp. physiol. Psychol.*, 1954, 47, 358–361.

Hagbarth, K. E., & Kerr, D. I. B. Central influences on spinal afferent conduction. *J. Neurophysiol.*, 1954, 17, 295–307.

Hagstrom, E. C., & Pfaffmann, C. The relative taste effectiveness of different sugars for the rat. *J. comp. physiol. Psychol.*, 1959, 52, 259–262.

Harlow, H. F. Motivations as a factor in the acquisition of new responses. In *Current theory and research in motivation*. Lincoln: Univer. Nebraska Press, 1953. Pp. 24–49.

Head, H., & Holmes, G. Sensory disturbances from cerebral lesions. *Brain*, 1911, 34, 102–254.

Hebb, D. O. Alice in wonderland or psychology among the biological sciences. In H. F. Harlow & C. N. Woolsey (Eds.), *Biological and biochemical bases of behavior*. Madison: Univer. Wisconsin Press, 1958. Pp. 451–467. (a).

Hebb, D. O. *A textbook of psychology*. Philadelphia & London: Saunders, 1958. (b).

Hernandez-Peon, R. Central mechanisms controlling conduction along central sensory pathways. *Acta. neurol. latino. Amer.*, 1955, 1, 256–264.

Hughes, L. H. Saccharine reinforcement in a T maze. *J. comp. physiol. Psychol.*, 1957, 50, 431–435.

Keller, F. S., & Schoenfeld, W. N. *Principles of psychology*. New York: Appleton-Century-Crofts, 1950.

Kling, J. W., Horowitz, L., & Delhagen, J. E. Light as a positive reinforcer for rat responding. *Psychol. Rep.*, 1956, 2, 337–340.

Klüver, H. The temporal lobe syndrome produced by bilateral ablations. In *Neurological foundations of behavior*. Ciba Foundation Symposium. Boston: Little, Brown, 1958. Pp. 175–186.

LeMagnen, J. Le rôle de la receptivité gustative au chlorure de sodium dans le mécanisme de régulation de la prise d'eau chez le rat blanc. *J. Physiol. Path. gen.*, 1955, 47, 405–418.

Lindsley, D. B. Emotion. In S. S. Stevens (Ed.), *Handbook of experimental psychology*. New York: Wiley, 1951. Ch. 14.

McCleary, R. A. Taste and postingestion factors in specific hunger behavior. *J. comp. physiol. Psychol.*, 1953, 46, 411–421.

MacLean, P. D. The limbic system and its hippocampal formation in animals and their possible application to man. *J. Neurosurg.*, 1954, 11, 29–44.

MacLean, P. D., Horwitz, N. H., & Robinson, F. Olfactory-like responses in pyriform area to non-olfactory stimulation. *Yale J. Biol. Med.*, 1952, 25, 159–172.

MacLeod, S. A construction and attempted validation of sensory sweetness scales. *J. exp. Psychol.*, 1952, 44, 316–323.

Magoun, H. W. *The waking brain*. Springfield, Ill.: Charles C. Thomas, 1958.

Miller, N. E. Experiments on motivation. *Science*, 1957, 126, 1271–1278.

Miller, N. E. Liberalization of basic S-R concepts: Extensions to conflict behavior, motivation, and social learning. In S. Koch (Ed.), *Psychology: A study of a science*. Vol. 2. New York: McGraw-Hill, 1959.

Montgomery, K. C. Exploratory behavior and its relation to spontaneous alternation in a series of maze exposures. *J. comp. physiol. Psychol.*, 1952, 45, 50–57.

Olds, J. Self-stimulation of the brain. *Science*, 1958, 127, 315–324.

Olds, J. S., & Milner, P. Positive reinforcement produced by electrical stimulation of septal area and other regions of the rat brain. *J. comp. physiol. Psychol.*, 1954, 47, 419–427.

Penfield, W. The role of the temporal cortex in recall of past experience and interpretation of the present. In, *Neurological foundations of behavior*. Ciba Foundation Symposium. Boston: Little, Brown, 1958. Pp. 149–174.

Pfaffmann, C. Gustatory nerve impulses in rat, cat, and rabbit. *J. Neurophysiol.*, 1955, 18, 429–440.

Pfaffmann, C. Taste mechanisms in preference behavior. *Amer. J. clin. Nutr.*, 1957, 5, 142–147.

Pfaffmann, C. *Flavor research and food acceptance*. New York: Reinhold, 1958.

Pfaffmann, C. The afferent code for sensory quality. *Amer. Psychologist*, 1959, 14, 226–232.

Pick, H., & Kare, M. Certain aspects of taste preference in chickens and calves. Paper read at Eastern Psychological Association, Atlantic City, April, 1959.

Pilgrim, F. J. The components of food acceptance and their measurement. *Amer. J. clin. Nutr.*, 1957, 5, 142–147.

Richter, C. P. Self-regulatory functions. *Harvey Lectures*, 1942, 38, 63–103.

Richter, C. P., & Campbell, K. H. Taste thresholds and taste preferences of rats for five common sugars. *J. Nutr.*, 1940, 20, 31–46

Schlosberg, H. Three dimensions of emotion. *Psychol. Rev.*, 1954, 61, 81–88.

Schreiner, L., & Kling, A. Behavioral change following rhinencephalic injury in the cat. *J. Neurophysiol.*, 1953, 16, 643–659.

Sheffield, F. D., & Roby, T. B. Reward value of a nonnutritive sweet taste. *J. comp. physiol. Psychol.*, 1950, 43, 471–481.

Sheffield, F. D., Roby, T. B., & Campbell, B. A. Drive reduction versus consummatory behavior as determinants of reinforcement. *J. comp. physiol. Psychol.*, 1954, 47, 349–354.

Sherrington, C. *The integrative action of the nervous system*. London: Constable, 1906.

Shuford, E. H., Jr. Palatability and osmotic pressure of glucose and sucrose solutions as determinants of intake. *J. comp. physiol. Psychol.*, 1959, 52, 150–153.

Skinner, B. F. *Science and human behavior*. New York: Macmillan, 1953.

Smith, M., & Duffy, M. The effects of intragastric injection of various substances on subsequent bar pressing. *J. comp. physiol. Psychol.*, 1955, 48, 387–391.

Smith, M., & Duffy, M. Evidence for a dual reinforcing effect of sugar. *J. comp. physiol. Psychol.*, 1957, 50, 242–247.

Soulairac, A. La physiologie d'un comportement: L'Appétit glucidique et sa régulation neuro-endocrinienne chez les rongeurs. *Bull. biol.*, 1947, 81, 273–432.

Spence, K. W. *Behavior theory and conditioning*. New Haven, Conn.: Yale Univer. Press, 1956.

Spiegel, E., Miller, H., & Oppenheimer, J. Forebrain and rage reactions. *J. Neurophysiol.*, 1940, 3, 538–548.

Sprague, J. M., Chambers, W. W., Stellar, E., Liu, C. N., & Robson, K. Chronic reticular and lemniscal lesions in cats. *Fed. Proc.*, 1958, 17, 154.

Stellar, E., Chambers, W. W., Liu, C. N., Levitt, M., & Sprague, J. M. Behavior of cats with chronic reticular and lemniscal lesions. *Fed. Proc.*, 1958, 17, 156.

Stellar, E., Hyman, R., & Samet, S. Gastric factors controlling water and salt solution drinking. *J. comp. physiol. Psychol.*, 1954, 47, 220–226.

Troland, L. T. *The fundamentals of human motivation.* New York: Van Nostrand, 1928.

Warren, R. P., & Pfaffmann, C. Early experience and taste aversion. *J. comp. physiol. Psychol.*, 1958, 52, 263–266.

Young, P. T. *Motivation of behavior.* New York: Wiley, 1936.

Young, P. T. Psychologic factors regulating the feeding process. *Amer. J. clin. Nutr.*, 1957, 5, 154–161.

Young, P. T. The role of affective processes in learning and motivation. *Psychol. Rev.*, 1959, 66, 104–125.

Young, P. T., & Greene, J. T. Quantity of food ingested as a measure of relative acceptability. *J. comp. physiol. Psychol.*, 1953, 46, 288–294.

Young, P. T., & Shuford, E. H., Jr. Intensity, duration, and repetition of hedonic processes as related to acquisition of motives. *J. comp. physiol., Psychol.*, 1954, 47, 298–305.

Young, P. T., & Shuford, E. H., Jr. Quantitative control of motivation through sucrose solutions of different concentrations. *J. comp. physiol. Psychol.*, 1955, 48, 114–118.

X Brain Mechanisms and Reinforcement

Although it had always been assumed that reinforcers
ultimately had their effects via some brain mechanism,
it was the finding (Olds and Milner, 1954) that the electrical
stimulation of certain subcortical brain structures could act as
a potent reinforcer which led to the search for the reinforcing
mechanism inside the head. Examples of experimental
exploration of this phenomenon are provided here by the
papers of Olds and Valenstein. The behavioural facts which
any neural model would need to explain have been summarized
by Bindra. Miller has tried to specify the type of neural
mechanism that might be common to all reinforcers.

Self-Stimulation Experiments and Differentiated Reward Systems

Reproduced in full from H. H. Jasper, *et al.* (Eds.), *Reticular Formation of the Brain*, Little, Brown & Co., Boston, 1958, pp. 671–87.

In self-stimulation experiments (1–4) electrodes are chronically implanted in the brain, and a circuit is arranged so that the experimental animal can deliver the shock to himself.

For rats, we use the electrode arrangement shown in the upper left of Figure 1. The plastic block is screwed to the skull, and a pair of insulated silver wires penetrates the brain to stimulate only at the tips. Electrodes in place in an intact animal are shown in the X-ray photograph of Figure 1. The circuit is shown in the lower left. Here the rat steps on a pedal to deliver to his brain a shock of 60-cycle current which lasts for about $\frac{1}{2}$ second. The shock level ranges from 10 to 150 microamperes, as will be shown. The electrode track following a completed experiment appears as the darkened area of the photomicrograph in Figure 1.

When electrodes are in certain places, animals stimulate their brains more than 5000 times an hour. With electrodes in other places, a negative effect can be achieved. Once the animal learns how to get the shock, he avoids it from then on.

The positive effect can be achieved in extreme or mild form through electrodes placed anywhere within a broad system of structures centered in the hypothalamus and including most of the rhinencephalon plus parts of the thalamus, tegmentum, and caudate nucleus (see lined areas in Figure 2). The negative or punishing effect is much less extensive, according to our studies. Animals avoid the electric shock when electrodes are in certain lateral and posterior parts of the diencephalon and in certain lateral parts of the tegmentum (see stippled area in Figure 2). Our studies of over 200 electrodes placed in all parts of the brain have indicated that about 60 per cent of all electrodes placed are motivationally neutral – the animal neither approaches nor avoids the shock. Only about 5 per cent are motivationally negative – the animal avoids the shock; the other 35 per cent are motivationally positive – the animal approaches the shock.

In the case of positive effects, we wished to establish categorically that we were dealing with a rewarding process rather than with automatism or compulsion. For this purpose we trained rats in a complicated maze and an obstruction box with electrical brain shock as the only reward. We compared results so obtained with results obtained when food was the reward for hungry rats (Figure 3).

The time to run the maze declined rapidly in the first three days whether the reward was food or electric stimulation. On the fourth day, when the reward was withdrawn, both groups showed extinction of the running response. The first runs of the day showed a steady decline during the four days (see insert, Figure 3). This

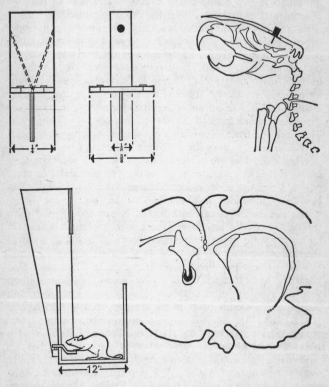

Figure 1 Electrode implants for self-stimulation experiments. Upper left, electrode placement used for rats. Upper right, electrodes in place. Lower left, circuit for self-stimulation. Lower right, electrode track as darkened area, after stimulation

indicates that no 'priming' with an hors d'oeuvre is necessary to start a rat self-stimulating.

In the obstruction box experiment done with Mr J. Sinclaire (Figure 4) the rat got three self-stimulations at one end, then had to cross the grid for three more, and so forth. Here we also ran hungry rats with food for reward. They were pretrained for a month to eat three bites at one end, then three at the other, and back and forth. Then shock was introduced by electrifying the grid, and was increased day by day until the rats would no longer cross the grid for food. It is clear from the data on the left in

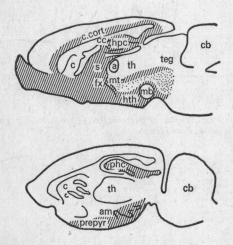

c.cort: cingulum cortex	mt: mammillo-thalamic fasciculus
cc: corpus callosum	hth: hypothalamus
s: septum	cb: cerebellar
hpc: hippocampus	mb: mammillary body
a: anterior commissure	am: amygdala
th: thalamus	prepyr: prepyriformis cortex
fx: fornix	

Figure 2 Lined areas indicate brain areas where positive effects can be achieved with electrodes. Stippled area represents regions of avoidance effects

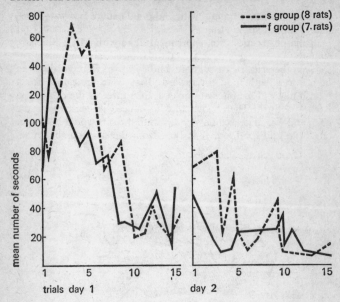

Figure 3 Maze results when rat is offered food (f group, solid line) or electric stimulation (s group, dotted line)

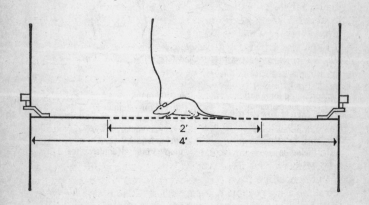

Figure 4 Obstruction box experiment

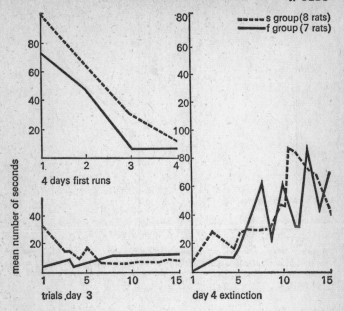

Figure 5 that most of the rats were stopped in their quest for food by about 50 to 60 microamperes, but a few rats kept going until given almost 300 microamperes.

The chart on the right in Figure 5 (one rat running for self-stimulation) shows microamperes along both the ordinate and the abscissa. From left to right are increasing microamperes of head shock (reward). From bottom to top are increasing microamperes of foot shock (obstruction). At 100 microamperes of shock to the head, this rat crossed an area through which he received about 200 microamperes of shock to the feet. At 150 to the head he crossed about 280 to the feet, and at 200 to the head, he crossed more than 420 to the feet. A shock of 420 microamperes is very high and painful for rat or human.

Our conclusion from these preliminary experiments is that we are stimulating genuine reward systems in the brain. We believe that the effect derives from no mere compulsion or automatism, but from stimulation of cells actually involved in food, sexual, or

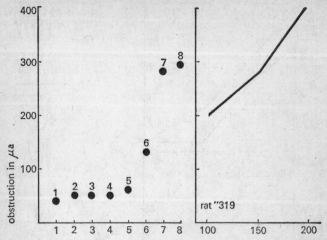

Figure 5 Obstruction box experiment with eight hungry rats with food reward (left), and one rat running for self-stimulation only (right). Height of each circle represents amount of electric current (in microamperes) required to stop the rat

other reward processes. We have therefore hoped that a study of the variables affecting self-stimulation may lead us toward a knowledge of the differentiations within these reward systems and the mechanisms involved in the control of behavior by rewards.

A brief glance suggests that the primary variables are (1) the location of the stimulating electrode, (2) the amount and kind of electric shock, and (3) the state of the neural units and pathways that mediate the effect.

Relationship of Location of Stimulating Electrode to Animal's Response

In the posterior hypothalamus (except for the mammillary bodies) self-stimulation rates are very high. Figure 6 shows cumulative response curves for a rat with a posterior electrode. Each sawtooth represents 500 responses, and each block represents an hour. Here we see a very stable rate of 4500 responses per hour maintained for 15 days of testing. Such rates are maintained for many months.

Figure 7 shows much slower rates when the electrodes are in the anterior hypothalamus. Within the tegmental hypothalamic

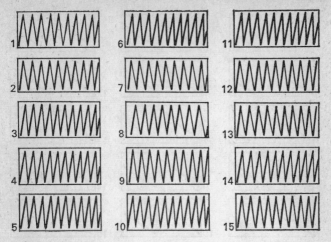

fifteen days of responding
posterior hypothalamic electrode#315

Figure 6

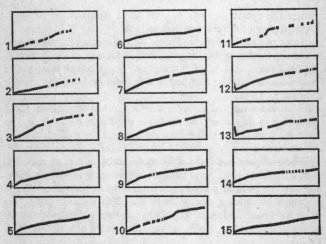

fifteen days of responding
middle hypothalamic electrode#124

Figure 7

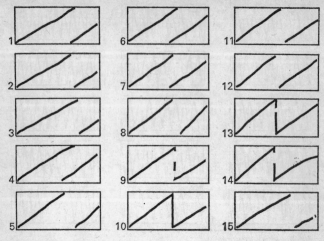

fifteen days of responding
forebrain electrode #215

Figure 8

system the decline in rates appears to be steady as we progress forward along the ventromedial surface.

Rates rise again slightly (Figure 8) in the preoptic region and posterior forebrain, but they are not as high as in the posterior hypothalamus, and they fall sharply to about 200 an hour as the electrodes are moved forward into cortical parts of the rhinencephalon.

In all cases we find extreme stability of self-stimulation rates from day to day when the electrode stays in a given place, the electric shock is set at 60 microamperes, and the animals are run for an hour a day.

When animals are run for 24 to 48 hours in a row. we often find that those with hypothalamic electrodes will self-stimulate steadily for 24-hour periods and even longer. The steady rise in Figure 9 indicates a rate of more than 2000 pedal responses an hour for about 24 hours. The flattening then indicates about 20 hours of sleep, after which the rat starts again at a rate of 2000 an hour.

Figure 10 shows similar response curves for a group of animals with forebrain electrodes and another group with hypothalamic ones. It is quite apparent that slowing in the second group is

304

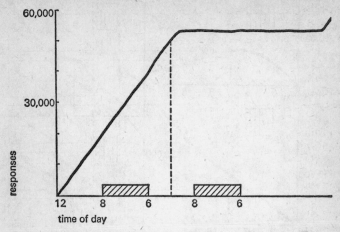

Figure 9 *Self-stimulation response of a rat with hypothalamic electrodes, run continually for over 24 hours*

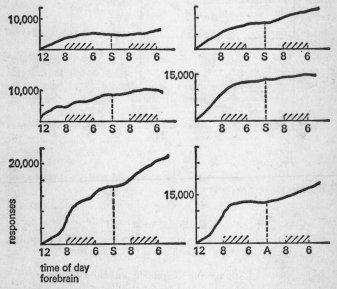

Figure 10 (*Continued on Next Page*)

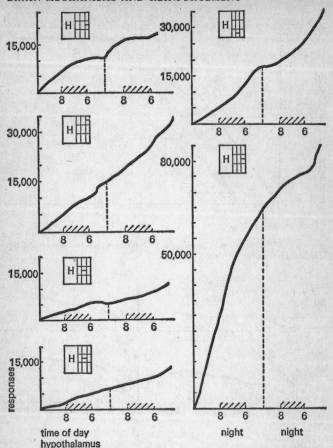

Figure 10 *Self-stimulation response for animals with forebrain electrodes and with hypothalamic electrodes*

moderate and could be attributed to general fatigue. Slowing in the animals with forebrain electrodes, however, is usually abrupt and suggests that some mechanism of neural satiation is at work.

Relationship of Stimulating Current to Animal's Response

Figure 11 shows three general types of curves. In the first (steep, asymptotic curves), the response rate mounts steadily and then levels off at a very high point. These results appear to be achieved with electrodes in the anterior or posterior portions of the medial forebrain bundle, and the rates appear to rise steadily with increases in electric shock to the head. The point of leveling off may be due to some limit of skill, and declines at the tops of the curves are usually accounted for by seizures. We assume that in these cases our electrode sits in a region of positive motivational units, and that all the cells in a millimeter sphere surrounding the electrode tip are homogeneous in this positive effect. We have some evidence from obstruction experiments that these rats will continue to increase their willingness to take pain for higher brain shocks after response rate has leveled off.

The second type of curve (undulating) suggests that the electrode is placed in a set of cells or fibers giving positive results, but that increases in electric current bring in a lamina of negative

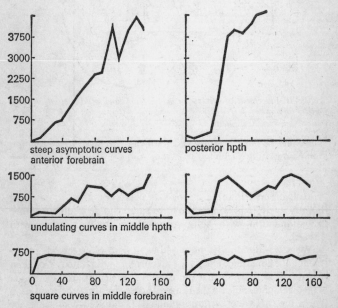

Figure 11 Self-stimulation responses with varying amounts of electric current. The current increases in 10-microampere steps along the abscissa, and response rate increases along the ordinate

motivational units, after which there are more positives. This result is achieved from electrodes placed in parts of the middle hypothalamus where we have previously found rewarding and punishing effects from neighboring electrodes.

The third type of curve (square) suggests that the electrodes are placed directly in a tract of fibers with positive motivational effects, but that all other cells in the region are neutral. So far, this result has been obtained only with electrodes placed in the diagonal band within the septal areas (Figure 12). This suggests that in this septal area proper, the diagonal band is the only active structure.

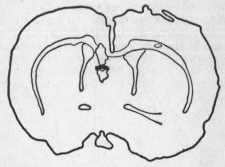

Figure 12 Placement of electrodes in diagonal band within septal areas of middle forebrain

The State of Neural Units and Pathways Involved in Self-Stimulating Behavior

Hunger

We have run the same animals first hungry, then sated, then hungry again, and so on. We have sought to determine whether self-stimulation with some placements might increase with hunger.

What we found quite surprised us at first. No electrode placement gave consistent effects for all current levels tested. We see in Figure 13 again rates that increase as the current level increases. The black bars indicate the range of scores for three different days when the rats were 24 hours hungry. The dotted bars represent ranges for three days on which animals were sated. Each bar represents the range for just one voltage level. The rat whose scores are on the left shows a marked difference between hunger and sated conditions only at 10 microamperes. At all other levels the scores overlap. The rat whose data are on the right shows clearcut differences only at the top of the microampere scale.

We have surmised here, as before, that increases in electric current widen the circle of cells stimulated. Cells far outside the circle will not be affected even when their thresholds are low; those deep within the sphere are stimulated by a suprathreshold current. Cells close to the boundary, however, are questionable, and drive variations may change the threshold of these cells to move them into or out of the ring. We must surmise, then, that only when this boundary includes hunger-sensitive cells can we expect a hunger difference to appear.

To look for a pattern, we plotted on a brain map the current levels at which hunger differences occur. We have, of course, found areas, particularly in the anterior hypothalamus, where there were apparently no hunger differences at all. Hunger differences are, however, particularly frequent in the posterior hypothalamus (Figure 14). It is apparent from the arrows that the points at which there is a clearcut hunger difference converge

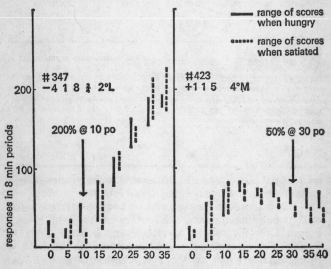

Figure 13

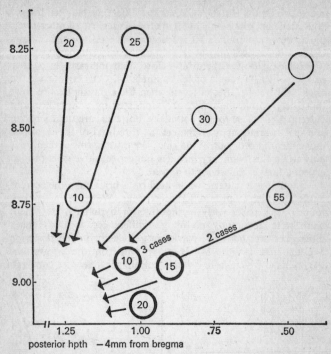

Figure 14 Hunger differences shown on diagrammatic cross-section of ventral posterior hypothalamus. The right side of the square is about at the midline, the base at the ventral surface (9½ mm. from top). The area is about 1½ mm. square. Number within circle indicates amount of current required to give clearcut hunger difference

on a ventral region about 1¼ mm. lateral to the midline. This is again the region of a part of the medial forebrain bundle.

On the basis of this diagram, we have attempted to draw a picture of our suprathreshold electric field for different electric current levels (Figure 15). This picture suggests that a current of 20 microamperes reaches about ¾ mm. down from the electrode tip but less than ½ mm. to either side. A 60-microampere stimulus reaches cells in a circle of about 1·5 mm. centered at a point about ½ mm. below the electrode tip. This work is preliminary, but it

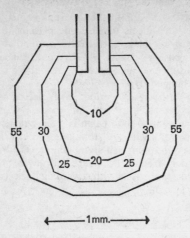

←——— 1mm. ———→

Figure 15 Suprathreshold electric field for different electric current levels

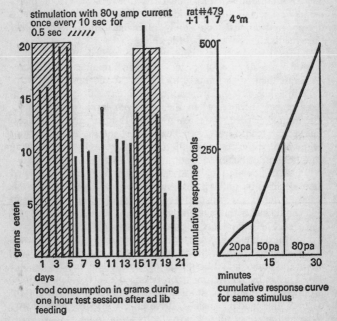

stimulation with 80γ amp current
once every 10 sec for
0.5 sec ///////

rat #479
+1 1 7 4°m

grams eaten

days

food consumption in grams during
one hour test session after ad lib
feeding

Figure 16

cumulative response totals

minutes

cumulative response curve
for same stimulus

gives us a useful tool for further analysis and suggests that in order to study the effects of electrode placement, we must be careful in specifying the level of electric current.

Other work on hunger with Mr R. Wendt has led to the surprising conclusion that an apparently rewarding stimulus often increases the hunger drive. In Figure 16 we see records of food intake during an hour test period. With electric stimulation of about 80 microamperes applied for about $\frac{1}{2}$ second every 10 seconds, the amount of food eaten is much greater than during comparable periods without stimulation. Yet with the same stimulus at the same point, self-stimulation rates are about 800 responses per hour. Wendt's later data indicate that this combination of drive increase effects with rewarding ones is very frequent in the hunger system.

Androgens

In studies done with Mr C. V. Critchlaw from Dr C. H. Sawyer's laboratory, we found that with some electrode placements and certain low electric shock, self-stimulation responses disappeared almost completely after castration. With other placements, there was very little change.

Figure 17 shows the daily response record of a castrated animal. Each day he was tested, first for 8 minutes at 15 microamperes, then for 8 minutes at 20, 25, 30 and up to 55 microamperes. The first record was taken 7 days after cessation of replacement therapy, when the androgen level was still high. The animal self-stimulated even at the 15-microampere current. The second record was taken 3 days later, and the animal did not begin until stimulated with 25 microamperes. On the following day, he did not begin until stimulated with 55 microamperes.

On the following 6 days, after androgen levels had completed their decline, he did not respond for any of the current levels tested. After this we injected 5 mg. of testosterone propionate in oil. The day after the injection, responding occurred at 55 microamperes. The second day, responding began at 45 microamperes. On the third day, there was responding again at 15 microamperes.

The electrode which produced this effect was lodged in cells along the dorsomedial boundary of the caudate nucleus (Figure 18). This is by far the most pronounced effect which we have produced in our drive studies, and it suggests that in certain parts of the caudate nucleus, drive effects may be more clearly separated anatomically than in the hypothalamus.

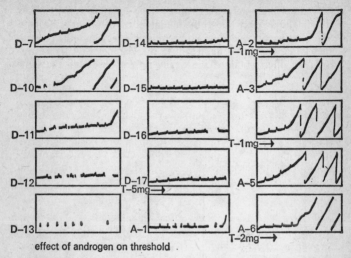

effect of androgen on threshold .

Figure 17

Figure 18 Arrow indicates electrode placement along the dorsomedial boundary of the caudate nucleus for testing the effect of androgens on self-stimulation

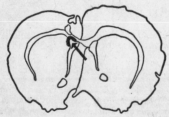

Figure 19 Electrode placed in the mesial reticular formation, to test androgen effect

Another androgen effect shown by a different technique was found with an electrode in the mesial reticular formation (Figure 19). Here we obtained a rapid but unstable response rate prior to castration, using a stimulus of 65 microamperes. After castration, we often obtained practically no response with the same

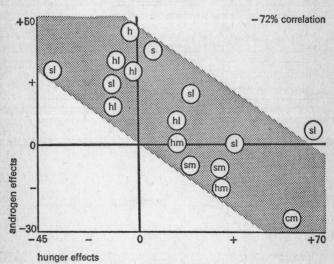

Figure 20 Negative correlation of androgen and hunger effects. Each circle stands for one animal. The letters inside the circles indicate electrode placement: s, septal; h, hypothalamic; c, caudate; l, lateral; m, medial. Animals are assumed to differ from one another only in electrode placement. The y axis indicates per cent improvement of self-stimulation rates by giving androgens to the castrated animals; the x axis indicates per cent improvement of self-stimulation rates by starving the animal for about 23 hours

Figure 21 Sections through the ventral portion of the diencephalon and telencephalon of the rat, showing places of extreme and mild inhibition of self-stimulation rates by chlorpromazine (2 mg./kg.). The numbers inside the circles indicate the number of 8-minute intervals of testing during which self-stimulation was abolished by the drug. (Thus a 1·5 would mean that half of the normal output was inhibited for one 8-minute interval and the whole normal output for another interval after drug injection.) Triangles indicate mild effects (depression of 1·5 or less); circles indicate moderate effects (depressions of 1·5 to 3 intervals); squares indicate extreme effects (depressions of more than 3 intervals)

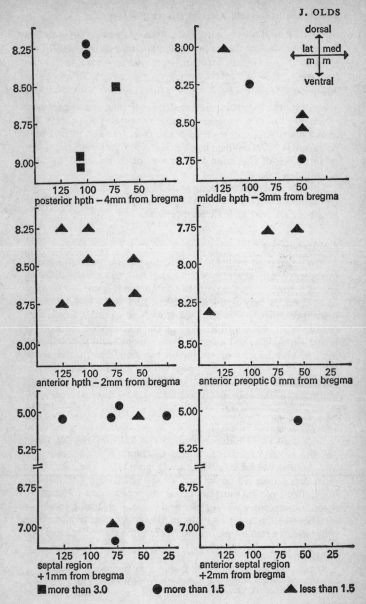

■ more than 3.0   ● more than 1.5   ▲ less than 1.5

stimulus. About a week after the commencement of replacement therapy, the animal was responding regularly again at about 1500 an hour.

Hunger and Androgens

When a series of animals was tested for both hunger and androgen effects, we found a remarkable negative correlation (Figure 20). When androgens improved response rates, hunger often had a detrimental effect. When hunger increased response rates, the performance of the same animal was often impaired by high androgen levels.

This certainly gives strong ground for expecting to find an anatomic differentiation of hunger reward systems from those positively affected by male sex hormone.

Chlorpromazine

In studies started with Dr K. Killam, chlorpromazine injected intraperitoneally at a rate of 2 mg./kg. had very greatly differing effects depending on the point of stimulation (Figure 21). In some cases it had a very slight effect for a very short time. In other cases it completely abolished self-stimulation at all current levels tested. When we map these effects on a schematic map of the posterior, middle, and anterior hypothalamus and the posterior, middle, and anterior septal region, we find that the heavy inhibitory effects collect in the posterior hypothalamus and anterior septal region. There are almost no effects on self-stimulation with electrodes in the anterior hypothalamus.

LSD

Studies with Dr S. Eiduson showed that LSD 0·2 mg./kg. never has the massive inhibitory effects of chlorpromazine, but does give very dependable inhibitions (Figure 22). The effects are most pronounced in some parts of the septal region. The inhibitory effects of LSD are abolished by preliminary injection of serotonin, except when the electrodes are deep in the forebrain just beyond the anterior commissure. In this same place, and only here, we found that Brom-LSD had the same effect as LSD.

References
1. Olds, James, and Milner, Peter. Positive reinforcement produced by electrical stimulation of septal area and other regions of rat brain. *J. Comp. Physiol. Psychol.*, 47:419, 1954.

2. Olds, James. A preliminary mapping of electrical reinforcing effects in the rat brain. *J. Comp. Physiol. Psychol.*, 49:281, 1956.
3. Olds, James. Runway and maze behavior controlled by baso-medial fore-brain stimulation in the rat. *J. Comp. Physiol. Psychol.*, 49:507, 1956.
4. Olds, James, Killam, K. F., and Bach-y-Rita, P. Self-stimulation of the brain used as a screening method for tranquilizing drugs. *Science*, 124:265, 1956.

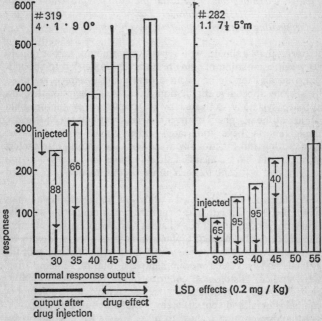

Figure 22 LSD effects on self-stimulation. Response output during successive 8-minute intervals is plotted as the electric current is raised from 30 to 55 microamperes. The open rectangles denote normal output; the black bars represent output under the effects of the drug

41 E. S. Valenstein and T. Valenstein

Interaction of Positive and Negative
Reinforcing Neural Systems

Reproduced in full from *Science*, 1964, Vol. 145, pp. 1456–58.

Abstract. – *Evidence is presented indicating that the repetitive turning on and off of reinforcing brain stimulation is not a special property of restricted hypothalamic and tegmental areas. Results from a sample of 22 diverse hypothalamic, septal, amygdala, and hippocampal sites suggest that such behavior can be obtained from most neural areas from which self-stimulation behavior may be elicited. Questions thus arise about the location of aversive neural systems when aversion is considered as being expressed by the act of terminating positively reinforcing brain stimulation.*

Reports that animals will repetitively initiate and terminate electrical stimulation of some brain areas (1) has led to speculation that an aversive or negative reinforcing system is activated by prolonged positive stimulation. It has been suggested that this aversive system is activated by a summation of subthreshold stimuli at the periphery of the influenced neural area (2). Because these reports have implicated either the hypothalamus or neighboring and functionally allied tegmental areas, interpreters of such data have concluded that aversive and positive neural systems are adjacent to each other in this relatively delimited area (3).

We have recently completed a study which suggests that animals will repetitively initiate and terminate reinforcing brain stimulation from most if not all neural areas from which self-stimulation behavior may be elicited. Eighteen rats were implanted with bipolar electrodes of a type previously described (4). As four of the animals had two electrodes implanted, a total of 22 neural sites were studied. Histological confirmation of these sites which included diverse hypothalamic, septal, amygdala, and hippocampal (dorsal and ventral) areas is illustrated in Fig. 1 (5).

Animals were first trained to press a lever for continuous reinforcement with 0·5-second trains of biphasic rectangular pulses (duration, 0·2 msec; frequency, 100 pulse-pairs per second). After this initial training animals were placed in a plexiglas testing

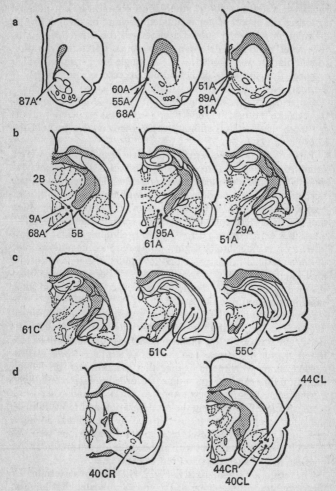

Figure 1 Cross sections of the rat brain after de Groot (6), illustrating placement of the electrodes

chamber with two levers 10 cm apart, mounted on the front wall. Pressing the left (onset) lever initiated the stimulation train, and responses on the right (offset) lever terminated the train. Animals

319

rapidly learned to turn the stimulation on and off, but in three instances the experimenter facilitated learning by turning off the stimulation when the animal approached the offset lever. This 'two-lever' method of determining an animal's preferred duration of stimulation was favored over the 'single-lever' method which requires that the lever be held down to receive stimulation. A comparative study of the two methods indicated that animals often terminated the stimulus with the 'single-lever' method simply because motoric side effects or the general excitement resulting from the electrical stimulus made them unable to hold the lever down (7).

The animals were given five practice tests in the two-lever situation at each of three stimulus intensities. During each 15-minute test only one intensity was presented. Different intensities were presented in a random sequence with an interval of at least 1 hour between tests. A 1-minute 'warm-up' period during which time no data were collected preceded each 15-minute test. The intensities selected were derived from preliminary tests: the low intensity was judged to be slightly above reinforcement threshold; the intermediate intensity yielded maximum response rates; the high intensity, which was approximately 75 per cent higher than the intermediate figure, resulted in great excitement and in some cases marked motoric side effects.

After the practice tests the animals were given an additional five tests at each of the three stimulus intensities, with all conditions as described for the practice tests. Two of the animals were tested at four intensities. The number of stimulus trains was recorded, along with the total time that the stimulus was left on (duration time) and off (reset time) (recorded in 0·1-second units) during each 15-minute test. Average duration and reset times were calculated by dividing the total duration and reset times by the number of stimulus trains initiated by the animal during a session. During a few tests, clonicotonic convulsions were induced in some animals, but with an observer always present it was possible to end such tests and repeat them later.

The results are summarized in Fig. 2. All the animals terminated the stimulus, and the slope of the curves indicates that animals terminated the stimulus more rapidly at the higher intensities. It is of considerable interest that, although the stimulus was terminated earlier at the higher intensities, it was also turned on again earlier. Some appreciation of the quality of the response pattern can be gained from inspection of the quantitative data. At the intermediate intensities the average duration of stimulation for all sites was 4·3 seconds, and the average reset time was 3·2 seconds. Thus, during the 15-minute tests animals were oscillating back and forth between the onset and offset levers. At the higher stimulus intensities this oscillation rate tended to be considerably faster (average duration, 2·8 seconds; average reset time, 2·6 seconds).

Some additional qualitative observations were made. For a few animals the reset time increased at the highest intensities. In some of these cases it was noted that a motoric response (for example, jumping), associated with the offset of the stimulus, appeared to interfere with the animals' ability to turn the stimulus on again. With ventral hippocampal electrode placements there was a significantly longer reset time. These animals tended to press the offset lever repeatedly before turning the stimulus on again. We could not determine with certainty whether some effects persisted after termination of the stimulus, so that experience of an abrupt offset was lacking; or whether after hippocampal stimulation the animals were confused and did not know which lever to press.

It was suggested (2) that animals receiving hypothalamic stimulation terminate the stimulus earlier at higher intensities as a consequence of more rapid activation of an aversive system. In contrast, it was also hypothesized that animals with septal electrodes may not exhibit this tendency because stimulation in this area does not activate an aversive system; in such animals the stimulus would be terminated only as a result of a loss of its effectiveness resulting from adaptation. It would be expected that adaptation would occur more slowly at higher intensities. The data from the present experiment directly oppose this hypothesis. The differences in duration and reset times attributable to these two neural areas seem to indicate that animals with septal electrodes terminate the stimulus faster at higher intensities than do animals with electrodes located in the hypothalamus. For the eight hypothalamic sites studied, the average duration and reset times were 7·1 and 1·6 seconds (intermediate intensity) and 3·0 and 1·2 seconds (highest intensity), respectively; for the seven septal placements the comparable averages were 1·5 and 2·3 seconds (intermediate intensity) and 0·9 and 1·1 seconds (highest intensity), respectively.

Several conclusions may be drawn from data which suggest that most, if not all, self-stimulating animals will repetitively turn a stimulus on and off when enabled to control duration. The position that these positive reinforcing areas have neighboring aversive areas would be difficult to maintain, however, in the absence of supporting evidence. In the past, when applied only to hypothalamic areas, this argument could be justified in view of the claims that medial hypothalamic stimulation produced ambivalent or avoidance reactions (8). According to another, perhaps more defensible conclusion, it is assumed that most positive systems have the potential to activate an aversive system or systems located at some unknown distance from the stimulation site.

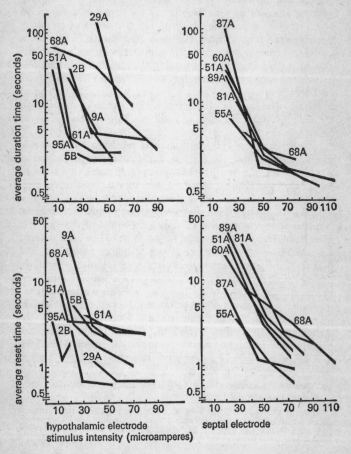

hypothalamic electrode
stimulus intensity (microamperes)

septal electrode

If this is true it is evident that any conclusion about the location of such an assumed aversive system(s) cannot be based solely upon the act of terminating positive brain stimulation. In fact, it would not be unreasonable to postulate that aversive consequences of prolonged stimulation may result from afferent feedback from systemic effects. Animals may terminate stimulation to obtain a respite from shifts in heart rate, body temperature,

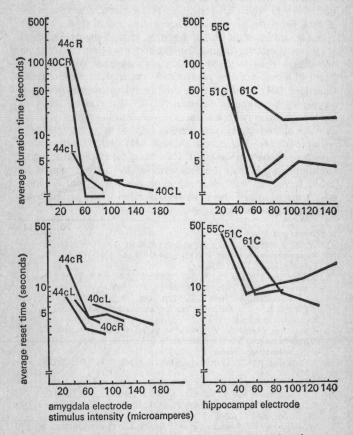

Figure 2 Average time animals left the stimulus on (duration time), and average time the stimulus was left off (reset time). Data obtained from five tests at each intensity

respiratory rhythm, and numerous other changes in bodily states known to be produced by central stimulation.

From another vantage point it may be asked whether termination of a stimulus should be considered sufficient evidence of the existence of an aversive system. It has been reported (9) that animals repeatedly turn on and off any appropriate stimulus placed under their control. With respect to reinforcing brain stimulation, more recent data raise some questions about interpretations in which an activation of an aversive system is assumed. From the present experiment it is evident that, although animals terminate the stimulus sooner at high intensities, there is no resistance to turning the stimulus on again. In fact, the stimulus is reset faster at the higher intensities. We have also fixed stimulation trains many times longer than the preferred durations, but even under these conditions there was no hesitancy in turning the stimulus on again (10). Similarly, it has been reported that when stimulus trains longer than the preferred duration are offered as a reward, animals respond at higher rates on a variable-interval reinforcement schedule (11), and at higher ratios on a progressive ratio test (12). This strong evidence that stimulus durations longer than those determined by the animals themselves have high reinforcement value raises a critical question about the nature of the presumed aversion which results from prolonged positive stimulation.

References and Notes

1. W. W. Roberts, *J. Comp. Physiol. Psychol.* 51, 400 (1958); G. H. Bower and N. E. Miller, *ibid.* 51, 669 (1958).
2. L. Stein, *ibid.* 55, 405 (1962).
3. J. Olds, *Am. J. Physiol.* 199, 965 (1960); J. Olds, R. P. Travis, R. C. Schwing, *J. Comp. Physiol. Psychol.* 53, 23 (1960).
4. E. S. Valenstein, W. Hodos, L. Stein, *Am. J. Psychol.* 74, 125 (1961).
5. We are indebted to Barbara Case for assistance in preparation of histological material.
6. J. deGroot, *Verhandel, Koninkl. Ned. Akad. Wetenschap. Afdel. Natuurk. Sect. II* 52, No. 4 (1959).
7. E. S. Valenstein, *Psychol. Rev.*, in press.
8. J. Olds, *ibid.*; M. E. Olds and J. Olds, *J. Comp. Neurol.* 120, 259 (1963).
9. J. L. Kavanau, *Science* 143, 490 (1964).
10. E. S. Valenstein and T. Valenstein, *Am. Psychol.* 18, 436 (1963).
11. R. E. Keesey, *J. Comp. Physiol. Psychol.*, in press.
12. W. Hodos, *Am. Psychol.* 18, 437 (1963).
13. Supported by NIH research grant M-4529, career development award MH-4947, and NASA research grant NsG-437.

Characteristics Required in a Reinforcing Mechanism

Excerpt from D. Bindra, *Motivation, a Systematic Reinterpretation*, Ronald Press, New York, 1959, Chapter 5.

If drive reduction is not the unique positive reinforcer (nor drive increment the unique negative reinforcer), the concept of drive ceases to be crucial in a discussion of the nature of reinforcers. In attempting to discover the essential feature of positive reinforcers, one must consider not only the positive reinforcing properties of drive reduction, but should also pay attention to the positive reinforcing effects of consummatory responses, some forms of exteroceptive stimulation, and certain types of intracranial stimulation. The problem of the nature of reinforcers can thus be formulated without any specific reference to the concept of drive or drive reduction.

In view of the similar effects they have on habit strength, it seems reasonable to assume that various types of positive reinforcers share a common mechanism. Let us call such a hypothetical mechanism the *positive reinforcing mechanism* or PRM. How does this mechanism operate? Our discussion so far suggests some of the rules according to which PRM must operate:

1. PRM must so act as to increase the over-all habit strength of those responses that accompany it.

2. PRM must be capable of operating at different levels or intensities, low levels producing small increments in habit strength and high levels producing larger increments in habit strength.

3. PRM must operate at a relatively high level under any one of the following conditions:
   a) certain instances of *decrease in sensory stimulation*, that is, decrease in receptor discharge or drive reduction, arising either proprioceptively (e.g. stomach-fistula experiments) or exteroceptively (e.g. escape training using termination of noxious stimulation as a reinforcer);
   b) certain instances of *increase in sensory stimulation*, that is, increase in receptor discharge or drive increment, arising either proprioceptively (e.g. consummatory-response experiments) or exteroceptively (e.g. light stimulation and visual exploration experiments); and
   c) the stimulation of certain subcortical structures (e.g. intracranial self-stimulation experiments).

4. PRM must so operate that 'neutral' stimuli associated with its operation can acquire (secondary) reinforcing properties.

It is likely that the statements made in relation to positive re-inforcers apply, with appropriate modifications, to negative re-inforcers as well.

Mechanism of Reinforcement: An Hypothesis

Excerpt from N. E. Miller, 'Some reflections on the law of effect produce a new alternative to drive reduction'. In M. R. Jones (Ed.), *Nebraska Symposium on Motivation*, University of Nebraska Press, Lincoln, 1963, pp. 65–112.

In one scene of a motion picture (Miller and Hart, 1948), an experimentally naïve rat has been scrambling around on an electrified grid for a while without securing more than momentary relief. Finally, he happens to rotate a wheel which turns off the shock. This initial response is not vigorous. But immediately afterward, almost like an actor doing a 'second take', he starts to rotate the wheel furiously.

My interpretation of such observations has been that the sudden reduction in pain strengthened the connection from pain, fear, and all of the other functioning cues in the situation, to the response of rotating the wheel. In other words, I assumed that the reinforcement produced by drive reduction caused the increase in vigor of this response. This may be true. But what happens if one assumes that the causal relationship runs in the opposite direction?

Let us explore the assumption that the sudden relief from pain produces an automatic increase in the activity of any neural circuits that have just been firing. Let us further assume that it is this energization that is responsible for the strong performance (in this case appearing as vigorous overt rehearsal) which in turn is responsible for learning by contiguity. Such energization could involve the reticular activating system or it could involve something as different as a DC potential. Let us see where such speculations can lead us.

There are a number of ways of proceeding from this point. At one extreme, one can assume that each of the stimulus situations in the long list known to be empirically rewarding is individually wired up so that it will have its own separate network (DC potential or other means) for facilitating any ongoing activity, including the trace of an immediately preceding activity. At the other extreme, one can assume that there is a single 'go network' or 'go mechanism'. It is obvious that the latter would be much more parsimonious to construct, but natural selection does not always result in maximum parsimony.

Let us make the following tentative assumptions:

1. *That there are one or more 'go' or 'activating' mechanisms in the brain which act to intensify ongoing responses to cues and the traces of immediately preceding activities, producing a stronger intensification the more strongly the 'go mechanism' is activated.*

2. *That this 'go mechanism' (or 'mechanisms,' as will be understood but not repeated hereafter) can be activated in a variety of ways, such as by reduction in noxious stimulation, by the taste of food to a hungry animal, possibly by feedback from still more central effects of eating, by the release of a stimulated but inhibited response from blocking, by the removal of a discrepancy between an intention and an achievement, etc.* The similarity between the 'go' mechanism and the 'confirming response' will be recognized, but it is assumed that the primary effect of the 'go' mechanism is to intensify current activities, including dynamic or other traces, rather than *directly* to strengthen connections. As will be seen from 3 and 4 below, however, a secondary effect of such intensification is to strengthen connections, or in other words, habits.

3. *That all responses, including the activation of this 'go mechanism' are subject to conditioning with contiguity being sufficient.* Note that this is a crucial difference from Mowrer (1960a and 1960b) which avoids the fatal weakness that has already been pointed out.

4. *That the strength of the CR is determined to a great degree by the strength of the UCR (including the intensified trace which automatically serves as a UCR since the activities are similar), but also by the number of pairings.* This is a key assumption, which together with the preceding ones, means that more strongly rewarded responses will be prepotent over competing less strongly rewarded ones. The number of pairings could act to build up more functional units in an all-or-none way as Guthrie (1952) assumes; we do not need to decide that point now.

5. *That when a chain of cues leads to a UCS for the 'go mechanism', it is most strongly conditioned to those nearer to the UCS, but can be conditioned (perhaps via lingering traces and/or by successive higher-order conditioning) to those farther away with a progressive decline in strength.*

6. *That every time a CR (including a conditioned 'go response') is repeated without reinforcement from the UCS (or perhaps it*

should be, a CS is presented without a UCS, or the CR is stronger than the UCR), it is subject to a certain amount of weakening, or in other words, experimental extinction. With instrumental responses it will be remembered that the intensified trace serves as the UCS, so that non-intensification of the trace will, according to the present assumption, produce experimental extinction.

It can be seen that, after various conditioning trials in its environment, an organism or other device, constructed along these principles, would tend to be guided cybernetically toward the UCS for the 'go system', and that it would tend to drop out sequences that doubled back on themselves (blind alleys). It also would learn specific S-R connections[1] which could be the basis for immediate choice, without the necessity for sampling various cues, or in other words, showing VTE's before every choice. Thus the theory avoids the fatal weakness of Mowrer's (1960a and 1960b) formulation. Such an organism would learn fear by classical conditioning, but would not learn to approach pain, because it is only the offset of pain that is the UCS for the 'go' mechanism.

In developing this line of speculation I use the extended definitions of stimulus and response, including central activities and attention, which were advanced before such notions were fashionable (Miller and Dollard, 1941), and have been repeated and extended recently (Miller, 1959, pp. 238–252; 1963b), including the extension to different 'programs' suggested in this paper. The key assumption is that all of these apparently diverse processes follow the same basic laws of learning (Miller, 1959, p. 243).

Some similarities and differences with other theories

The present hypothesis has obvious resemblances to Mowrer (1960a, 1960b) except for the crucial fact that, like the original analysis of copying (Miller and Dollard, 1941), it does *not* rule out connections between cues and motor responses, and therefore does have a way of eliciting immediate responses. Thus, it overcomes a fatal weakness of Mowrer's theory.

1. Please note carefully that the word 'connection' is used in the sense defined by Miller and Dollard (1941 p. 21): 'The word "connection" is used to refer to a causal sequence, the details of which are practically unknown, rather than to specific neural strands.' There is nothing to prevent a 'connection' from being a modulation of an ongoing activity, a complex processing of information, or a complex pattern of permanent traces in different parts of different networks, provided that the end result is that under specified conditions a cue has a tendency to be followed by a response, as we have broadly defined both of these terms.

The present formulation also resembles Sheffield's (1954) drive-induction hypothesis, and some of the recent emphasis by Spence (1956) on the incentive value of the anticipatory goal response, except that it does *not* limit itself to incentives based on the conditioning of peripheral consummatory responses, and does specifically include an incentive based on the termination of noxious stimulation.[2] While Spence, who has primarily used the empirical law of effect, prudently has not clearly made up his mind, the present formulation differs from what seems to be Spence's present position in that it clearly and definitely does not assume different processes for appetitive and aversive learning, or for the acquisition of habit strength and incentive strength.

While the present formulation does use association by contiguity, it differs from Guthrie (1952) in using the booster or 'go mechanism' to explain the obvious selectivity of learning, instead of relying on stimulus change to protect certain elements of completely indiscriminate learning from being unlearned. It also differs from Guthrie in having a specific assumption about experimental extinction. Conceivably, this assumption can later be derived from the more basic phenomenon of habituation, or from the learning of interfering activities, but this is a tricky problem.

The present formulation is similar to Tolman (1932) in that reward serves to elicit performance and that there is a possibility of learning by contiguity. It differs, however, in (a) that activated performance clearly is essential for the learning of responses, including central ones, that must compete with other strong responses at the time of such learning or that are strong enough to do so during performance, and (b) that it is assumed that direct responses can be learned without always having an expectancy as a mediating link. It is similar to Tolman's and different from most other CR formulations in that it does not place all of its emphasis on peripheral mediating responses, but allows for the possibility of central perceptual, imaged or other processes

2. In his latest version of his drive-induction hypothesis, Sheffield (1960) is moving toward a 'central response' position, more similar to the one advanced in the present paper, but he still seems to emphasize the consummatory response. In discussing the problem of what aspect of the consummatory response is conditionable and what aspect moves forward to produce consummatory excitement, he says: '... we will all have to give up the idea that what moves forward is some overt or peripheral portion of the consummatory response. I am already thinking instead of a central-nervous-system phenomenon which may show up in various ways at the behavioral level.'

utilizing the myriad potential interconnections in the brain. It is different from Tolman in that it conceives of these central processes as obeying the same fundamental laws as overt responses, and hence refers to them as cue-producing 'responses'.

The central responses, which have been a part of my thinking for a long time, obviously resemble Hebb's (1949) cell assemblies and phase sequences, but in the 'go mechanism' and experimental extinction, the present formulation has selective factors which are essential to prevent Hebb's cell assemblies and phase sequences from continuing to grow from association by contiguity until they elicit one grand convulsion.

In short, while certain assumptions of the present tentative formulation necessarily resemble previous theories, I believe that this particular combination of assumptions is unique and that it is precisely this particular combination that actually will work. Certainly, difficulties will be encountered and revisions or extensions will be needed. Only a few lines of further development may be briefly suggested here.

Look for direct evidence of 'go' mechanism

One of the first things that should be done is to try to secure some direct evidence that something like the 'go mechanism' outlined in the first assumption actually exists and, if it does, to investigate the degree to which it can be demonstrated to intensify or prolong the activity of neural traces or overt motor activity. What are the effects in different parts of the brain when a given response first gives sudden relief from prolonged pain or causes food to be delivered to a hungry animal which has been thoroughly trained to promptly seize and eat it in the experimental situation? What are the effects during the first trial on which a CS, to which the investigatory response has been habituated, is paired with the UCS of food? We know that after several trials, the CS shows no habituation and that effects of it are more intense and widespread than they otherwise would be. The occurrence of such effects during the very first trial would be evidence for the type of 'go' or 'booster' mechanism we have postulated. If, however, such effects occurred only on the second trial, this would be evidence for the more conventional conception of a retroactive effect of reward on the strengthening of a connection.

Experimental tests of cybernetic guidance

We also need to know the extent to which drive induction and reduction can cybernetically guide responses as emphasized by

Mowrer (1960a). Is such guidance very effective on the very first trial, or only after S-R connections have been strengthened either by the new process we have just proposed or by some other means? Let us place a rat in an open-field apparatus, wearing a little headlight casting the brightest beam directly ahead. Place a photocell at a given point in the field and have the illumination of this photocell reduce the intensity of electric shock delivered via body electrodes (or electrodes on an aversive area of the brain) placed so that the shock elicits a minimum of interfering motor responses. Will the rat be guided efficiently to that point on the very first trial? Will it be more effective to turn the shock off completely whenever the rat starts to move in the desired direction? If this is done, will the beneficial effects appear only as the strength of the shock is gradually built up again? We need to know more facts about the possibilities, and difficulties, of such guidance as contrasted with learning specific directional responses to specific directional cues.

It seems reasonable to assume that the areas in which Olds (1958) secured self-reward are either a part of the 'go mechanism' or are directly connected with it. On the behavioral side, it would be interesting to see whether or not one can guide a rat cybernetically toward a goal by playing 'you're getting hotter or colder' with an area in which the animal will hold a bar down continuously in order to get continuous brain stimulation.

The fact that there are so many areas in which the rats do not give themselves continuous stimulation by holding down such a bar continuously, and where they will even perform a second response to turn the stimulation off (Roberts, 1958; Bower & Miller, 1958), poses certain problems for such an experiment, and perhaps also for the hypothesis. Perhaps responses are facilitated, not by the absolute level of activity of the 'go system', but only by increases in its level of activity. Perhaps a succession of brief episodes of rises and falls in motivating stimulation will be found to be more effective in cybernetic shaping than continuous feedback.

Relationships between 'go' and 'stop' mechanisms

While we are clumsily groping along, it is tempting to endow our organism with one or more 'stop' mechanisms which have effects directly opposite to those of the 'go' one. But this might cause trouble. Desirable as it may be to have pain and fear stop behavior under certain circumstances, as indeed it seems to do in the CER, there are other circumstances, namely escape and avoidance learning, in which it is desirable to have them elicit vigorous activity. The same seems to be true of frustration. Perhaps we might want to have a generalized freezing mechanism with connections from pain and fear that could be strengthened if it was active when their termination activated the 'go' mechanism by sudden reductions in pain, fear, and frustration.

Although it does not seem desirable to assume a 'stop' mechanism with effects on all responses that are directly opposite to those assumed for the 'go' mechanism, it does seem worthwhile to make the following additional assumption which is more tentative than the preceding ones:

7. *That there is a certain amount of reciprocal inhibition between the central mechanisms involved in pain, fear, and frustration and the 'go' mechanism, or mechanisms.*

Such inhibition would explain the counterconditioning of fear, which it will be remembered is badly in need of additional detailed experimental study. The activation of the 'go' mechanism would tend to inhibit fear, rather than to boost it. The converse aspect of such inhibition would cause pain at the goal to tend to subtract from the effectiveness of reward there. Furthermore, the activation of the 'go' mechanism by the termination of pain would be prevented by the inhibiting effects of the pain from being strongly conditioned to cues occurring during the pain. This would account for the apparent difficulty of establishing strong secondary reinforcement based on the termination of pain. (If such secondary reinforcement were strong enough, it could even lead to the performance of responses leading to pain.) The particular responses energized by the termination of pain would not, however, be subject to such inhibition and hence could become anticipatory. Before being too explicit about the inevitability, symmetry, and strength of such reciprocal inhibition, however, it will be wise to have more exact experimental evidence concerning the phenomena to be accounted for. We have already suggested some experiments which might contribute to this goal.

Speed vs. prepotency

As one tries to apply the hypothesis to a greater variety of situations, problems arise. For example, how can one account for the experiment in which Egger and I (1962) found that, if a first and second cue always are immediately associated with food, the redundant second one has relatively little secondary reinforcing value, and at the same time have the subject take the shortcut of choosing the second cue when subsequently confronted with both simultaneously? A careful analysis of the stimulus changes involved may provide the answer.

Another difficulty arises from the fact that, if rats are specifically rewarded for running slowly down one alley, and allowed to run rapidly down another, they will learn to run at different speeds in the two alleys, but if they are given better rewards for running slowly, they will choose the slow alley (Logan, 1962). In short, the most vigorous response in terms of speed (and presumably amplitude also) is not necessarily the one that is strongest in terms of prepotency. Therefore, we probably shall have to be careful to define strength in terms of prepotency, rather than speed and amplitude.

The lesson is that it is dangerous to regard one hypothesis as more promising than another when it has not been worked out in as much detail. Nevertheless, each hypothesis has to start out in a tentative manner and there is an advantage in trying to work from the general to the specific by a strategy analogous to that employed in the game of 'twenty questions'.

Changes in rewards

We know that performance declines when one shifts from a larger reward to a smaller one. Such a decline would be expected if we assume that extinction occurs whenever the CR is stronger than the UCR, or than some given fraction of the UCR.

There is also some disturbance when an animal is shifted from one reward to another, although the laws of such disturbance need to be experimentally determined in more detail, especially since many experiments have confounded shifts in the type of reward with shifts to a less preferred one. We need to find out the extent to which the disturbance is a function of the goal responses elicited by the reward, biting dry food versus lapping sweet water, and the extent to which it can also be produced by distinctive changes in the flavor of food without apparently introducing any change into the motor responses of eating. To what extent do such disturbances become greater as one advances from the rat to the dog to the monkey? Perhaps we shall have to assume a number of 'go' mechanisms, or that different strengths of the 'go' mechanism function as incompatible responses, or that a conflict between an image and a perceptual response produces a disturbance. In the absence of better data, there is not much point in making overly specific theoretical assumptions.

Furthermore, the problems of sensory preconditioning and

latent learning seem to me to be closely related to the foregoing ones.

You will note that in a previous context I said 'functioning cues'. Having been one of the few stimulus-response psychologists who used the concept of 'attention' before our entry into World War II (Miller & Dollard, 1941), I use functioning cues to mean ones that are receiving at least some attention, a concept that has been given a physiological basis by recent work on the reticular formation (Magoun, 1958) and has been extended and clarified by detailed experimental work such as that which Broadbent (1948, 1962) has summarized in support of his filter theory.

References

Bower, G. H., & Miller, N. E. Effect of amount of reward on strength of approach in an approach-avoidance conflict. *J. comp. physiol. Psychol.*, 1960, 53, 59–62.

Broadbent, D. E. *Perception and communication*, New York: Basic Books, 1958.

Egger, M. D., & Miller, N. E. Secondary reinforcement in rats as a function of information value and reliability of the stimulus. *J. exp. Psychol.*, 1962, 64, 97–104.

Guthrie, E. R. *The psychology of learning.* (Revised.) New York: Harper, 1952.

Hebb, D. O. *The organization of behavior.* New York: Wiley, 1949.

Logan, F. A. Conditional-outcome choice behavior in rats. *Psychol. Rev.*, 1962, 69, 467–476.

Magoun, H. W. *The waking brain*, Springfield, Ill. : Charles Thomas, 1958.

Miller, N. E. Liberalization of basic S-R concepts: extensions to conflict behavior, motivation and social learning. *Psychology: a study of a science.* Study 1, vol. 2, S. Koch (Ed.). New York: McGraw-Hill, 1959.

Miller, N. E. Some implications of modern behavior theory for personality change and psychotherapy. P. Worchel & D. Byrne (Eds.), *Personality change.* New York: Wiley, 1963b.

Miller, N. E., & Dollard, J. *Social learning and imitation.* New Haven: Yale Univ. Press, 1941.

Miller, N. E., & Hart, G. Motivation and reward in learning. Film, Psychological Cinema Register, Penn. State Univ., 1948.

Mowrer, O. H. *Learning theory and behavior.* New York: Wiley, 1960a.

Mowrer, O. H. *Learning theory and symbolic processes.* New York: Wiley, 1960b.

Olds, J. A. Self-stimulation of the brain used to study local effects of hunger, sex, and drugs. *Science*, 1958, 127, 315.

Roberts, W. W. Both rewarding and punishing effects from stimulation of posterior hypothalamus with same electrode at same intensity. *J. comp. physiol. Psychol.*, 1958, 51, 400–407.

Sheffield, F. D. A drive-induction theory of reinforcement. Mimeographed MS of paper read at Psychology Colloquium, Brown University, Nov. 1954.

Sheffield, F. D. New evidence on the drive-induction theory of reinforcement. Mimeographed MS of paper read at Psychology Colloquium, Stanford University, Nov., 1960.

Spence, K. W. *Behavior theory and conditioning*. New Haven: Yale Univ. Press, 1956.

Tolman, E. C. *Purposive behavior in animals and men*. New York: Appleton-Century-Crofts, 1932.

Further Reading

Amsel, A., The role of frustrative non-reward in non-continuous reward situations, *Psychol. Bull.*, 1958, Vol. 55, pp. 102–19. (For Chapter IV.)

Amsel, A., Frustrative non-reward in partial reinforcement and discrimination learning: Some recent history and a theoretical extension, *Psych. Rev.*, 1962, Vol. 69, 306–28. (For Chapter IV.)

Atkinson, J. W. (Ed.), *Motives in Fantasy, Action, and Society*, Van Nostrand, New York, 1958. (For Chapter IV.)

Atkinson, J. W., *An Introduction to Motivation*, Van Nostrand, New York, 1964, Chapter 5 (For Chapter V); Chapter 7 (For Chapter III).

Baumeister, A., Hawkins, W. F., & Cromwell, R. L., Need states and activity level, *Psychol. Bull.*, 1964, Vol. 61, 438–53. (For Chapter III.)

Beach, F. A., The descent of instinct, *Psych. Rev.*, 1955, Vol. 62, 401–10. (For Chapter I.)

Berlyne, D. E., *Conflict, Arousal and Curiosity*, McGraw-Hill, New York, 1960. Chapters 4, 5 and 6 (For Chapter IX).

Bindra, D., *Motivation: A Systematic Reinterpretation*, Ronald Press Co., New York, 1959. Chapter 3 (For Chapter V); Chapter 5 (For Chapter VII).

Bindra, D., An interpretation of the 'displacement' phenomenon, *Brit. J. Psychol.*, 1959, Vol. 50, 263–68. (For Chapter I.)

Bolles, R. C., The usefulness of the drive concept. In M. R. Jones (Ed.), *Nebraska Symposium on Motivation*, University Nebraska Press, Lincoln, 1958. (For Chapter III.)

Brown, J. S., & Farber, I. E., Emotions conceptualized as intervening variables – with suggestions toward a theory of frustration, *Psychol. Bull.*, 1951, Vol. 48, 465–95. (For Chapter III.)

Brown, J. S., *The Motivation of Behavior*, McGraw-Hill, New York, 1961, Chapters 2 to 5 (For Chapter III).

Butler, R. A., Discrimination learning by rhesus monkeys to visual-exploration motivation, *J. Comp. Physiol. Psychol.*, 1953, Vol. 46, 95–8. (For Chapter IX.)

Cofer, C. N., & Appley, M. H., *Motivation: Theory and Research*, Wiley, New York, 1964. Chapter 10 (For Chapter III.)

Delgado, J. M. R., Roberts, W. W., & Miller, N. E., Learning motivated by electrical stimulation of the brain, *Amer. J. Physiol.*, 1954, Vol. 179, 587–93. (For Chapter X.)

Guttman, N., Operant conditioning, extinction, and periodic reinforcement in relation to concentration of sucrose used as reinforcing agent, *J. Exp. Psychol.*, 1953, Vol. 46, 213–24. (For Chapter IX.)

FURTHER READING

Hall, J. F., *Psychology of Motivation*, Lippincott, New York, 1961, Chapter 2 (For Chapter I); Chapter 3 (For Chapter II).

Harlow, H. F., & McClearn, G. E., Object discrimination learned by monkeys on the basis of manipulation motives, *J. Comp. Physiol. Psychol.*, 1954, Vol. 47, 73–6. (For Chapter IX.)

Hinde, R. A., Factors governing the changes in strength of a partially inborn response, as shown by the mobbing behaviour of the chaffinch (Fringilla coelebs): I. The nature of the response, and an examination of its course, *Proc. Royal Soc.*, B., 1954, Vol. 142, 306–31. (For Chapter I.)

Hinde, R. A., Factors governing the changes in strength of a partially inborn response, as shown by the mobbing behaviour of the chaffinch (Fringilla coelebs): II. The waning of the response, *Proc. Royal Soc.*, B., 1954, Vol. 142, 331–48. (For Chapter I.)

Lehrman, D. S., A critique of Konrad Lorenz's theory of instinctive behavior, *Quart. Rev. Biol.*, 1953, Vol. 38, 337–63. (For Chapter I.)

Lehrman, D. S., The organization of maternal behavior and the problem of instinct, In *L'instinct dans les comportement des animaux et de l'homme*, Masson, Paris, 1956, 475–520. (For Chapter I.)

Logan, F. A., The free behavior situation. In D. Levine (Ed.), *Nebraska Symposium on Motivation*, University Nebraska Press, Lincoln, 1964, 99–128. (For Chapter III.)

Malmo, R. B., Measurement of drive: an unsolved problem in psychology. In M. R. Jones (Ed.), *Nebraska Symposium on Motivation*, University Nebraska Press, Lincoln, 1958, 229–65. (For Chapter III.)

Mandler, G., The interruption of behavior. In D. Levine (Ed.), *Nebraska Symposium on Motivation*, University Nebraska Press, Lincoln, 1964, 163–219. (For Chapter IV.)

Melzack, R., Irrational fears in the dog, *Canad. J. Psychol.*, 1952, Vol. 6, 141–47. (For Chapter II.)

Miller, N. E., Learnable drives and rewards. In S. S. Stevens (Ed.), *Handbook of Experimental Psychology*, Wiley, New York, 1951, 435–72. (For Chapter III.)

Mowrer, O. H., A stimulus-response analysis of anxiety and its role as a reinforcing agent, *Psychol. Rev.*, 1939, Vol. 46, 553–65. (For Chapter III.)

Mowrer, O. H., *Learning Theory and Behavior*, Wiley, New York, 1960, Chapters 4 and 5 (For Chapter III).

Nissen, H. W., The nature of the drive as innate determinant of behavioral organization. In M. R. Jones (Ed.), *Nebraska Symposium on Motivation*, University Nebraska Press, Lincoln, 1954, 281–321. (For Chapter I.)

Olds, J., & Milner, P., Positive reinforcement produced by electrical stimulation of septal area and other regions of rat brain, *J. comp. physiol. Psychol.*, 1954, Vol. 47, 419–27. (For Chapter X.)

Premack, D., Toward empirical behaviour laws: I. Positive reinforcement, *Psychol. Rev.*, 1959, Vol. 66, 219–33. (For Chapter VIII.)

Roberts, W. W., & Kiess, H. O., Motivational properties of hypothalamic aggression in cats, *J. Comp. Physiol. Psychol.*, 1964, Vol. 58, 187–93. (For Chapter II.)

Seward, J. P., Drive, incentive, and reinforcement, *Psychol. Rev.*, 1956, Vol. 63, 195–203. (For Chapter III.)

Sheffield, F. D., Wulff, J. J., & Backer, R., Reward value of copulation without sex drive reduction, *J. Comp. Physiol. Psychol.*, 1951, Vol. 44, 3–8. (For Chapter VIII.)

Solomon, R. L., Kamin, L. J., & Wynne, L. C., Traumatic avoidance learning: The outcomes of several extinction procedures with dogs, *J. abnorm. soc. Psychol.*, 1953, Vol. 48, 291–302. (For Chapter IV.)

Solomon, R. L., & Brush, E. S., Experimentally derived conceptions of anxiety and aversion. In M. R. Jones (Ed.), *Nebraska Symposium on Motivation*, University Nebraska Press, Lincoln, 1956, 212–305. (For Chapter III.)

Sommerhoff, G., *Analytical Biology*, Oxford University Press, London, 1950. (For Chapter V.)

Spence, K. W., A theory of emotionally based drive (D) and its relation to performance in simple learning situations, *Amer. Psychologist*, 1958, Vol. 13, 131–41. (For Chapter IV.)

Spence, K. W., *Behavior Theory and Learning*, Prentice-Hall, Englewood Cliffs, N. J., 1960. (For Chapter IV.)

Stein, L., & Ray, O. S., Brain stimulation reward 'thresholds' self-determined in rat, *Psychopharmacologia*, 1960, Vol. 1, 251–56. (For Chapter X.)

Stellar, E., The physiology of motivation, *Psychol. Rev.*, 1954, Vol. 61, 5–22. (For Chapter II.)

Stewart, J., Reinforcing effects of light as a function of intensity and reinforcement schedule, *J. Comp. Physiol. Psychol.*, 1960, Vol. 53, 187–93. (For Chapter IX.)

Thorpe, W. H., *Learning and Instinct in Animals*, (2nd Ed.), Methuen, London, 1963. (For Chapter I.)

Tinbergen, N., On aims and methods of ethology. *Zeitschrift für Tierpsychologie*, 1963, Vol. 20, 4, 410–33.

Valenstein, E. S., Problems of measurement and interpretation with reinforcing brain stimulation, *Psychol. Rev.*, 1964, Vol. 71, 415–37. (For Chapter X.)

von Holst, E., & van Saint Paul, U., On the functional organisation of drives, *Anim. Behav.*, 1963, Vol. 11, 1–20. (For Chapter II.)

Welker, W. I., Escape, exploratory and food-seeking responses of rats in a novel situation, *J. Comp. Physiol. Psychol.*, 1953, Vol. 46, 95–8. (For Chapter IX.)

Young, P. T., & Shuford, E. H., Jr., Quantitative control of motivation through sucrose solutions of different concentrations, *J. Comp. Physiol. Psychol.*, 1955, Vol. 48, 114–18. (For Chapter III.)

Young, P. T., *Motivation and Emotion*, John Wiley, New York, 1961. (For Chapter II.)

Acknowledgements

Acknowledgements are due to the following for permission to publish extracts in this volume: American Psychological Association, *Psychological Review*, E. C. Tolman, 'Purpose and Cognition: The Determiners of Animal Learning', 1925, D. O. Hebb, 'Drives and the C.N.S. (Conceptual Nervous System)', 1955, C. Pfaffmann, 'The Pleasures of Sensation', 1960, P. T. Young, 'The Role of Affective Processes in Learning and Motivation', 1959, H. W. Nissen, 'Instinct As Seen by a Psychologist', 1953, K. S. Lashley, 'Experimental Analysis of Instinctive Behavior', 1938; *American Psychologist*, K. W. Spence, 'A Theory of Emotionally Based Drive (D) and its Relation to Performance in Simple Learning Situation', 1958; Appleton-Century-Crofts, H. Spencer, *The Principles of Psychology*, C. L. Hull, *Principles of Behavior*, copyright by D. Appleton-Century Co. Inc., 1943; Basic Books Inc., Hogarth Press, *The Complete Psychological Works of Sigmund Freud*, revised and edited by James Strachey, Vol. 4, 1925; *British Journal of Animal Behaviour*, H. M. B. Hurwitz, 'Conditioned Responses in Rats Reinforced by Light', Vol. 4, 1956; Cambridge University Press, *Symposia of the Society for Experimental Biology*, K. Lorenz, 'The Comparative Method in Studying Innate Behaviour Patterns', Vol. 4, 1950, R. A. Hinde, 'Energy Models of Motivation', Vol. 14, 1960; Charles Scribner's Sons and Methuen & Co. Limited, W. McDougall, *Outline of Psychology*, copyright Charles Scribner's Sons 1923, renewal copyright 1951 Anne A. McDougall; Clarendon Press Oxford, N. Tinbergen, The Study of Instinct, 1951; Columbia University Press, R. S. Woodworth, *Dynamic Psychology*, 1918; D. Van Nostrand Co., Inc., L. T. Troland, *The Principles of Psychology*, 1932; *Journal of Comparative and Physiological Psychology*, N. Guttman, 'Equal Reinforcement Values for Sucrose and Glucose Solutions Compared with Equal Sweetness Values', 1954, N. E. Miller and M. L. Kessen, 'Reward Effects of Food via Stomach Fistula Compared with Those of Food via Mouth', 1952, K. C. Montgomery, 'The Role of Exploratory Drive in Learning', 1954, F. D. Sheffield and T. B. Roby, 'Reward Value of a Non-Nutritive Sweet Taste', 1950; *Journal of Experimental Psychology*, A. Amsel and J. Roussel, 'Motivation Properties of Frustration: Effect on a Running Response of the Addition of Frustration to the Motivational Complex', 1952, N. E. Miller, 'Studies of Fear as an Acquirable Drive: 1. Fear as Motivation and Fear-Reduction as Reinforcement in the Learning of New Responses', 1948; Little, Brown & Co., H. H. Jasper, et al. (Eds.), *Reticular Formation of the Brain*, J. Olds, 'Self-Stimulation Experiments and Differentiated Reward Systems', 1958; Macmillan & Co., B. F. Skinner, *Science and Human Behaviour*, copyright 1953, E. L. Thorndike, *Animal Intelligence*, copyright 1911; Methuen & Co., W. McDougall, *An Introduction to Social Psychology*, 1908; P. A. Norstedt & Soner, *Acta Physiologica Scandinavia*, B. Andersson and S. M. McCann, 'A Further Study of Polydipsia Evoked by Hypothalamic Stimulation in the Goat', Vol. 33, 1955; *Science*, E. S. Valenstein and T. Valenstein, 'Interaction of Positive and Negative Reinforcing Neural Systems', Vol. 145, 1964, D. Premack, 'Reversibility of the Reinforcement Relation', Vol. 136, 1962, Copyright by the American Association for the Advancement of Science 1962, 1964, A. E. Fisher, 'Maternal and Sexual Behavior Induced by Intracranial Stimulation', Vol. 124, 1956; The Ronald Press Company,

Subject Index